Implementing a
National
Assessment of
Educational
Achievement

National Assessments of Educational Achievement

VOLUME 3

Implementing a National Assessment of Educational Achievement

Editors
Vincent Greaney
Thomas Kellaghan

THE WORLD BANK
Washington, DC

1 2 3 4 15 14 13 12

This volume is a product of the staff of The World Bank with external contributions. The findings, interpretations, and conclusions expressed in this volume do not
necessarily reflect the views of The World Bank, its Board of Executive Directors,
or the governments they represent.

The World Bank does not guarantee the accuracy of the data included in this
work. The boundaries, colors, denominations, and other information shown on any
map in this work do not imply any judgment on the part of The World Bank concerning the legal status of any territory or the endorsement or acceptance of such
boundaries.

ISBN (paper): 978-0-8213-8589-0
ISBN (electronic): 978-0-8213-8590-6
DOI: 10.1596/978-0-8213-8589-0

Library of Congress Cataloging-in-Publication Data
Implementing a national assessment of educational achievement / editors,
    Vincent Greaney, Thomas Kellaghan.
    p. cm. — (National assessments of educational achievement ; v. 3)
    Includes bibliographical references and index.
    ISBN 978-0-8213-8589-0 (alk. paper) — ISBN 978-0-8213-8590-6
    1. Educational tests and measurements—United States.   2. Educational
evaluation—United States.   I. Greaney, Vincent.   II. Kellaghan, Thomas.

    LB3051.I463 2011
    371.26'2—dc22

                                                                2010036024

Cover design: Naylor Design, Washington, DC

*Microsoft, Access, Excel, Office, Windows, and Word are either registered trademarks
or trademarks of Microsoft Corporation in the United States and/or other countries.
SPSS is a registered trademark of IBM.
WesVar is a registered trademark of Westat.*

CONTENTS

Part I
The Logistics of a National Assessment
Sarah J. Howie and Sylvia Acana

Part II
School Sampling Methodology
Jean Dumais and J. Heward Gough

Part III
Data Preparation, Validation, and Management
Chris Freeman and Kate O'Malley

Part IV
Weighting, Estimation, and Sampling Error
Jean Dumais and J. Heward Gough

EXERCISES

FIGURES

TABLES

PREFACE

Measuring student learning outcomes is necessary for monitoring a school system's success and for improving education quality. Student achievement information can be used to inform a wide variety of education policies and decisions, including the design and implementation of programs to improve teaching and learning in classrooms, the identification of lagging students so that they can get the support they need, and the provision of appropriate technical assistance and training where it is most needed.

This *National Assessments of Educational Achievement* series of publications, of which this is the third volume, focuses on state-of-the-art procedures that need to be followed in order to ensure that the data (such as test scores and background information) produced by a large-scale national assessment exercise are of high quality and address the concerns of policy makers, decision makers, and other stakeholders in the education system.

Volume 1 in the series describes the key purposes and features of national assessments of educational achievement and is mainly aimed at policy makers and decision makers in education. Volume 2 addresses the design of two types of data collection instruments for national assessment exercises: student achievement tests and background questionnaires.

This third volume in the series, *Implementing a National Assessment of Educational Achievement*, focuses on the practical tasks involved in implementing a large-scale national assessment exercise, including detailed step-by-step instructions on logistics, sampling, and data cleaning and management. Like Volumes 2 and 4 in the series, this volume is intended primarily for the teams in developing and emerging economies who are responsible for conducting a national assessment exercise.

Volume 4 in the series deals with how to generate information on test items and test scores and how to relate the test scores to other educational factors. Finally, Volume 5 covers how to write reports that are based on the national assessment findings and how to use the results to improve the quality of educational policy and decision making. Volume 5 should be of particular relevance to those with responsibility for preparing assessment reports or for communicating or using the findings from them.

As readers make their way through this third volume in the *National Assessments of Educational Achievement* series, it should become evident that the successful implementation of a national assessment exercise is a complex task that requires considerable knowledge, skill, and resources. At the same time, research has shown that the payoff from well-implemented national assessments can be substantial in terms of the quality of the information provided on levels of student achievement and on school and nonschool factors that might help raise those achievement levels. (Conversely, the "cost" of a poorly implemented national assessment may be inaccurate information about student achievement levels and related factors.) Good quality implementation can increase the confidence of policy makers and other stakeholders in the validity of assessment findings. It also can increase the likelihood that policy makers and other stakeholders will use the results of the national assessment to develop sound plans and programs designed to enhance educational quality and student learning outcomes.

Marguerite Clarke
Senior Education Specialist
January 2012

ABOUT THE AUTHORS AND EDITORS

Sylvia Acana directs Uganda's National Assessment of Progress in Education (NAPE). She is a former secondary school science teacher and subject officer at the Uganda National Examinations Board. Arcana has provided technical support in assessment to the Economic Policy Research Centre and to Save the Children. She is an executive committee member of the International Association for Educational Assessment (IAEA) and vice chairperson of the Board of Governors, Loro Core Primary Teachers' College. She holds a master's degree in educational measurement and evaluation.

Jean Dumais is chief of the Statistical Consultation Group at Statistics Canada and a survey statistician at its methodology branch. He has a particular interest in educational assessment. In recent years Dumais has overseen the implementation of the sampling and estimation activities of the International Association for the Evaluation of Educational Achievement comparative study of teacher education (TEDS-M), and the Organisation for Economic Co-operation and Development (OECD) Teaching and Learning International Survey (TALIS). He has also served as sampling referee for a number of international comparative educational assessments.

Chris Freeman is research director at the Australian Council for Educational Research. His work has focused on aspects of large-scale assessments in most Australian states and territories. National-level work includes the National Assessment Program Literacy and Numeracy, surveys in science-related curricular areas, and directing the implementation of OECD programs. He has also been closely associated with national monitoring programs in the South Pacific and in the Middle East. His current areas of interest include the impact of guessing in large-scale national assessments.

J. Heward Gough is a sample survey statistician and was until recently senior statistical consultant in the Statistical Consultation Group at Statistics Canada. He has extensive experience in survey methodology development and statistical consulting, including five years at the UN Latin American Demographic Centre (CELADE). Gough has taught courses on statistical methods, sampling techniques, and survey methodology within Statistics Canada, for external clients across Canada, and for national statistical offices in Colombia, Cuba, Eritrea, Peru, and Zambia. He participated in a statistical capacity-building project in Burkina Faso.

Vincent Greaney is an educational consultant. He was lead education specialist at the World Bank and worked in Africa, Asia, and the Middle East. A former teacher, research fellow at the Educational Research Centre at St. Patrick's College in Dublin, and visiting Fulbright professor at Western Michigan University in Kalamazoo, Greaney is a member of the International Reading Association's Reading Hall of Fame. Areas of interest include assessment, teacher education, reading, and promotion of social cohesion through textbook reform.

Sarah J. Howie is director of the Centre for Evaluation and Assessment and professor of education at the University of Pretoria. In South Africa, she has coordinated international assessments in reading literacy, mathematics, science, and information and communications technology. In addition to providing training in research in a range of countries, Howie has participated in international and national committees concerned with monitoring and evaluating educational quality. Areas of professional interest include large-scale assessment, student assessment, and performance and program evaluation.

Thomas Kellaghan is an educational consultant. He was director of the Educational Research Centre at St. Patrick's College, Dublin, and is a fellow of the International Academy of Education. He has worked at the University of Ibadan in Nigeria and at the Queen's University in Belfast. Areas of research interest include assessment and examinations, educational disadvantage, and home-school relationships. Kellaghan served as president of the International Association for Educational Assessment. He has worked on assessment issues in Africa, Asia, Latin America, and the Middle East.

Kate O'Malley is a research fellow at the Australian Council for Educational Research. She has been closely associated with a series of national assessments in Australia and with the triennial civics and citizenship and ICT literacy assessments, the annual National Assessment Program Literacy and Numeracy (NAPLAN), and the Essential Secondary Science Assessment (ESSA). O'Malley coordinated the Australian component of IEA's Second Information Technology in Education Study (SITES), and OECD's Teaching and Learning International Survey (TALIS) and coauthored the reports for these two projects.

ACKNOWLEDGMENTS

A team led by Vincent Greaney (consultant, Human Development Network, Education Group, World Bank) and Thomas Kellaghan (consultant, Educational Research Centre, St. Patrick's College, Dublin) prepared the series of books titled *National Assessments of Educational Achievement*, of which this is the third volume. Other contributors to the series are Sylvia Acana (Uganda National Examinations Board), Prue Anderson (Australian Council for Educational Research), Fernando Cartwright (Statistics Canada), Jean Dumais (Statistics Canada), Chris Freeman (Australian Council for Educational Research), J. Heward Gough (Statistics Canada), Sara J. Howie (University of Pretoria), George Morgan (Australian Council for Educational Research), T. Scott Murray (Data Angel, Canada), Kate O'Malley (Australian Council for Educational Research), and Gerry Shiel (Educational Research Centre, St. Patrick's College, Dublin).

The work was conducted under the general direction of Ruth Kagia, director of education, and of her successor Elizabeth King, and Robin Horn, manager, Human Development Network, Education Group, all at the World Bank. Robert Prouty initiated the project and managed it up to August 2007. Marguerite Clarke has managed it since then through review and publication.

We are grateful for contributions of the review panel: Al Beaton (Boston College), Zewdu Gebrekidan (Assessment Consultant, Ethiopia), Eugenio Gonzalez (Educational Testing Service), Kelvin Gregory

(New South Wales Board of Studies), Louis Rizzo (Westat), and Carlos Rojas (World Bank). Marguerite Clarke and Robin Horn provided additional helpful comments.

Hilary Walshe helped prepare the various drafts of this document. We also received input and support from Peter Archer, Jung-Hwan Choi, Mary Rohan, Hans Wagemaker, and Hana Yoshimoto.

We wish to thank the following organizations for permission to reproduce material: the Australian Council for Educational Research, the International Association for the Evaluation of Educational Achievement, and Statistics Canada.

Book design, editing, and production were coordinated by Janice Tuten and Paola Scalabrin of the World Bank's Office of the Publisher; printing was coordinated by Nora Ridolfi.

The Australian Council for Educational Research, the Bank Netherlands Partnership Program, the Educational Research Centre in Dublin, the Irish Educational Trust Fund, Statistics Canada, and the Russia Education Aid for Development (READ) Trust Fund have generously supported preparation and publication of the series.

ABBREVIATIONS

DM	data manager
IAEA	International Association for Educational Assessment
ID	identifier
IEA	International Association for the Evaluation of Educational Achievement
ISCED	International Standard Classification of Education
JK	jackknife
MOS	measure of size
NAMA	National Assessment of Mathematics Achievement
NC	national coordinator
NSC	national steering committee
PASW	Predictive Analytic Software
PPS	probability proportional to size
PSU	primary sampling unit
SAS	Statistical Analysis Software
SPSS	Statistical Package for Social Sciences
SRS	simple random sampling
SUDAAN	Survey Data Analysis
SYS	systematic random sampling
TIMSS	Trends in International Mathematics and Science Study

INTRODUCTION

The importance of obtaining evidence about the quality of education, not just of provision but also of student learning, has been a major theme of education policy throughout the world since the 1990s. For a considerable time, impressionistic evidence has suggested that many children derive little benefit from their experience of schooling, in particular if that experience is limited to only a few years in the education system. However, governments now recognize the need for more objective and systematic information on how successful schools are in transforming resources into student learning. Such information is required (a) to obtain an adequate picture of national levels of learning achievement, especially in key curriculum areas; (b) to compare the achievement levels of subpopulations (for example, boys and girls, language or ethnic groups, urban and rural students), which can have important implications in judging the equity of the system; (c) to monitor change in achievement over time; and (d) to guide policy and management decisions regarding the provision of resources.

The procedure used to assess student learning at the system level is called a *national assessment*; its administration is a complex activity requiring a variety of skills and facilities. The centerpiece of the assessment is the collection of data in schools, primarily through responses to assessment instruments and questionnaires from students in groups.

However, activities begin well before data collection and extend well after it. An institution with responsibility for collecting data has to be appointed, decisions have to be made about the policy and research issues to be addressed, and tests and questionnaires have to be designed and tried out. In preparation for the actual testing, populations and samples of schools and students have to be identified, schools have to be contacted, and test administrators need to be selected and trained. Following test administration, much time and effort will be required to prepare data for analysis, to carry out analyses, to write reports, and to disseminate the findings of the assessment.

Although many education systems since 1990 have committed themselves to carrying out a national assessment, few had the wide range of technical skills required to undertake the many tasks involved. As a result, many assessments have been of poor quality. This series of publications, National Assessments of Educational Achievement, of which this is the third volume, was planned to address the issue of improving the quality of national assessments. The focus of the series is on state-of-the-art procedures that need to be followed in implementing the components of an assessment to ensure that the data they provide on student learning are of high quality and address the concerns of policy makers, decision makers, and other stakeholders in the education system.

Volume 1, *Assessing National Achievement Levels in Education* (Greaney and Kellaghan 2008), describes key national assessment concepts and procedures and is intended primarily for policy and decision makers in education. Issues addressed are the purposes and main features of a national assessment, the reasons for carrying out an assessment, and the main decisions that have to be made in the design and planning of an assessment. International assessments of student achievement, which share many procedural features with national assessments (such as sampling, administration, and methods of analysis), are also described.

Volumes 2, 3, and 4 provide step-by-step details on the design and implementation of a national assessment and the analysis of data collected in the assessment. They are intended primarily for the teams in developing countries responsible for carrying out an assessment. Volume 2, *Developing Tests and Questionnaires for a National Assess-*

ment of Educational Achievement (Anderson and Morgan 2008), describes the development of achievement tests, questionnaires, and administration manuals. The book has an accompanying CD that contains achievement and questionnaire items released from national and international assessments and a test administration manual.

Volume 4, *Analyzing Data from a National Assessment of Educational Achievement* (Cartwright and Shiel forthcoming), has two parts. The first is designed to help analysts carry out basic analyses of the data collected in a national assessment. The second half of the book deals with the generation of item-level data using classical test theory and item-response modeling. A CD is provided that allows users to apply statistical procedures to data sets and to check their mastery levels against solutions depicted on screenshots in the text.

Volume 5, *Using the Results of a National Assessment of Educational Achievement* (Kellaghan, Greaney, and Murray 2009), the final book in the series, provides guidelines to describe the findings of a national assessment in technical reports, press releases, briefings for policy makers, and reports for teachers and specialist groups. It also considers how national assessment findings can be used to guide policy and educational management, to influence curriculum and classroom practice, and to raise public awareness of educational issues. Its contents should be of particular relevance to (a) those who have responsibility for preparing assessment reports and for communicating and disseminating findings and (b) users of findings (policy makers, education managers, and school personnel).

This volume, *Implementing a National Assessment of Educational Achievement*, like volumes 2 and 4, focuses on the practical tasks involved in running a large-scale national assessment program. It has four parts. Part I ("The Logistics of a National Assessment") provides an overview of the tasks involved: how the essential activities of an assessment are organized and implemented, what personnel and resources are required, and what tasks follow the collection of data.

Part II ("School Sampling Methodology") presents a methodology for selecting a sample of students that will be representative of students in the education system. Principles underlying sampling are described, as well as step-by-step procedures that can be implemented in nearly any national assessment. Readers should be able to follow the sampling procedures by working through a realistic set of training materials and checking their progress by referring to screenshots and data files with solutions.

An accompanying CD contains supporting data files. To reproduce the various steps in the demonstration assessment, the user will require SPSS (Statistical Package for the Social Sciences),[1] including the Complex Samples add-on module, and Westat's WesVar. SPSS is also used for some analysis sections in volume 4 of this series. The software WesVar and its user's guide may be downloaded from Westat's web site.[2]

A description of how the population of interest is defined is followed by the steps involved in creating a sampling frame. The case of a fictitious small country (Sentz), data from which will be used for the various exercises, is introduced. This part of the volume concludes with a description of basic concepts and methods of probability sampling.

Part III ("Data Preparation, Validation, and Management") describes procedures for cleaning and managing data collected in a national assessment. These procedures are essential elements of a quality assurance process. It also describes how to export and import data (that is, make data available in a format that is appropriate for users of statistical software such as Microsoft Access, SPSS, WesVar, and Microsoft Excel). The primary objective of this section is to enable the national assessment team to develop and implement a systematic set of procedures to help ensure that the assessment data are accurate and reliable.

Following sampling, test administration, and data entry and cleaning, the next step is to prepare data for analysis. Part IV ("Weighting, Estimation, and Sampling Error") describes a series of important preanalysis steps, including producing estimates, computing and using survey weights, and computing estimates. The exercises build on the earlier work carried out on the Sentz data set (in part II). The section dealing with the computation of estimates describes how they and their sampling errors are computed from simple and complex samples, such as those prepared for Sentz. Finally, a range of special topics, including nonresponse and issues relating to oversize and undersize schools, is addressed.

The procedures described in this volume (and in volumes 2 and 4) are designed to ensure the quality of a national assessment. The importance of adopting appropriate procedures is reiterated throughout part I when it addresses the various components of an assessment:

- Recruiting a competent team to carry out the assessment
- Deciding on the staffing, facilities, and equipment required to carry out a large-scale survey
- Monitoring the quality of items produced by item writers
- Training and monitoring the performance of the individuals who collect data in schools
- Monitoring the accuracy of scoring and data recording
- Ensuring that statistical analyses of data collected in the assessment are appropriate and address issues of concern to policy makers, education managers, and other stakeholders

The quality of some components of a national assessment is often taken for granted, presumably on the assumption that personnel responsible for the components have the required expertise. However, that assumption may not always be warranted. For example, although one might assume that individuals with experience in the development of public examinations would have the skills required for a national assessment, very different approaches are required in developing tests for selection of students and developing tests to describe the achievement levels of the education system. Whatever the background, knowledge, or skills of personnel who carry out a national assessment, a need exists for studies or reviews, carried out perhaps by an external consultant, to assess the quality of some of the components of the assessment (for example, the tests used to assess students' achievement or the appropriateness of the sampling procedures that were used).

Quality assurance requires a planned and systematic set of actions to provide evidence that a national assessment has been implemented to a high professional standard. In chapter 5 of volume 1 of this series, *Assessing National Achievement Levels in Education*, a number of issues are identified that are relevant to the confidence that stakeholders can have in the results of an assessment. Activities for five components of a national assessment (design, implementation, data analysis, report writing, and dissemination and use of findings) are identified, and suggestions are made of activities that should serve to enhance confidence. Common errors in national assessments for each component are also identified. The issues could be used to form a checklist that a national assessment team could use to assess the quality of its work.

Specific quality assurance measures are usually built into several components of a national assessment: test development, administration of tests in schools, the scoring of test items, data entry, and data cleaning. Measures for training test developers and scorers and for checking the quality of scoring are described in volume 2 of this series, *Developing Tests and Questionnaires for a National Assessment of Educational Achievement*. Issues relating to the quality assurance of test administration in schools, which requires particular scrutiny because it is an area in which departure from standards can easily occur, are addressed in chapter 4 of this volume. Procedures to address issues of quality in data recording, data cleaning, and data management are described in part III (chapters 9 to 13).

Although standards exist for conducting a national assessment, those responsible for implementation will at varying times need to exercise judgment (for example, in sampling and analysis). They may, on occasion, also require the advice of more experienced practitioners in making their judgments. And they should always be prepared to adapt their practice in light of developments in knowledge and technology that will inevitably occur in the coming years.

NOTES

1. In 2009–10, the premier software for SPSS was called Predictive Analytic Software (PASW).

2. The Web site is http://www.westat.com/westat/statistical_software/WesVar/index.cfm.

THE LOGISTICS OF A NATIONAL ASSESSMENT

Sarah J. Howie and Sylvia Acana

Part I provides an overview of the tasks involved in implementing a national assessment. It describes the important role a national steering or advisory committee, with representatives of the major stakeholders in the education system, can play in the design, planning, and implementation of an assessment and in the communication of its findings. The personnel and the facilities that are required to carry out an assessment are identified, and activities involved in preparation for an assessment, in its administration in schools, and following administration are outlined. Choices will be required at varying points in the assessment, depending on local circumstances, but the procedures adopted always have to meet basic standards. Otherwise, the quality of the assessment and, hence, the value of its findings, will be compromised.

Many of the topics dealt with in part I are considered in greater detail in later parts of this volume, as well as in other volumes in the series.

CHAPTER 1

PREPARING FOR THE NATIONAL ASSESSMENT: DESIGN AND PLANNING

This chapter describes the main issues to be considered in designing a national assessment. It outlines the value of establishing a committee to oversee design and implementation, and then identifies important planning issues, concluding with a description of budgetary issues.

NATIONAL STEERING COMMITTEE

In many, but not all, national assessments, the ministry of education appoints a national steering committee (NSC) or advisory committee to oversee design and implementation of the assessment. Such a committee has several advantages. First, the committee can help ensure that the assessment has status and will have credibility in the eyes of government agencies, teacher education institutions, organizations that represent teachers, and other key stakeholders in the broader community. Second, it can contribute to the identification of key policy questions to be addressed in the assessment. Third, it can act as a channel of communication between key educational stakeholders, an important consideration in both designing an assessment and increasing the likelihood that its results will play a role in policy formation and decision making. Fourth, an NSC can help resolve administrative and financial problems that might arise during implementation of the assessment. Finally, the committee can have an important role in dealing with possible negative reactions to the assessment from politicians, who may fear that publication of the findings will give rise to political debate that reflects on their stewardship, or from teacher representatives, who may perceive the assessment as a new form of accountability.

Composition of an NSC will vary from one education system to another, depending on the organization and power structure of the system. One would expect to see on the committee representatives of the ministry of education (especially policy analysts and curriculum bodies); of the agency implementing the assessment; of teachers, teacher educators, and parents; and of major ethnic, religious, and linguistic groups (see volume 1, *Assessing National Achievement Levels in Education*).

The size of the committee should reflect the need for a balance between the minimum number of stakeholders that should be represented and the costs and logistical efforts necessary to organize committee meetings. The latter is especially relevant in a country where committee members have to travel long distances and stay overnight to attend meetings. As noted in volume 1, the NSC should have a limited number of meetings. The need for meetings is likely to be greatest at the initial and final stages of the assessment.

DESIGN OF A NATIONAL ASSESSMENT

The team appointed to carry out an assessment should, from the outset, work closely with the NSC, if one has been established. The national assessment team and the NSC, together with the funding agency (usually the ministry of education), should reach agreement on the objectives, general design, and scope of the assessment, taking into account available resources, including personnel and budget. The actual drafting of the design might be entrusted to the NSC or to the national assessment team. The design should encompass the following decisions:

- Indicate the policy questions to be addressed.
- Specify the target population to be assessed.
- Indicate whether the assessment is to be based on a sample or on the entire target population (census).
- Identify the curriculum areas or constructs to be assessed.
- Describe the data collection instruments (tests and questionnaires) as well as the methods to be used to collect the data.
- Assign responsibility for developing tests and questionnaires.
- Specify the specific questions to be addressed in analyses.
- Assign responsibility for preparing final reports and other documents (for example, reports for policy makers), and decide on the number of copies of each report.
- Specify dissemination activities to ensure that the education system learns about—and benefits from—the results of the assessment.

One issue that should be taken into account in the design of a study is whether to monitor change over time by repeating an assessment at a future date. Also, it is important to consider whether the assessment will be carried out at more than one grade level to provide information on achievement at different levels of the education system. Account should also be taken of the budget that has been allocated and support services that can be provided at no additional cost.

PLANNING

A detailed plan for implementing the national assessment should build on and reflect the overall design. A *project plan* is a document that outlines the activities, tasks, duration, time frames, and people involved. The plan should do the following:

- Specify the scope of the national assessment.
- Identify major activities and tasks.
- Allocate resources for each activity in terms of the individuals responsible.
- Develop a schedule with start and completion dates for each activity.

The plan should serve as a reference for the entire project and as a basis for monitoring its progress. The NSC, for example, may use the plan to check discrepancies between achieved and planned deadlines, which would assist in managing the assessment.

Table 1.1 presents an example of a section of the project plan developed for South Africa. The overall plan, which covered many more activities than are presented here, applied to a period extending from early 2004 to December 2006.

The plan for the national assessment should take into account the timing of the release of funds. Recruiting personnel and procuring services and equipment are unwise until funds for recurrent and capital costs are guaranteed.

Many national assessment plans have unrealistic time estimates. In developing countries, in particular, a wide range of problems should be anticipated relating to delays in hiring personnel; finding qualified experts; obtaining up-to-date, accurate data on schools and student numbers; training local staff members on specific tasks (for example, item writing, sampling, statistical analysis); piloting and developing final versions of achievement tests; getting permission to administer tests and questionnaires; printing materials; and cleaning data. Time estimates that are based on international studies of achievement or studies in industrial countries are likely to be inappropriate, because such studies do not normally encounter problems such as inadequacies in communication and transport systems, interruptions in the supply of electricity, and work practices and constraints that limit the amount of time individuals can devote to national assessment tasks.

BUDGETING

Having a realistic budget and obtaining sufficient funding for large-scale assessments are fundamental. Several national assessment efforts have failed because of gross underbudgeting. Because no established formula exists for estimating the cost of a national assessment, the national assessment team might start with a crude budget based on the various phases of the project and then begin to refine it. The design of the assessment should reflect the available budget. Alternatively,

TABLE 1.1

Excerpt from a National Assessment Project Plan

Main activity and subactivities	Duration	Hours of work needed	Start date	Finish date	Person
Plan and convene NSC meeting.	1 month	40	05/01/04	05/02/04	
Identify and contact participants.					
Determine suitable date for meeting.					
Organize transportation, venue, accommodation, meeting, and refreshments.					
Send out invitations.					
Specify an assessment framework.	1 month	120	05/01/04	05/02/04	
Select sample of schools.	2 months	160	05/02/04	05/04/04	
Specify target population.					
Contact Department of Education for school data.					
Prepare school and within-school sampling procedures.					
Draw sample.					
Finalize sample.					
Develop instruments.	4 months	640	20/02/04	30/06/04	
Develop, edit, and finalize items and scoring guides.					
Identify item writers.					
Appoint item writers.					
Train item writers.					
Draft test items, sample items, and administration manual.					
Review test items.					
Pilot test items.					

(continued)

TABLE 1.1

Excerpt from a National Assessment Project Plan *(continued)*

Main activity and subactivities	Duration	Hours of work needed	Start date	Finish date	Person
Develop scoring guides.					
Score test items.					
After formal review, select final set of test items and sample items.					
Complete artwork and test layout.					
Estimate time allowed for each test.					
Prepare administration manual and scoring guides.					

Source: Adapted from Howie 2004.

given a predetermined budget, adaptations can be made to an initial design. If possible, assessment experts and financial decision makers should be involved in budgetary discussions.

In developing a budget, all major activities in the assessment design should be listed, and timelines and costs should be allocated to each item (activity and subactivity or task) (see Greaney and Kellaghan 2008; Ilon 1996). This process may take several days to complete. Conditions and costs will vary widely from country to country. National pay rates for specific task types are normally taken into consideration. In some instances, adjustments may have to be made to reflect skill shortages in key professional areas (such as statistical analysis). Budgetary provision should be made for likely salary increases over the life of the assessment (normally two to three years), for inflation, and for unexpected events (contingencies).

Funding Checklist

The checklist presented in table 1.2 lists the major expense items normally associated with a national assessment. Because circumstances will vary from country to country, some items may not be relevant in

TABLE 1.2

National Assessment Funding Checklist

Items	Source of funding		
	Dedicated national assessment funds	Other funds	Not funded
Personnel			
Facilities and equipment			
Design of assessment framework			
Instrument design and development			
Training (for example, item writing, data gathering)			
Pilot-testing			
Translation			
Printing			
National steering committee			
Local travel (to schools)			
Data collection			
Data scoring (open-ended)			
Data recording			
Data processing and cleaning			
Data analysis			
Report writing			
Printing of reports			
Press release and publicity			
Conference on results			
Consumables			
Communications			
Follow-on activities			

Source: Authors' compilation.

some assessments. In some countries, data gathering in a national assessment has taken up to 50 percent of the budget, whereas in one country, data recording used approximately 20 percent of the budget. The costs to be borne by existing agencies should be established at the outset. For example, the ministry of education might carry the costs of the time school inspectors spend in administering the assessment instruments, or a national census bureau might provide the services of a sampling expert.

CHAPTER **2**

PERSONNEL AND FACILITIES REQUIRED IN A NATIONAL ASSESSMENT

If one accepts that the reason for carrying out a national assessment is to provide valid information about the achievements of students in the education system, then decisions regarding the personnel who will carry out the assessment and the facilities they will need are crucial. All sorts of problems can be anticipated if personnel are not competent or if facilities are inadequate. For example, the test used may not provide valid and reliable information about student achievement in the curriculum area or construct being assessed; the sample that is selected may not adequately represent the target population; the students that take the tests may not be the ones who were selected; test administrators may not follow precisely directions for test administration; data collected in schools may not be correctly entered in the database; the statistical analysis of data may not be appropriate; unwarranted conclusions (for example, regarding causation) may be drawn; and reports may provide inadequate information on technical aspects of the study, content of achievement tests, methods used, or error and bias in estimates. This chapter describes the staffing and the basic facilities and equipment required in a national assessment to help prevent these problems, thus contributing to the quality of the exercise. Planning for quality control needs to start with project planning.

STAFF REQUIREMENTS

As a general principle, not only should personnel have specialist skills; they should also be committed and open-minded, attentive to detail, and willing to put in additional hours beyond the normal workday. From the point of view of technical adequacy and efficiency, these attributes are more important than seniority within a government department or within an academic institution.

The level of funding provided for the national assessment will determine to a considerable extent the number and skill levels of key staff members. The design or planning proposal can help clarify the roles and functions of staff members. Thus, identification of the target population (for example, grade level) and of the curriculum areas or constructs to be assessed will indicate the knowledge and skills that will be required of item writers, whereas a decision to base the assessment on a sample rather than on the whole population will point to the need for a person skilled in probability sampling. Some staff members (for example, item writers, test administrators, or data entry personnel) will be employed on a temporary basis at various stages. This section describes the role of key or core staff members (for example, the national coordinator) as well as the roles of additional personnel, such as test administrators, who will be required to carry out the assessment.

National Coordinator

The national coordinator (NC)[1] should give general direction and provide leadership throughout the planning and implementation stages of the national assessment. The NC should help ensure that the assessment

- Addresses the key policy questions requested by the ministry
- Is technically adequate
- Is carried out on time and within budget

The NC should be respected within the educational community and should have access to key educational stakeholders and to the main sources of funding. He or she should be able to see the "big picture." NCs have been recruited from public examination boards, national ministries of education, universities, and research institutions. NCs should be familiar with key concepts in educational measurement and with the curriculum or construct being assessed. They should have extensive experience in test development as well as in project management and in management of large groups of people. They should have strong leadership and good communication skills. Some of the key responsibilities of the NC might include

* Liaising with national organizations and bodies concerned with education and reporting to a national steering committee
* Managing the personnel and budget at each phase of the assessment
* Providing training and leadership for item writers
* Reviewing tests, questionnaires, and related materials to ensure that contents are appropriate and free of bias (for example, relating to males and females, urban and rural students, or ethnic group membership)
* Providing advice on the interpretation of test results
* Coordinating and ensuring the quality of publications that follow the national assessment
* Managing public relations, including the conduct of awareness and sensitization seminars during and after the national assessment

Assistant National Coordinator

An assistant national coordinator may be required depending on the structure of the education system, the scope of the assessment, the time demands on the NC, and the availability of funding. The assistant NC should have many of the attributes required of the NC and should support and serve as a substitute for the NC when necessary. He or she might be assigned primary responsibility for particular aspects of the assessment, such as test development or data management, or might focus on operational and logistical issues. Detailed knowledge of the overall national assessment implementation plan is essential.

Regional Coordinators

In large countries with regional administrative systems, the national assessment team should consider appointing regional coordinators to organize testing and to liaise with schools and test administrators. Such coordinators would be responsible for allocating and delivering materials to the test administrators and should check the contents of boxes coming from the central office. They would also be responsible for materials returned from schools following test and questionnaire administration. Under this arrangement, the coordinator's office would become the regional office and the storage facility for assessment instruments.

Item Writers

Experience suggests that practicing teachers with a good command of the curriculum make effective item writers. It is a good idea to ensure that teachers are drawn from different types of schools, including rural and remote schools. Academics, public examination officials, and school inspectors have been used to draft pilot items for some national assessments. The experience has not always been positive, however, because these individuals often lack contact with classroom realities and may have unrealistically high expectations of student achievement standards.

Item writers should be trained in how to analyze the curriculum, develop learning objectives, identify the common misconceptions and errors of students, write items that provide diagnostic information, and judge the quality of pilot-test items in terms of both content and statistical properties. They are normally recruited on a part-time basis. After a trial period, the test development coordinator may have to dispense with the services of some individuals who fail to produce good items or who are careless in terms of attention to detail or in filing.

Statistician

A statistician is responsible for the technical adequacy of statistical analyses. He or she is likely to be involved in designing an assessment, in developing a national sampling frame, and in drawing the representative sample used in the national assessment. He or she also helps interpret pilot and final test results, may be involved in database construction, and guides or carries out analyses of the results of the assessment. Volume 4 in this series, *Analyzing Data from a National Assessment of Educational Achievement*, describes many of the statistical tasks involved in an assessment. The statistician should be competent in the use of SPSS (Statistical Package for the Social Sciences), WesVar, Excel, and Access.

The services of a statistician may not be required on a full-time basis. The statistical workload is likely to be heavy at the initial stage, when the focus is on the design and, in particular, on the sampling and piloting of instruments, and again after data have been collected and cleaned.

Sources of competent statisticians include universities and some government departments. The national census bureau can be a particularly good source. In some instances, recruiting the services of an external, nonnational statistician may be necessary to assist in sampling, analysis, and interpretation of results. If an external statistician is recruited, he or she should be expected to help develop technical capacity within the national assessment team.

Data Manager

Ultimately, the data manager (DM) bears a good deal of responsibility for the quality of the data used in analyses. In particular, he or she is responsible for the accuracy of data—specifically for the correct coding, cleaning, and recording of test and questionnaire data. He or she will have a working knowledge of Microsoft Word, Excel, and Access as well as SPSS and WesVar. Ideally, he or she should also have extensive data management experience, should be appointed at the beginning of the assessment, and should be involved in sampling and in designing and coding instruments.

With the agreement of the NC, and together with the survey statistician working on the sampling frame and design, the DM prepares the numbering scheme and procedures that will be used during the assessment. This scheme should apply to schools, classes, and students.

The numbering scheme is a key component of quality control. It is required for sampling activities and must be implemented, at the latest, at the time of sample selection. The DM should ensure that individual student booklets, questionnaires, and answer sheets (if used) can be identified by numbering them before sending out materials for administration. Prior numbering is critical for monitoring student participation rates and for checking on the security of the materials.

School identifier numbers from the education management information system may be used to identify schools selected for an assessment. An alternative is to catalog schools by using a numbering system that identifies the province or region, school, and individual pupil. Box 2.1 gives examples of two such numbering systems. The first identifies individual schools; the second identifies not just individual schools but also participating students within schools.

A computer programmer, or someone with sufficient knowledge of and experience with setting up and managing databases, will be required at critical points during the assessment. In some instances, the same person may be called on to play various roles: programmer and data manager, or data manager and statistician, depending on the expertise available locally. Part III deals with data cleaning and management, key skills required of a DM.

BOX 2.1

Numbering Systems Used in National Assessments

The following are examples of numbering systems used in national assessments:

1. A four-digit figure is used. The first digit represents the region, the second the zone, the third the district, and the last the school. Number 5342 refers to school number 2, which is located in district 4, in zone 3, in region 5.

2. Six digits are used. The first digit indicates the province, the next three digits indicate the school number, and the last two digits are the pupil's identification code. For example, pupil number 200537 refers to a student located in province 2, in the fifth school on the list, and he or she is the 37th pupil on the class list.

Source: Authors' compilation.

Designer or Graphics Person

A designer or graphics person has responsibility for giving a professional appearance to all tests, questionnaires, manuals, and reports associated with the national assessment. He or she should provide the pictorial representations linked to test items as well as charts and graphs and other visuals used in reports. Sources of experienced personnel include publishing firms and printing houses. A designer or graphics person should be available when needed and should be given sufficient notice of likely time demands. The CD that accompanies volume 2, *Developing Tests and Questionnaires for a National Assessment of Educational Achievement*, contains examples of well-presented test items with supportive pictorial and graphical material.

Translators

Many countries have large populations of students who do not share a common language, in which case instruments may need to be translated. Clearly, translators should have a high level of competence in the languages involved in the translation and should be familiar with the content of the material they are translating. A minimum of two translators per language is advisable. Both may translate the same test simultaneously, compare results, and where inconsistencies arise, reach agreement through discussion. This process is termed *simultaneous translation*. An alternative is to have one person translate from the first language into the second and then give the translated test to the other translator who then translates from the second language back into the first. Versions are compared, and again through a process of discussion, discrepancies are resolved. This process is termed *back translation*. Despite the best efforts of translators, for a variety of reasons, including differences between languages in their structure, achieving precise equivalence between a test and its translated version may prove very difficult or even impossible.

Pilot tests provide a good opportunity for removing linguistically difficult terms or words. In Ghana, for example, pupils were asked to translate some words (from English) into local languages during a pilot test to identify commonly misunderstood words. In a somewhat similar fashion, South African children underlined words they did not understand during the pilot-testing phase; this information helped modify items for the main study. The services of translators are normally required only during the preparation of the pilot and final versions of tests and questionnaires and when reports are being prepared for publication.

School Liaison Person

The school liaison person or school coordinator could be a teacher or guidance counselor in a school, but he or she should not be teaching students selected for the assessment. Frequently, the school principal serves in this role. The school liaison person serves as a contact point in schools for the national assessment team and helps ensure that school personnel are aware of the assessment. He or she arranges the test venue, sets testing times and dates with pupils and their teachers, and meets the assessment team on the day of testing. The school liaison person should coordinate the completion of student tracking forms and distribute teacher and school questionnaires. He or she is responsible for ensuring that all testing materials are received and kept secure and are returned to the national or regional center following test administration. He or she should also strive to ensure that the classroom used for the assessment is sufficiently large to accommodate all students selected to take the tests, allowing adequate space between them to prevent communication with others and copying. The school liaison person essentially supports the assessment team by making all the arrangements necessary to ensure the orderly conduct of the assessment in a school.

Data Recorders

Some national assessment teams use professional data entry personnel to record or capture data from tests and questionnaires. Individuals selected to perform this task should have experience and a record of speed and precision in entering data. Careless data recording can undermine the quality of the assessment. An alternative to in-house data recording is contracting the work to an external agency. In this case, one or more members of the assessment team should routinely check the quality of the work. Whether data recording is conducted in house or is outsourced, quality control is essential. Electronic scanners are increasingly being used to record test and questionnaire data, which are then filed for data cleaning and analysis. In some countries, however, access to scanners or to necessary backup maintenance services is not available.

Test Administrators

In some countries, classroom teachers administer national assessment tests to their own students. More often than not, however, teachers other than those who teach the students who are taking the test or individuals who are external to the school are entrusted with this task. Local work practices, levels of financial reward, and availability of personnel play important roles in selecting test administrators. Test administration personnel have included teachers (including retired teachers), school inspectors, teacher trainers, public examination officials, and university students (especially students in education and psychology programs). In some countries, data collection is contracted to a body that specializes in that activity. Potential administrators should have the following characteristics:

- Good organizational and communication skills
- Experience working in schools
- Reliability, and ability and willingness to follow instructions precisely

Some possible advantages and disadvantages of using personnel from different backgrounds are summarized in table 2.1. Providing clear guidelines and intensive training can help address any disadvantages that exist.

Because faulty test administration tends to be the most common source of error in a national assessment, particular attention should be paid to selecting, training, and supervising test and questionnaire administrators. Above all, persons assigned this position should be trustworthy, responsible, and committed.

Test administrators should

- Ensure that teachers and other staff members are not present in the room when tests are being administered.

TABLE 2.1

Advantages and Disadvantages of Categories of Personnel for Test Administration

Category	Advantages	Disadvantages
Teachers	Are professionally qualified	May have difficulty unlearning usual practices (for example, helping students) and learning new ways of dealing with pupils
	Are familiar with the children	May feel they are also being assessed and may try to help the children (if their own class is being assessed)
	May be less expensive than others, especially in terms of travel and subsistence	May be difficult and costly to organize and train
	Are likely to be fluent in the area or local language	
Inspectors and teacher trainers	Are likely to have classroom experience	Might be overly authoritarian
	Will become involved as partners in the national assessment, which may give them an interest in the outcomes	Might be tempted to conduct inspection activities in addition to administering tests
	Are likely to know the location of most schools	Are likely to be more costly than teachers
		May feel they need not follow the detailed instructions in the manual
University students	Are readily available, especially during university vacations	May not be very reliable
	Are likely to follow instructions	May lack the authority required to deal with managers, principals, and others
	Are more likely than others to withstand harsh travel conditions	Are difficult to hold accountable
	Can often use a work opportunity	May not be fluent in the local language
	Are relatively inexpensive	May not communicate a sense of respect and authority in front of students

(continued)

TABLE 2.1

Advantages and Disadvantages of Categories of Personnel for Test Administration *(continued)*

Category	Advantages	Disadvantages
Assessment or examination board personnel	Are professionally qualified	May be too authoritarian, especially if they are used to supervising public exams
	Are directly accountable to the appointing authority	May lack recent classroom experience and therefore not exude a sense of authority in front of students
	Tend to be reliable	May lack experience at the particular educational level being tested
	Are good at recordkeeping	Are expensive to maintain in the field
	Tend to consult before making major decisions	May not be fluent in the local language

Source: Authors' compilation.

- Check to see that only students selected in the sample take the tests.
- Be familiar with and follow *precisely* test administration guidelines.
- Give loud and clear instructions.
- Ensure that students understand the procedure for recording their answers.
- Stick strictly to time limits.
- Guard against copying or other forms of communication between students.
- Collect all materials when testing is complete.
- Note and report any irregularities before, during, and after testing.

Test Scorers

In many national assessments, the responses to all or most items are entered into the data entry system and are scored by computer. When items are open ended, the services of scorers are required.

Test scorers should have an adequate knowledge of the subject matter being tested. In many countries, teachers are used for scoring. Recruiting teachers can be difficult during school term, however, when they may be available only outside school hours. Some national assessments use examination board personnel. Others engage the services of ministry of education staff or university students. Irrespective of their backgrounds or status, scorers must be trained specifically to score the particular national assessment tests. A member of the core team should monitor the quality of scoring on a daily basis and should dispense with the services of inaccurate scorers.

FACILITIES

Those involved in the administration of a national assessment need space for work and a range of equipment.

Space for Personnel

Core staff members require offices that are secure and equipped with computers. Space is needed for books and files. Part-time staff members also require some office space. Because national assessments tend to involve many meetings with subject-matter specialists, item writers, and others, access to a room that is large enough to accommodate group meetings is advisable.

Space for Organizing and Storing Instruments

Adequate provision needs to be made for the space requirements associated with packing tests for distribution to schools. Some national assessments hire a hall or other space in an institution of learning. The space requirements can be substantial (see box 2.2). Unpacking at least one school's test booklets and other required materials can be useful to obtain an idea of how much space will be needed to provide for all schools in the national assessment.

A large storage facility is required both before and after scoring, data entry, and data cleaning. If possible, a specific room should be set aside for data recording. It should provide adequate desktop working space, including computer space, for each of the data recorders. Ad-

---

BOX 2.2

Storage Requirements

The dimensions of the test booklets and questionnaires affect the height and depth of the shelving used for storage. Test booklets are typically printed on A4-size paper (210 × 297 millimeters or 8.27 × 11.69 inches). Most often, booklets are grouped by class and by school. If a test booklet in one subject area is 1.5 millimeter in thickness and the national sample includes 5,000 pupils, a minimum of 7.5 meters of storage space is required. Additional storage space will be needed for test booklets in other curriculum areas, for pupil and teacher questionnaires, and for administration and school coordinators' manuals, as well as for correspondence, packing material, and other documents associated with the national assessment.

Source: Authors' compilation.

---

ditional space will be needed for storing and organizing booklets that are being processed. Test booklets and questionnaires should be readily accessible because some items may have to be checked.

Equipment and Supplies

The amount and nature of equipment and supplies that are needed will vary depending on the size of the national assessment and local conditions. Essential basic equipment includes

- Telephones, desks, chairs, filing cabinets, shelving, packing tables, cupboards, and trolleys for transporting instruments
- Normal office supplies (stationery, pads, print cartridges, discs, tapes, punches, scissors, staplers, pens, pencils, packing tape, string, labels, glue, and thick pens)
- Packing paper and boxes or bags
- Vehicles for transporting tests and other materials as needed

The available budget will help determine the amount and quality of technical equipment. Some national assessment teams (for example, in ministries of education or in universities) may have access to electronic equipment such as computers, software (such as Microsoft Office and SPSS), printers, photocopiers, scanners, and fax machines. Other teams may have to purchase or rent some equipment. Appropriate software can enhance accuracy and efficiency, especially in areas such as data recording, entry, cleaning, and analysis, as well as graphic design.

NOTE

1. Other terms may be used in some countries.

PREPARATION FOR ADMINISTRATION IN SCHOOLS

The national coordinator should inform schools that they have been selected for the national assessment as soon as possible after sample selection. Inviting them to participate is a courtesy. Experience to date suggests that the vast majority of public schools in developing countries are willing to take part in a national assessment. In some countries, schools have the option of refusing to participate. Most likely private schools (which are not included in many national assessments) would have such an option. In many jurisdictions, the refusal option is not open to public schools.

In some countries, the permission of parents is required for their children's participation in an assessment, in which case arrangements must be made to obtain it. Asking parents to respond only if they are refusing permission may be sufficient. In this case, if parents do not respond, their agreement is assumed.

This chapter describes preparatory steps in the administration of a national assessment. These steps involve contacting schools, organizing instruments, and preparing schools.

CONTACTING SCHOOLS

If required, the permission of the ministry of education or regional education authority should be obtained before schools are contacted.

When schools are contacted and invited to participate, they should be asked to acknowledge receipt of the invitation. The initial communication should be followed up on a regular basis right up to the day before testing. The school should be asked to appoint a contact person, school liaison person, or coordinator for the assessment. The national assessment team should strive to ensure that it establishes and maintains a good rapport with local education authorities, if they exist.

Informing Schools

Many schools, especially at primary level, prefer letters, which they can file. In Uganda, the national assessment agency sends letters to all selected schools as well as to each district education office. This step is followed by telephone calls (using mainly cell phones) and notes delivered by *bodaboda* (bicycle and motorcycle riders hired to transport people or luggage).

The first communication should inform schools that they have been selected to participate in a national assessment (see box 3.1). It should also include provisional dates for test administration. A reminder note, which should reach the schools about a month before testing, should give the exact date and more details about the actual assessment exercise. Confirming the school's participation two weeks prior to testing, and again the day before the event, is advisable.

The national assessment team should keep an updated list or tracking form of participating schools to help monitor fieldwork progress. The form will provide information on schools, such as school name, size, and contact information (see table 3.1).

Replacing Schools

Insofar as possible, after schools have been selected, they should not be changed or replaced. Despite the best efforts of a national assessment team, however, some school replacements may be necessary. Should the need to replace schools be anticipated, that possibility should be discussed with the sampling statistician so that adequate sampling procedures are implemented and replacement schools are properly

BOX 3.1

Example of a Letter to Schools

Dear _____,

I am writing to seek your support for the 2012 National Assessment of Mathematics Achievement (NAMA), which is being conducted by the National Research Center for Educational Research.

As you may know, the level of student achievement in mathematics in the education system is assessed every five years. In October 2012, data will be collected from sixth-grade students in 160 schools across the country. Students will be tested for two 1-hour periods during the third week of October. Your school has been randomly selected to participate in this important national study.

Your local school inspector will visit you over the next two months to answer any questions you may have and to discuss your school's participation. The precise dates of testing will be confirmed over the local radio. A representative of the National Research Center for Educational Research will administer the test and a short questionnaire to the students and will also request you and the class teacher to complete questionnaires. All information collected in your school will be treated in confidence, and results for individual students or schools will not be made available to anyone. Rather, information collected will be used by the Ministry of Education to help identify the strengths and weaknesses of learning in the system. The ministry requires the information to help it improve the quality of learning of our students, and NAMA has the support and approval of the National Union of Teachers.

You do not need to make elaborate preparations for the assessment, but please inform the pupils the week before the assessment. Students do not need to prepare for the test. Each student will be given a pencil to complete the test and questionnaire and will be allowed to keep the pencil after the assessment has been completed.

Yours sincerely,

Director
National Research Center for Educational Research

Source: Authors' compilation.

TABLE 3.1

National Assessment: School Tracking Form

Priority of school[a]	School ID	Name, address, phone number of school	Name and phone number of school coordinator	School size	Status (participant or nonparticipant)	Date materials sent	Date materials received	Date of testing
1								
1								
1								
1								
1								
1								
1								
1								
1								
2								
2								
2								
2								
2								

Source: Adapted from TIMSS 1998c.

a. Schools selected from the sample are priority 1. Replacement schools are priority 2.

selected. Under no circumstances should the selection of replacement schools be left to the discretion of the test administrator or local school official. This topic is discussed further in part II of this volume.

ORGANIZING INSTRUMENTS

The national coordinator or his or her appointee should check the quality of all tests, questionnaires, and manuals to ensure the following:

- Spelling and typographical errors are removed.
- Font size in test booklets is sufficiently large. Large font sizes are particularly important for young children. A 14-point font is recommended for grades 3 and 4, and a 12-point font for higher grades. One set of national achievement tests uses a 16-point font for grades 1 and 2; a 13-point font for grades 3, 4, and 5; and a 12-point font for grade 6. Question or item numbers should use a larger font.
- Adequate spacing is used between lines of text.
- Diagrams are simple and clear. Where possible, they should be on the same page as the relevant text.

A qualified data entry person who is familiar with computer packages such as Microsoft Office should type tests, questionnaires, and other materials. Manuscript secretaries employed by examination boards have considerable experience, both in laying out questions and accompanying graphics and in ensuring the security of tests. Cost-saving measures that should be considered at this stage include

- Preparing test booklets to fit on an even number of pages
- Careful proofreading, especially of final drafts, which can help prevent reprinting of test booklets necessitated by serious typographical or graphical errors
- Giving the printer adequate time to print tests and questionnaires to avoid paying overtime rates when the assignment has to be completed over a relatively short time or when the printer has other priorities

Three people should independently proofread final drafts of all the materials used in a national assessment. This system is preferable to asking the same proofreader to examine each document three times. When print runs are ordered, additional copies should be requested for each school package in anticipation of the need for replacement schools and of some spoilage. Volume 2 of this series, *Developing Tests and Questionnaires for a National Assessment of Educational Achievement*, has an extensive section on layout and printing.

PREPARING SCHOOLS

Effective national assessment team leaders plan thoroughly and well in advance of administration of the assessment in schools. They also tend to delegate responsibility while retaining overall control of the preparation process through quality control measures, in particular spot-checking the work of others.

Packing

A set of packing procedures should be established and documented. Box 3.2 provides a sample set. A packing checklist is required. National assessment staff members should sign and date the appropriate boxes in the "Packed" and "Returned" columns in the packing checklist. The school liaison person is expected to do the same in the boxes in the "Received" columns after checking the material sent from the national assessment office. Table 3.2 presents a copy of a checklist used in the South African assessment.

Delivery

Local circumstances will determine the most appropriate and cost-effective method of delivering and collecting materials for the national assessment. In some instances, materials are delivered to central offices that are secure (for example, district education or local government offices), and test administrators collect them using public transportation. In other cases, where secure and reliable delivery systems exist, materials are delivered to test administrators' homes. Sometimes, teams of administrators travel together in a van and are dropped off with the necessary materials at schools.

BOX 3.2

Packing Instruments

The following are typical procedures for packing instruments:

- Group booklets in units of 20.
- Arrange units in order before packing into envelopes.
- Manually check a number of samples when booklets are machine counted.
- Include additional tests for unexpected circumstances (for example, additional pupils).
- Use strong but affordable packing materials (for example, plastic envelopes).
- Record the contents of each package and add packers' signatures to the sheets as each set of items is packed.
- Label each package clearly and boldly.
- Add a colored sticker or mark to show that packing has been completed.
- Label each carton on at least two sides.
- Prepare a packing checklist (see table 3.2) so that test administrators can check that they have the necessary materials.
- Make one bundle of materials for each school.
- Pack the materials for one district in a strong carton or bag.

Source: Authors' compilation.

Test Administration Manual

In the interest of efficiency and to limit the number of documents test administrators have to carry, the key information related to timing, student preparation, packing and returning of tests and question-naires, and instructions for administration should be included in one document—the test administration manual. Instructions that are read aloud to pupils should be in large, bold print. A person entrusted with training test administrators should go through the entire manual with at least a sample of test administrators prior to formal training of the selected administrators. No matter how well they claim to be quali-fied, test administrators should not be left to go through the manual on their own. In volume 2, *Developing Tests and Questionnaires for a National Assessment of Educational Achievement*, the development of the test administration manual is described in some detail.

TABLE 3.2

Packing Checklist

Number	Item	Packed	Received	Returned
40	Student booklets			
40	Student questionnaires			
45	Pencils			
45	Erasers			
5	Extra booklets			
5	Extra questionnaires			
45	Rubber bands			
3	Self-addressed envelopes			
2	Test administration forms			
1	Student tracking form			

Source: Authors' compilation.

Training Location

The location for training test administrators will depend mainly on the size of the country and the number of administrators. If possible, it is best to provide training in one central location. In a large country, training may have to be carried out in a number of locations.

CHAPTER 4

ADMINISTRATION IN SCHOOLS

This chapter outlines the role of the test administrator. Then it describes problems frequently encountered in test administration and procedures to enhance the quality of the exercise.

THE TEST ADMINISTRATOR

Test administrators, if external to the school, should follow conventional procedures for school visits, including reporting to the school principal's office (if it exists).

In some national assessments, test administration is carried out at the same time in all schools, usually over one or two days. In others, test administrators travel from school to school over a short period. In the latter case, care has to be taken to maintain the security of test materials and to ensure that test-related information is not exchanged between schools. The temptation to obtain information about tests before administration is likely to be particularly strong in education systems that have a tradition of high-stakes testing, because in this situation some teachers may feel that they or their schools are being evaluated. This situation can arise even when the initial letter to schools and announcements in the public media make clear that the education system as a whole, not individual teachers or schools, is being evaluated.

When test administrators travel to a region and test in a number of schools in the same locality in one week, they will normally carry only those materials they need to use during a single day of testing.

The national assessment team should ensure that each test administrator has, or has access to, a timing device to be used during test administration. In one national assessment that overlooked this requirement, almost 50 percent of test administrators were found not to have access to a watch or clock during test administration. The role of the test administrator during testing is described in volume 2 of this series, *Developing Tests and Questionnaires for a National Assessment of Educational Achievement*. Issues related to test instructions, level of assistance to students, timing, and materials allowed in the testing location are addressed.

The test administrator is responsible for ensuring that teachers do not help students and that students do not copy from each other or bring unauthorized materials into the room. School conditions will dictate seating arrangement options. The test administrator should check that desks are free of books and other materials prior to testing. National assessments that use more than one form of a test reduce the possibility of copying by requiring students seated near each other to take different versions of the test.

Student Tracking Form

The design of a national assessment will specify how students are to be selected within a school. If selection of an intact class is specified, it may be done in advance of administration by the national assessment center, or instructions may be given to the test administrator on how to select the class. If the design of the assessment specifies the selection of students from across all classes at the relevant grade level, again the national assessment center may select the students prior to administration or the test administrator will be instructed on how they are to be selected.

During test administration, the test administrator should complete a student tracking form, which is sent to schools with test booklets

BOX 4.1

Student Tracking Form

School name: _____

School ID	Class ID	Class name	Grade

Student name	Student ID	Date of birth	Gender	Excluded	Drop-out	Session	Replace-ment session

Source: Authors' compilation.

and questionnaires. Information from this form will be needed at the data cleaning and analysis stages (for example, in weighting data). Information recorded on the tracking form usually includes each student's name, assigned identifier (ID) number, date of birth, gender, and record of attendance at individual testing sessions and, where applicable, replacement sessions (see box 4.1). If the testing requires more than one session, the student's presence should be noted for each session.

The form in box 4.1 includes a column that identifies excluded students. These students may have a disability, may be recent immigrants, or may be unfamiliar with the language used in the test and are excused on the grounds that the assessment would be unfair to them. The form also includes a column that identifies dropouts—that is, students who were listed in the population compiled at the beginning of the school year but who subsequently left the school.

Return of Instruments

The test administrator must ensure that all tests and questionnaires, used and unused, are kept secure and are returned to the national assessment center. This step is important because items, and in some instances an entire test, might be used in a subsequent national assessment. If some teachers and students have prior access to those items, the credibility of the subsequent assessment would be undermined. The paper or rough notes used by students while doing the tests should also be returned to the national assessment office. Packing instructions should be provided for test administrators (see box 3.2). Methods of returning materials tend to be the same as methods of delivery.

Clear instructions should be provided on how returns from schools to the national assessment center should be organized. A large space is required to accommodate returns. Returned instruments should be sorted and placed on clearly labeled shelves. Tests and questionnaires should be stored so that they can be easily retrieved for data entry and data cleaning. All returns should be recorded in a returns book or in a computer database (not on a piece of paper).

COMMON ADMINISTRATION PROBLEMS

Problems associated with administering a national assessment tend to vary from country to country in both nature and magnitude. The more serious the problem, the more it undermines the entire national assessment enterprise. From the outset, the national assessment team should ensure that the sampled schools are in fact the ones in which students are being assessed. In one country, district officials are known to have insisted, after the national sample had been drawn, that different political constituencies be represented in the final selection. Some teams have discovered "ghost" (bogus) schools after using national data sources for sampling purposes. The test administrator and the school liaison person should establish that the pupils who take the tests are in fact the pupils who were selected for participation. School lists or enrollment data may be inflated, especially in situations where school grants are based on pupil enrollment data. It is not uncommon for teachers to want to substitute pupils on the basis that "only dull ones were selected."

The following are other problems that have been identified in administration:

- Date of testing clashing with a school event
- Pupils completing the first section of the test and leaving school before the second section
- Teachers and pupils arriving late
- Teachers, and even the principal, insisting on remaining in the class while students are taking the test
- Lack of adequate seating arrangements for test taking
- Failure to stick to time limits
- Test administrator or others giving assistance to students
- Copying by pupils

Low Participation Rates

High levels of participation are required in a national assessment to provide valid information on student achievement in the education system. International Association for the Evaluation of Educational Achievement (IEA) studies, for example, require (a) a participation rate of at least 85 percent for both schools and students or (b) a combined rate (the product of school and student participation) of 75 percent (see part IV). IEA also sets the upper limit of exclusions (on grounds such as school remoteness and disability) at 5 percent of the desired target population. In an effort to improve the level of school cooperation in one country, replacement sessions were held at a later date for students who had been absent for the initial testing session. This experience suggested that students and schools tended to cooperate more fully when they realized that the test administrators would keep returning until all selected pupils had been tested.

QUALITY ASSURANCE

To monitor the quality of test administration, the test administrator should complete a test administration form (box 4.2) after work in an

BOX 4.2

Test Administration Form

Complete one form per testing session.

Name of test administrator: _____

School ID: _____

School name: _____

Class name: _____

School liaison person: _____

Original testing session: _____

Replacement testing session (if applicable): _____

Date of testing: _____

Time of testing

Start time	End time	Details
		Administration of test materials
		Testing session 1
		Testing session 2
		Testing session 3
		Testing session 4

1. Did any special circumstances or unusual events occur during the session?

   NO _____

   YES _____ *Please provide the details.*

   _____

2. Did students have any particular problems with the testing (for example, tests too difficult, not enough time provided, language problems, tiring, instructions not clear)?

   NO _____

   YES _____ *Please provide the details.*

   _____

3. Were there any problems with the testing materials (for example, errors, blank pages, inappropriate language, omissions in the student tracking forms, inadequate numbers of tests or questionnaires)?

   NO _____

   YES _____ *Please provide the details.*

   _____

Source: TIMSS 1998a. Reprinted with permission.

individual school has been completed. The form will provide a record of the extent to which proper administrative procedures were followed.

To check further if testing has been carried out following prescribed procedures, many national assessments appoint a small number of quality control monitors to make unannounced visits to schools. Although all test administrators should know that a possibility exists that they will be monitored, in practice, usually only 10 to 20 percent of schools are visited. Quality control personnel should be familiar with the purpose of the national assessment, the sampling design and its significance, the roles of the school coordinator and test administrator, the content of tests and questionnaires, and the classroom observation record. They should be briefed on how to conduct school visits without disrupting the actual assessment. Monitors should complete a form on administrative and other conditions in each school visited. Examples of the activities for which information is recorded in the form used for TIMSS (Trends in International Mathematics and Science Study) are provided in box 4.3.

BOX 4.3

Examples of Questions Addressed by Quality Control Monitors in TIMSS

1. **Preliminary activities of the test administrator**

   Did the test administrator verify adequate supplies of test booklets?

   Were all the seals intact on the test booklets prior to distribution?

   Was there adequate seating space for the students to work without distraction?

   Did the administrator have a stopwatch or timer?

   Did the test administrator have an adequate supply of pencils and other materials?

2. **Test session activities**

   Did the test administrator follow the test administrator's script exactly in (a) preparing the students, (b) distributing materials, and (c) beginning testing?

(continued)

BOX 4.3 *(continued)*

Did the test administrator record attendance correctly?

Did testing time equal the time allowed?

Did the test administrator collect test booklets one at a time from the students?

3. **General impressions**

During the testing session, did the test administrator walk around the room to ensure that students were working on the correct section of the test and behaving properly?

In your opinion, did the test administrator address students' questions appropriately?

Did you see any evidence of students attempting to cheat on the tests (for example, by copying from a neighbor)?

4. **Interview with the school coordinator**

Did you receive the correct shipment of items?

Was the national coordinator responsive to your questions or concerns?

Were you able to collect completed teacher questionnaires before test administration?

Were you satisfied with the accommodation (testing room) for the testing?

Do you anticipate that makeup sessions will be required at your school?

Did students receive any special instruction, motivational talk, or incentive to prepare them for the assessment?

Were students given any opportunity to practice questions like those in the test before the testing session?

Source: TIMSS 1998b. Reprinted with permission.

CHAPTER 5

TASKS FOLLOWING ADMINISTRATION

In this chapter, the tasks that remain following administration of instruments in schools and their return to the national assessment center are described: test scoring, data recording, data analysis, and report writing.

TEST SCORING

Some national assessments use multiple-choice items exclusively, and in a few, answer sheets are electronically scanned. Other assessments combine multiple-choice and open-ended items and score both by hand, which requires a considerable amount of time.

If a test includes more than one type of item, the order of the scoring or marking must be decided on. Whatever order is used, scoring for one region (state or province) is usually completed before moving on to the next region. Ideally, the material in a room at one time should be limited to one region. As each region is completed, the scored tests can be sent for data entry.

Monitoring the number of instruments being hand-scored or being entered into a database to be scored electronically over a one-hour period allows one to estimate how long the process is likely to take.

BOX 5.1

Instrument Tracking Form

Name of school: _____

School number: _____

Number of instrument A: _____

Number of instrument B: _____

Start time: _____

Finish time: _____

Name and code of the scorer: _____

Name and code of quality assurer: _____

Source: Authors' compilation.

This method can also help provide a reasonable estimate of cost. A simple form (such as the example in box 5.1) can keep track of scoring speed and accuracy when scoring all the tests from the same school.

Use of Scoring Guides

The test development team prepares the scoring guides. Guides for scoring (marking) open-ended items should clearly specify types of responses that are acceptable and types that are not. However, the guides may have to be modified slightly after test administration because some students may have given answers that were not listed at the test development stage. In that case, the task of modifying the guide should not be left to the discretion of scorers or those entering data into a computer. The test development team is ultimately responsible for indicating whether unexpected responses to an open-ended item are adequate. A separate scoring guide, which must be finalized before the start of the scoring process, should be provided for each language used in the assessment. The CD that accompanies volume 2, *Developing Tests and Questionnaires for a National Assessment of Educational Achievement*, contains examples of guides used to score items.

Scoring

Scorers and data entry personnel require adequate space to sit comfortably. Having a clear system in place for handling materials is important, given the large amount of material that is being processed and to avoid clutter. Allowing two scorers to work side by side has been found to be more efficient and to result in less gossip during scoring. It also permits an individual scorer to clarify issues with a colleague. The scoring room should have sufficient tables and boxes for packing tests after scoring so that they can be sent for data recording.

The national coordinator has ultimate responsibility for the quality of the scoring of items. He or she should establish a quality assurance procedure to ensure the accuracy and consistency of scoring. This procedure involves rescoring a sample of tests, the size of which varies from one national assessment to another. In some cases, lead raters check 50 percent of the test booklets, whereas in other cases, as few as 10 percent are checked. Factors to be considered in deciding on the size of the quality control sample include the experience of scorers, the number of pupils being tested, the time available, and the size of the budget. Responses to test items that are computer scored can be entered twice and the results compared.

In one national assessment, scorers marked multiple-choice answers in the test booklets. In the case of open-ended items, 100 percent of the items were checked. In another assessment, scores were recorded on a separate verification sheet, and a colleague marked the same items without seeing the previous scorer's marks. The two marks were then compared and discrepancies resolved. The verification sheet also helped identify individual scorers who made serious errors on a regular basis.

Breaks in work should be provided as the quality of scoring and data entry can suffer if scorers get tired and lose concentration. Adequate refreshment should also be provided. In one national assessment, government scorers threatened to strike on the grounds that they had not been provided with snacks between meals.

Sometimes, when multiple-choice items are hand-scored, scorers may not be able to read or understand some answers, or they may be confronted with double answers for a particular item. Rather than leave the resolution of these problems to the data recording stage, scorers should resolve such problems and record their decisions. In the event of lack of agreement, the lead rater should make the final decision. When multiple-choice items are scored by computer, procedures for dealing with double answers will be built into the scoring program.

DATA RECORDING

Attention to detail and careful recording of data will help reduce the amount of time spent cleaning data and rectifying errors. This section outlines general principles relating to the facilities and staff required for data recording, quality assurance, data cleaning, and data storage. Procedures for data cleaning and management are described in detail in part III of this volume (see also TIMSS 1998a).

Facilities for Data Recording

In planning data recording, one should bear in mind the available budget and the date by which data are required. By calculating the amount of time necessary to enter and verify data for each test (such as one mathematics test booklet and one language test booklet) and each questionnaire (such as student and teacher questionnaires), one can estimate the amount of time that will be needed to enter or type and verify all the data. This estimate will give a rough guide to how many data entry personnel will be needed to complete the task on time.

After determining how many staff members will be needed, one computer should be provided for each data entry person, as well as one for the supervisor. Ideally, computers should be linked to a network. Some national assessment teams use custom software (such as the International Association for the Evaluation of Educational Achievement's WinDem or EpiData) for data entry; others use database packages such as Access and Excel. Examples of data entry using Access are presented in part III of this volume.

Furniture requirements include good chairs for people who have to spend long hours entering data and long tables for organizing tests and questionnaires. Each data entry person should also have adequate workspace (a) for material that has to be entered; (b) for material that has been recorded; and (c) for problem documents to be discussed with the supervisor, data manager, or leader.

Staff for Data Recording

The data manager plays a crucial role in the data recording process and should be consulted constantly. He or she should, if possible, be involved in selecting data entry personnel. A competent data manager will generally pick up problems caused by poor work practices or inexperience. The data manager should have responsibility for procuring and ensuring the adequacy of both the hardware and software to be used in data entry. If possible, the national assessment team should employ experienced data entry personnel who are meticulous in their work. Although employing inexperienced individuals at low rates of pay may seem economical, they may cost more than professionals in the long run.

Data Recording and Quality Assurance

Data recording templates for each instrument should be prepared as soon as the instruments have been developed. The template is a matrix within which the data are typed. Templates look different in different data recording software. Part III of this volume goes into considerable detail on how to create and use a data entry template. Altering a template once data recording has commenced is not recommended.

Data entry personnel will make mistakes. As part of quality assurance, the national assessment team should decide (when estimating the budgetary requirements) what percentage (perhaps between 6 and 10 percent) of test records will be entered twice. Such double entry can determine whether a widespread problem exists or if most errors are attributable to one or two data entry personnel.

Data Cleaning

When data recording has been completed, tests and questionnaires should be carefully stored in a systematic way because some documents may have to be retrieved during data cleaning. Data cleaning, which is treated in detail in part III, is a tedious but very important part of data processing. It includes checking to ensure that data look plausible and that scores and response categories are within acceptable limits. It provides an opportunity to check problematic responses to test and questionnaire items. The data can also be checked for patterns that suggest cheating.

Data Storage

After the assessment has been completed, storage of data may be required for a number of years. Many research institutions regard five years as an appropriate length of storage time. In some countries, tests and questionnaires are scanned and data are stored in electronic form.

DATA ANALYSIS

In this section, some practical logistical issues that can have a bearing on the quality and efficiency of data analysis are raised. Volume 4, *Analyzing Data from a National Assessment of Educational Achievement*, focuses on generation of item statistics and test score results and on analysis to generate data for policy.

One core team member, with proven competence in statistics, including psychometrics, should be responsible for data analysis. Others may assist that person. Although employing a full-time statistician may not always be possible, a statistician's services will be required at many stages of the assessment process from the initial design to report writing.

The national assessment team will need the services of a data analyst at the pretest stage of test development. During that stage, test items are administered to a sample of students similar to those who will eventually take the test. Pretesting is covered in some detail in volume 2 of this series, *Developing Tests and Questionnaires for a*

National Assessment of Educational Achievement. The analyst should be able to apply appropriate computer software packages to analyze pre-test results. He or she should work closely with item writers and subject-matter specialists in selecting the items from the pool of pre-tested items that will be included in the test administered in the national assessment.

Experience suggests that selecting appropriate hardware and specialized software; getting release of government, donor, or other funds; ordering equipment and software (if necessary); and having it installed and operational can all take a considerable amount of time. The national assessment team should ensure that provision has been made in the budget to purchase and service hardware and for supplies such as paper and ink cartridges. Ideally, appropriate hardware and software should be in place before pretesting.

Many universities and government departments have access to various software packages and receive regular updates. At the time of writing, among the more widely used packages are SPSS (Statistical Package for the Social Sciences), which is used extensively in volume 4, *Analyzing Data from a National Assessment of Educational Achievement*; SAS (Statistical Analysis Software); and STATISTICA. Relevant specialist software, in addition to item and test analysis software, which was developed for this series and which is introduced in volume 4, includes

- Iteman (http://www.assess.com/xcart/product.php?productid=541)
- Conquest (https://shop.acer.edu.au/acer-shop/group/CON2/9)
- Winsteps (a free, less powerful version, Ministep, is available at http://www.winsteps.com/)

The data analyst should have access to a good-quality, high-speed printer, which is needed at many stages, but especially during data cleaning, item analysis, and more general data analysis, as well as for producing text, tables, charts, and graphs for the reports of the assessment.

REPORT WRITING

Because volume 5, *Using the Results of a National Assessment of Educational Achievement*, covers report writing in considerable detail, the

TABLE 5.1

Dummy Table Describing Characteristics of Primary School Teachers

	Gender		Age		Highest level of formal education achieved		
Province	Female	Male	Under 30	30 and over	Completed junior secondary level	Completed senior secondary level	Completed at least 2 years of postsecondary level
A							
B							
C							
D							

Source: Authors' compilation.

following paragraphs are limited to some logistical aspects associated with this key task.

The national coordinator and the core team should plan the report before conducting major analyses as the plan can help drive the analysis. To help develop ownership and to clarify analyses, designing dummy tables and checking whether the national assessment can provide data for each cell are a good idea. Members of the national steering committee and key policy makers can provide valuable insights at this stage and suggest headings for the tables. Table 5.1 presents an example of a dummy table based on questionnaire data.

Some weeks in advance of the release of results, the national coordinator should request trusted professional colleagues or likely key users to make time available to provide feedback on the first draft of each report (for example, press release, report summary, technical report, report for teachers). These individuals could include senior policy makers within the ministry of education, researchers, teacher trainers, and other key stakeholders. Practicing teachers should be included, especially if teacher newsletters based on the results are to be distributed. The national assessment team should review comments received, revise where necessary, and finalize reports for dissemination.

The national assessment team will have responsibility for ensuring that budgetary provision is made to cover the costs of typesetting and preparing tables, charts, and graphs, as well as printing copies of reports. The team will also have to coordinate the preparation and production of final reports and ensure that printers are given adequate time to have the published versions of reports available on a predetermined date. The team should proofread the manuscripts and follow up later to check that appropriate changes have been made. Experience suggests that in developing countries the process from the preparation of the first draft to the official launch of a final report can take three to six months.

The national assessment team should plan a press conference for the day when results are due to be released and invite key education stakeholders to attend. It should make budgetary provision to cover costs related to the press conference. In at least one country, reporters expect to have their expenses paid by the organizers of such events. If a national assessment team wishes to have the minister of education or other senior policy personnel attend the launch of a report, it should give adequate notice, given the busy schedules of these individuals.

PART **II** SCHOOL SAMPLING METHODOLOGY

Jean Dumais and J. Heward Gough

Part II describes how to define the population that is to be assessed in the national assessment. Different sampling approaches are described. Much of the section is devoted to the methodology for selecting a sample of students that will be representative of students in the education system. The emphasis is on "learning by doing." Readers are guided through the various sampling steps by working on a set of concrete tasks presented in the text and using data files in the accompanying CD. They can check their solutions by comparing them to correct solutions that are presented on screenshots in the text. The files are based on national assessment data from a fictional country, Sentz.

CHAPTER 6

DEFINING THE POPULATION OF INTEREST

This chapter introduces the terms *target population* and *survey population*, the first building blocks in the design of a probability survey. Later chapters describe a sampling frame (chapter 7) and probability sampling (chapter 8).

The first major task is to identify and define the population to be assessed in accordance with the goals of the assessment. This task involves specifying who (such as students, teachers, aides, principals, or parents), or what (for example, all schools or only publicly funded schools) the assessment will cover. The scope of the study helps define the populations of interest and determine whether the results can be compared with those of similar studies.

The *desired target population* comprises all the units of interest—the population for which information is sought and estimates are needed. In a national assessment, the population might be all students enrolled in grade 5 in all schools in the country or grade 5 students enrolled only in public schools. A desired target population could also be all teachers employed in primary schools.

Unfortunately, in some instances, practical reasons prevent the survey of some elements of a target population, in which case they may have to be excluded. Reasons for exclusion may relate to cost, absence of roads, geographic isolation (remote islands or mountainous regions), civil unrest, schools that serve very few students, or children with special needs. The remaining population elements will form the *defined target population*—the population that the national assessment team can reasonably cover. International studies of educational achievement routinely publish data on desired and defined target populations for each participating country.

Exclusions should be kept to a minimum and should not be used as a means of obtaining a "convenience" sample. International studies have routinely set the upper limit of exclusions at 5 percent of the desired target population; data on countries that fail to meet this criterion are usually reported with a cautionary note. Failure to meet the exclusion criterion in a national assessment could be highlighted by a comment such as the following: "Data for rural secondary schools in region Y should be treated with caution because three large remote areas were excluded from the survey."

The national steering committee should play a key role in making decisions about the population to be assessed. It could, for instance, define the desired target population as all students enrolled in grade 6 during any part of a specific or reference school year. However, it might specify that the defined target population should be limited to students enrolled in grade 6 on May 31 of a reference year in schools with at least 10 students in grade 6. From logistical and budgetary perspectives, assessing students in smaller schools would be impractical. Furthermore, the steering committee would be aware that some grade 6 students would have dropped out of school or migrated during the school year and that attempting to find and assess these students would not be practical.

Figure 6.1 depicts a fairly typical situation in which the *desired* target population is defined (left bar). The target population has been reduced by omitting certain categories of schools (such as remote or very small schools or schools serving children with special needs) and results in a new population, the *defined* target population (middle bar). The size of this population may be reduced further, mainly by finding excluded units (for example, special needs students) in participating schools on the day of testing, resulting in the *achieved* population (right column).

FIGURE 6.1

Percentages of Students in Desired, Defined, and Achieved Populations

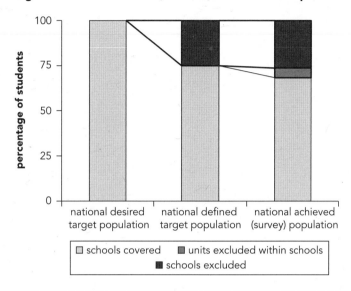

Source: Authors' representation.

The national steering committee may also wish to identify subnational groups of interest that it defines, for example, in terms of region or gender. Having determined the defined target population and possibly the subgroups of interest, the national assessment team or its sampling experts must then construct an appropriate sampling frame.

CHAPTER 7

CREATING THE SAMPLING FRAME

This chapter introduces the most basic tool for survey sampling: the sampling frame. The chapter addresses how the frame and the population can be very similar or completely different, as well as the properties of a "good" frame. Finally, the chapter introduces the demonstration assessment conducted in Sentz.

THE SAMPLING FRAME

Ideally, a sampling frame is a comprehensive, complete, up-to-date list that (a) includes the students of the defined target population and (b) contains information that helps access the students. In the case of a national assessment of educational achievement, the availability of a list of all the students enrolled in the school grades of interest would allow the sampling team to pick a sample of students directly.

In many countries, such a complete and up-to-date list is impossible to obtain, even when the central public administration (such as the ministry of education) conducts the assessment. Such countries may have to resort to alternative sources of information or construct their own complete and up-to-date frame.

One alternative to a comprehensive, complete, and up-to-date list of students is partial up-to-date coverage of the target population. Indirect access to a list of students may be achieved by first selecting schools and then their students. In effect, this means lists of students are required only for the schools selected to take part in the national assessment.

In many countries, the national ministry of education or an equivalent authority will be the primary source of information for constructing the sampling frame. Such a list will likely contain a national school identifier, the name and address of the school, the name of the school principal, a phone number, the grade levels covered, the size of staff, student enrollment, and possibly the source of funding and type of education provided.

In practice, the sampling frame will usually be imperfect to some degree because it will not cover exactly the defined target population. Some frame entries may not correspond to actual target population units. The school frame entries may contain more schools than are in the actual population, a situation known as *overcoverage*, which occurs, for example, when a school closes or merges with another between the time of frame creation and data collection. Furthermore, some elements of the target population may be missing from the frame (*undercoverage*), for example, when a school is not listed in the frame or is misclassified as out of scope. The elements actually covered by the frame constitute the population from which the survey sample is selected and are normally referred to as the *survey population*. Essential elements of a sampling frame are outlined in table 7.1.

Sampling frames can take many forms. The following example is based on a desired target population of all students enrolled in primary schools during any part of the reference school year and a defined target population of students enrolled in primary schools on May 31 of the reference year. In this instance, the sampling frame was based on the ministry of education's list of all students enrolled in primary schools on April 15 of the reference year. This approach should be adequate provided that the list is updated several times a year. However, the survey population defined by this frame might not cover the defined target population if some students leave and others enroll after April 15. If the ministry has an out-of-date or deficient list

TABLE 7.1

Essential Elements of a Sampling Frame for a National Assessment

Element	Description
Identification	Each school must be identified clearly (for example, by name or school number).
Communication	The national assessment team must have information to allow it to contact each school. Appropriate information might include postal addresses, telephone numbers, or both. If such information is lacking, contact might have to be made by direct field visits, which require knowing the school's physical location.
Classification	Classification information must be included in the sampling frame if a national assessment requires classification of schools (such as grouping of schools by geographic area, linguistic or cultural group, or public or private administration) for sampling, estimation, or reporting purposes.
Measure of size	A measure of size such as school enrollment or number of classrooms may be required if sampling involves unequal probabilities.
Update	The sampling frame should have details on when the information used to construct it was obtained or updated. This information will be considered in the event that the national assessment is repeated.

Source: Authors' compilation.

of schools, an alternative approach for constructing a sampling frame will be needed. This approach may require a more traditional and labor-intensive way of assembling lists of schools and lists of students by walking streets and roads and listing all schools and their students. Modern educational management information systems, especially those that have a computer link to the ministry, will greatly facilitate the task of developing up-to-date sampling frames.

In creating the sampling frame, one must assign unique identification numbers to the frame units. Identification numbers may already exist on the source files of the ministry or equivalent authority. These official identification numbers should be kept on the frame to facilitate communication with the ministry about the data it provided. These numbers may well be sufficient for the needs of the assessment. However, as preparation work progresses, items and structures will be added (for example, information on school principals, teachers, tracks or classes within schools, and students within classes). The units of each layer should be properly identified as they are added to the frame or frames. The ultimate objective is to create a set of identifiers that allows location and tracking of each individual and each institution through the entire assessment process. Box 2.1 in part I has examples of identification numbering systems used in national assessments.

SENTZ CASE STUDY

The CD accompanying this manual contains a number of files with the necessary frame and sample data for the case study of Sentz. A summary description of the files can be found in annex II.A. Follow the case study (see exercise 7.1) step by step to become familiar with the necessary steps in designing and selecting a national assessment sample.

Sentz is about to embark on a multiyear program of national assessment of educational achievement. In Sentz, schooling is compulsory until the end of International Standard Classification of Education (ISCED) level 2 (lower secondary) (UNESCO 1997). The ministry wishes to establish the learning achievement levels of students at various stages of the education system, starting with eighth grade. It specified that literacy should be assessed during each assessment. The first national assessment should also assess student achievement in mathematics and science. Future assessments would include other curriculum areas.

Sentz has two distinct geographic regions, the Northeast and Southwest, which are separated by the Grand River (see figure 7.1). The national capital, Capital City, is located in the Southwest region. The Northeast consists of three provinces (provinces 1, 3, and 5) and 21 towns, while the Southwest has two provinces (provinces 2 and 4) with a total of 12 towns. (The term *town* includes cities, smaller towns, or rural areas consisting of farms and small villages.) Each province is divided into an urban and a rural section with the exception of province 4 in the Southwest, which has a rural section only. Each town is classified as either urban or rural.

Every child in Sentz can attend a local school up to and including ISCED level 2 (second stage of basic education: lower secondary education). The 227 schools offering instruction at this level comprise

EXERCISE 7.1

Getting Started

On your local hard drive or server, create a folder called **NAEA SAMPLING** (or something similar). Create five separate subfolders within **NAEA SAMPLING**. These subfolders are **BASE FILES**, **MYSAMPLSOL** (for My Sampling Solutions), **SRS400**, **2STG4400**, and **NATASSESS** (for an actual national sample assessment that we will use later). Copy the files for **BASE FILES**, **SRS400**, **2STG4400**, and **NATASSESS** subfolders from the **SPSS VERSION** folder in the CD that accompanies this book. You will use the **MYSAMPLSOL** folder to file your output after completing an exercise. The proposed file structure can be examined in figure II.A.1 of annex II.A (page 106). The various exercises are organized so that you should be able to work through the case study, building on the work already accomplished and saved under **MYSAMPLSOL**. However, you can always start from one of the permanent files (located in **SRS400** or **2STG4400**); doing so will prevent carrying out analyses on incomplete or inaccurate exercise files. To avoid a lot of wasted effort later, take considerable care at this stage in setting up the **NAEA SAMPLING** folder and the subfolders. Unless you are so instructed, *do not* use automatic save and *do not* write over the permanent files in the subfolders.

From this point on, you should be working from the files located on your hard drive or server. If you need to, you can open the answer files located on the CD to verify your work.

As you progress through the various tasks or exercises, you will be accessing, creating, and storing the equivalent files on your local drive or server. Note that SPSS17,[a] including the Complex Samples add-on modules, was used to create this case study; earlier versions of SPSS might show slight differences in menu presentation or options. The optional SPSS module Complex Samples is required to carry out some of the exercises.

The reasons behind the choices of stratification, sample allocation, sample selection scheme, and a number of other key concepts, as well as related terminology and abbreviations, are explained as they are introduced.

The survey manager for Sentz has been able to obtain from the ministry of education a list of the 227 schools in the country where eighth-grade education is offered. The list is organized by **region**, **province**, **density** (**urban** or **rural**), **town**, and **school**. Each school on the list has a unique identification number (**schoolid**) built using the province (left-hand digit), the town (second digit), and the school within the city (two right-hand digits). For example, the school identified by the number 1413 is located in province 1, town 4. Similarly, for classes within schools (in this case the grade 8 classes in a school), an identification number will be created for the class by adding a digit to the right of the school identifier: 14131, 14132, 14133, and so forth. Two more digits are added to identify the students within their class; if, for instance, the class has 43 students, you would use 1413101, 1413102, …, 1413143. For each school, the ministry has provided the number of eighth-grade classes (**nbclass**), the total number of children enrolled in eighth-grade classes (measure of size, or **school_size**), and the average class size (**avgclass**).

The file **SCHOOLS.SAV** is the provisional sampling frame of schools in Sentz. You can open it in the SPSS viewer by following the SPSS instructions given here. SPSS keywords and instructions are in **lowercase**.

(continued)

EXERCISE 7.1 *(continued)*

To read the school frame, from the menu bar, choose the following options:

File – Open – Data – Look in

   ...\BASE FILES\SCHOOLS.SAV

Open

Check that **Data View** and not **Variable View** is highlighted at the bottom of your screen. Check record number 6. You should see that school 1202 is in the Northeast region, province 1, town 2, and is school number 2 in that town. This school has three classes with a total of 153 students in grade 8, for an average class size of 51.0 students (exercise figure 7.1.A).

EXERCISE FIGURE 7.1.A   Sentz School Data

SCHOOLS.sav [DataSet1] - PASW Statistics Data Editor

File   Edit   View   Data   Transform   Analyze   Graphs   Utilities   Add-ons   Window   Help

1 : schoolid   1101

	schoolid	region	province	density	town	school	nbclass	school_size	avgclass
1	1101	NE	1	rural	1	1	2	89	44.5
2	1102	NE	1	rural	1	2	2	111	55.5
3	1103	NE	1	rural	1	3	4	221	55.3
4	1104	NE	1	rural	1	4	4	214	53.5
5	1201	NE	1	rural	2	1	2	109	54.5
6	1202	NE	1	rural	2	2	3	153	51.0
7	1203	NE	1	rural	2	3	3	146	48.7
8	1204	NE	1	rural	2	4	2	105	52.5
9	1301	NE	1	rural	3	1	3	143	47.7
10	1302	NE	1	rural	3	2	3	140	46.7
11	1601	NE	1	rural	6	1	4	208	52.0
12	1602	NE	1	rural	6	2	3	158	52.7
13	1603	NE	1	rural	6	3	3	159	53.0
14	1401	NE	1	urban	4	1	2	81	40.5
15	1402	NE	1	urban	4	2	3	91	30.3
16	1403	NE	1	urban	4	3	4	144	36.0
17	1404	NE	1	urban	4	4	4	130	32.5
18	1405	NE	1	urban	4	5	3	104	34.7
19	1406	NE	1	urban	4	6	3	108	36.0

Source: Authors' example within SPSS software.

SPSS will not allow an open session without an active data set. To be able to close the data set **SCHOOLS** without closing SPSS, click the commands **File – New – Data**, and a blank data set should show on the view screen. Then, bring the data set **SCHOOLS** back to the view screen, and click **File – Close** to effectively close **SCHOOLS**.

a. Version 17, used here, was originally published as SPSS. During 2009 and 2010, versions issued were published under the name Predictive Analytic Software (PASW).

27,654 students in 702 eighth-grade classes. ISCED level 3 (upper secondary education) is offered in the regional capital cities; ISCED level 4 (postsecondary nontertiary education) and level 5 (first stage of tertiary education) are available in Capital City only.

FIGURE 7.1

Map of Sentz

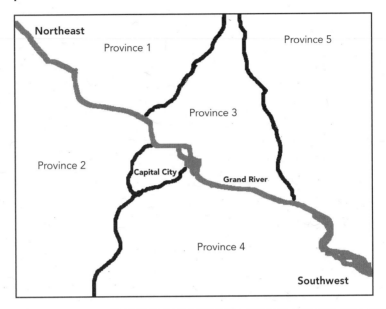

Source: Authors' representation.

In this case study, two sample designs are demonstrated. The first, a base case for reference, is a simple random sample of 400 students from the national list. This number has been selected because it is the effective target sample size in most national and international educational assessment surveys.[1] The folder ***SRS400*** on the CD contains the answer files for this sample. A simple random sampling (SRS) design is usually impossible to implement because of the lack of a complete and up-to-date list frame of all eligible students. Moreover, even if such a list were available, the SRS design would be very expensive, because it would involve selecting students in a very large number of schools, involving as few as one or two students in selected schools. Administration of tests and quality control measures would absorb a lot of the national assessment budget. The SRS example is used here mainly for pedagogical purposes and to allow comparison of the results using this approach with the results of an actual or recommended design.

The second design, referred to as the recommended design, is the standard real-life design used in most national assessments. The relevant answer files are in folder **2STG4400**, so called because the design will be a two-stage sample with an expected size of 4,400 students. The design includes geographic or administrative stratification, in this case the five provinces of Sentz. The sample design will involve initial selection of schools (stage 1) followed by selection of one class per selected school (stage 2). If researchers wanted to isolate the effect of the teachers on student performance from that of the school, more than one classroom would be selected. If they were only interested in the effect of the school, the sample of students should be selected from the entire target grade, regardless of their class. For reasons of budget and practicality, Sentz has decided to survey one entire classroom from each school. The desired size of the sample of students is based on the available information on class size, intraclass correlation, expected design effects, and the analytical and reporting needs of the assessment. In the first stage, schools are allocated in proportion to the number of eligible students in each province, and are selected using systematic probability proportional to size sampling (PPS). Then a simple random sample of one entire class per school is taken.

NOTE

1. In some major assessments (such as Trends in International Mathematics and Science Study, or TIMSS), psychometric scales are centered on 500 with a set standard deviation of 100; then, with a sample size of 400, the coefficient of variation of the estimated scores is about 1 percent, and confidence intervals for unknown characteristic prevalence are ±5 percentage points.

CHAPTER 8

ELEMENTS OF SAMPLING THEORY

This chapter describes the fundamental elements of sampling theory, including random sampling and some of the most important random sampling techniques, such as sample stratification and multistage and cluster sampling.

Probability sampling is normally used when reliable and valid estimates of certain population characteristics are needed from a sample, because it allows estimation of the precision (sampling variance or standard error) of those estimates. Those characteristics can be expressed as counts (for example, number of children between 10 and 15 years of age); as totals (for example, total enrollment in lower secondary schools); or as proportions (for example, proportion of children living in households whose annual income is below the national poverty line). Any and all of those characteristics can be estimated from a sample, as long as it has been selected with a probability sampling scheme and proper field procedures have been developed and implemented.

Probability sampling requires that each unit in the population of interest—the population for which estimates are sought—have a known nonzero probability of being selected into the sample. Probability sampling does not require that all units have the *same* probability of selection, just that they *have* a probability of being selected. In a national assessment, the relevant units are the students, their teachers, their principal, and their school.

SIMPLE RANDOM SAMPLING

When all units have the same probability of selection, the sampling scheme is part of a larger group of sampling schemes called *equal probability sampling methods*. The population of interest might be 10 schools. The school names are written on identical pieces of paper that are dropped into a box. The identical pieces of paper are shuffled and 2 of the 10 pieces of paper are drawn from the box. In theory, each school has 2 chances in 10, or 1 in 5, of being selected.

The starting point for all probability sampling designs is simple random sampling (SRS). SRS is a one-step selection method that ensures that every possible sample of size n has an equal chance of being selected. As a consequence, each unit in the sample has the same inclusion probability. This probability π is equal to n/N, where N is the number of units in the population and n is the size of the sample. In the example in the previous paragraph, since $n = 2$ and $N = 10$, $\pi = 1/5$. Figure 8.1 depicts a simple random sample of 7 schools drawn from a population of 45 schools.

Sampling may be done with or without replacement. Sampling with replacement allows a unit to be selected more than once; this method is not normally used in practice. Sampling without replacement means that once a unit (a school or a student) has been selected, it cannot be selected again. SRS with replacement and SRS without replacement are practically identical if the sample size is a very small fraction of the population size, because the possibility of the same unit appearing more than once in the sample is small. Generally, sampling without replacement yields more precise results and is operationally more convenient.

For a number of reasons, SRS alone is normally neither cost-effective nor practical in large-scale national surveys. Nowadays, computer programs such as Excel and SPSS (Statistical Package for the Social Sciences), among others, offer tools for drawing samples. These tools may be quite limited in scope, as in the case of Excel, or quite broad, as in the case of SPSS. Exercise 8.2 uses SRS as a learning tool

FIGURE 8.1

SRS without Replacement of Schools

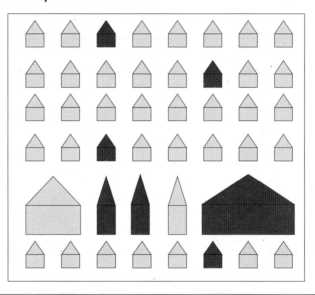

Source: Authors' representation.
Note: N = 45 schools; *n* = 7 schools (gray).

to draw a sample of 400 students from a hypothetical list of students for illustrative purposes.

SYSTEMATIC RANDOM SAMPLING

In *systematic random sampling* (SYS), units are selected from the frame at regular intervals. A sampling interval and a random start are required. When the population size, N, is a multiple of the sample size, n, every kth unit is selected where the interval k is equal to N/n. Simple adjustments to this method are available if N is not an exact multiple of n. The random start, r, is a single random number ranging from 1 to k. The units selected are then: $r, r + k, r + 2k, \dots r + (n - 1)\, k$. Like SRS, each unit has an inclusion probability equal to $1/k$, but unlike SRS, not every combination of n units has an equal chance of being selected. SYS can select only samples in which the units are separated by k. Thus, under this method, only k possible samples can be drawn from the population.

As an illustration of SYS, suppose a researcher in a province with a population of $N = 36$ schools has to draw a sample of size $n = 12$ schools. The sampling interval would be $k = N/n = 36/12 = 3$. Next, the researcher selects a random number ranging from 1 to 3, the value for k. Suppose it is 1. The schools selected for the sample are those numbered 1, 4, 7, ... , 31, and 34. With a population of size 36, only three possible SYS samples of size 12 exist, whereas more than 1.2 billion possible simple random samples exist of the same size.

SYS can be used when no list of the population units is available in advance. In this case, a conceptual frame can be constructed by sampling every kth unit until the end of the population is reached. For example, if a class of approximately 50 students is selected, but no class list is available, *and* a one-in-three sample of students is required, the test administrator can be given a random start number ranging from 1 to 3. Assume that the number is 2. When the administrator arrives at the selected classroom, he or she starts at a predetermined corner of the room (for example, left end of the front row), selects the second student, the fifth, and so on. If in actuality the class turns out to have 46 students, the sample will be students 2, 5, 8, ... , and 44. (No students are numbered 47 or 50.) If the class had 54 students, the sample would be extended to include students 47, 50, and 53. This technique is often used when a test administrator or interviewer can travel to the field only once. Note that the "random" part of the sampling is done before visiting schools. Figure 8.2 shows a systematic random sample of 7 schools drawn from a population of 45 schools.

CLUSTER SAMPLING

Cluster sampling is the process of randomly selecting complete groups (clusters) of population units from the survey frame. It is usually a less statistically efficient sampling strategy than SRS because it has a higher sampling variance for a given sample size. Cluster sampling, however, has several distinct advantages. First, sampling clusters can greatly reduce the cost of data collection, particularly if the school population is widely spread throughout a large country. For example, a national assessment that involves sampling 1,000 grade 3 students

FIGURE 8.2

Systematic Random Sample of Schools

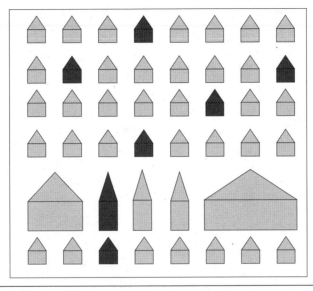

Source: Authors' representation.
Note: N = 45 schools; n = 7 schools (gray); step = 6; start = 4.

in schools at a rate of 25 in each of 40 selected schools will be much less expensive than sampling 1,000 grade 3 students scattered at random across the country. Second, sampling individual units from the population is not always practical. Sometimes sampling groups of the population units or clusters (for example, entire classrooms) is much easier, or it may be required for administrative reasons. Finally, cluster sampling supports the production of estimates (for example, average achievement per classroom or per school). Figure 8.3 provides an example of a sample of three school clusters involving 19 schools, taken from a population of 45 schools grouped into seven clusters.

Cluster sampling is a two-step process. First, the population is grouped into clusters. (Natural clusters such as schools or classrooms might already exist.) Second, a sample of clusters is selected, and all units within the selected clusters are included in the survey (for example, all are administered tests). The survey frame may dictate the method of sampling. If the units of the population are naturally grouped together, creating a frame of these groups and sampling them is often easier than trying to create a list of all individual units in the

FIGURE 8.3

Cluster Sample of Schools

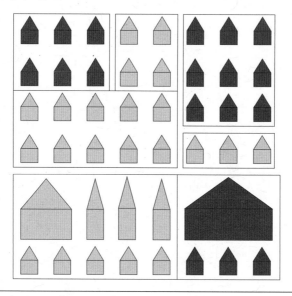

Source: Authors' representation.
Note: N = 7 clusters (45 schools); n = 3 clusters (19 schools = unit).

population. For example, a list of schools may be the only data available to a national assessment team.

In figure 8.3, each of the seven rectangular areas separated by solid lines represents a school area. Three school areas have been selected by a random sampling method, and all the students in the selected areas (shown in gray) are to be tested. This sampling method requires visiting only three compact geographic areas but samples 19 schools. SRS, in contrast, would have required visiting seven widely scattered schools, as would SYS (see figures 8.1 and 8.2).

There are a number of considerations to bear in mind when doing cluster sampling. For estimates to be statistically efficient, the units within a cluster should be as different as possible. If the units within a cluster are very similar, they will tend to provide similar information. Unfortunately, units within a cluster frequently tend to have similar characteristics and are more homogeneous than units randomly selected from the general population. As a result, a larger sample is normally required to achieve a fixed level of precision than would be the case under SRS.

Some schools or education systems organize classes taking into account factors such as perceived student competence in curriculum subject areas. In such a situation, a school might, for instance, have sufficient student numbers at a particular level to form three classes. One class might consist of students who are expected (on the basis of previous years' results or their expressed interest) to continue their studies in mathematics or the sciences, another might consist of students who have an aptitude or preference for the humanities, and a third class might be formed from students who are not expected to persist much longer in school. In this situation, one would expect that most of the students in the first class would do well on mathematics tests, the second group perhaps less well at mathematics but well at languages, while quite likely the third group would appear relatively weak in both areas. In such circumstances, cluster sampling would be statistically quite inefficient: selection of a single entire class would suggest that the students are strong in mathematics and weak at languages, or the reverse, or weak in both areas. Such a situation suggests that from the point of view of sampling efficiency, selecting a few students from each of the three classes would be better to increase the chances of obtaining a balanced picture of student achievement levels in the school. However, practical reasons often exist—related to the research objectives, administrative constraints, or testing costs—for selecting intact classrooms. Reasons for selecting intact classes include a school principal's or manager's interest in minimizing the amount of disruption in a school during testing or a researcher's interest in applying a specific analytical model or in quantifying the relative influence of the school, teacher, or class on individual achievement.

The statistical efficiency of cluster sampling depends on how homogeneous the clusters are, how many population units are in each cluster, and the number of clusters that are sampled. A standard measure of this efficiency (really, inefficiency) is called the *clustering effect* or the *design effect*. A value of 1 means that the design in question is as efficient as SRS. If the design effect is much larger than 1, as is usually the case in cluster sampling, the design is less efficient. A cluster sample with a design effect of 5 would need to draw a sample size five times larger than that of a simple random sample to yield estimates of comparable precision.

The value of the design effect depends on two factors: (a) the number of units in the cluster (number of students in the class, in this instance) and (b) the degree to which students in the same class resemble each other more than they resemble those in other classes or schools with respect to some variable or variables to be measured. This latter measure is known as the *intraclass correlation*, commonly referred to as *roh* (*rate of homogeneity*) or sometimes as *rho*. In the case of test scores in mathematics, which this exercise takes as the most important assessment variable in Sentz's national assessment, this intraclass correlation is frequently as high as 0.25 or even 0.30. The value of *roh* would probably be different for other variables.

National assessment sampling or statistical personnel should use the following formula to calculate the design effect (*deff*) (Kish 1965; Lohr 1999):

$$deff = (1 + roh \times (M - 1)),$$

where M is the cluster (class) size and *roh* is the rate of homogeneity or intraclass correlation. For a *roh* = 0.25 and class size $M = 35$, *deff* = $(1 + 0.25 \times (35 - 1)) = 1 + 8.5 = 9.5$.

Estimates of *roh* may be obtained from previous national assessments of similar or adjacent grade levels. If such data are not available, estimates may be obtained from public examinations results or "borrowed" from neighboring country assessments conducted in a country with similar educational characteristics. When neighboring units are similar, selecting many small clusters is statistically more efficient than selecting a few larger clusters.

In the case of Sentz, the recommended design is to select a certain number of schools and then to take one entire class as a cluster in each selected school. Although this approach is used largely for administrative reasons, a substantial price is paid in terms of statistical efficiency because the intraclass correlations and large class sizes are likely to make the design effects quite high.

STRATIFICATION

SRS and SYS of elements and of clusters are simple, basic methods for drawing random samples, but they may not be the most efficient methods. A good strategy often makes use of available information on the units of interest by creating homogeneous groups of units—called *strata*—and then applies some basic sampling method within the strata.

Before sample selection, the national assessment team may want to organize sampling so that particular groups of units or specific areas of the country are covered with certainty. Policy makers, for instance, may wish to obtain estimates of learning achievement for provinces or regions, or they may wish to be able to look at data from different linguistic groups or from large and small schools. The team may hope that the random choices will yield a sufficient number of units in each province or region to allow for reliable estimates. Alternatively, it might arrange its sampling strategy by first listing the population of schools in groups (for example, provinces or linguistic groups) and then selecting part of the total sample from each of these groups. This strategy, termed *stratification*, can be used with any probability sampling method. Stratification requires a bit more work at the beginning of the national assessment, but the rewards often far outweigh the extra work required. Schools have been stratified in national assessments by location, language, religious affiliation, source of funding, and degree of urbanization.

Experience shows that stratifying on too many criteria proves counterproductive; in fact, the requirements imposed by fine stratification often increase the sample size. Furthermore, the number of units that end up in the "wrong" stratum may increase with the number of strata, especially those that are based on more volatile or less reliable information, such as number of staff members or student enrollment.

Depending on the situation, some national assessments use one, two, or more stratification variables. Stratification can improve both statistical and overall efficiency, reducing the size (and cost) of the sample while maintaining the level of reliability. This course of action requires the input of a survey statistician used to dealing with such problems. Figure 8.4 illustrates a stratified random sample of 45 schools using one 3-level stratification variable.

A population can be stratified by any variable for which data are available for all units of the frame prior to the assessment. This infor-

FIGURE 8.4

Stratified Random Sample of Schools

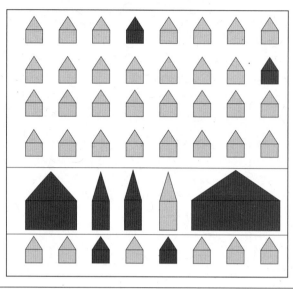

Source: Authors' representation.
Note: $H = 3$ strata; $N_1 = 32$; $N_2 = 5$; $N_3 = 8$; $n_1 = 2$; $n_2 = 4$; $n_3 = 2$.

mation could be as simple as the school address, which would support stratification by geographic location. Commonly used stratification variables in assessment surveys include geographic location (such as region, province, or town); private or public funding; type of educational program (primary versus secondary, academic versus vocational); and gender of students (girls, boys, mixed).

Three main reasons justify stratification. First, it makes the sampling strategy statistically more efficient than SRS or SYS. Second, it helps ensure adequate sample sizes for specific domains of interest for later analysis. Third, it protects against drawing a "bad" sample. The following sections look more closely at each of these reasons.

Enhancing Statistical Efficiency

For a given sample size and estimator, stratification may lead to lower sampling error or, conversely, for a given sampling error, to a smaller sample size. Although both cluster sampling and stratification are methods of grouping units in the population, in stratified sampling, samples of units are drawn within each stratum, whereas in cluster sampling, samples of clusters are drawn and everyone in the cluster is assessed. Stratification generally increases the precision of estimation with respect to SRS, whereas clustering generally decreases it (because neighboring units are usually similar).

For improved statistical efficiency of a sampling strategy with respect to SRS, strong homogeneity must exist within a stratum (that is, units within a stratum should be similar with respect to the variable of interest), and the strata themselves must be as different as possible (with respect to the same variable of interest). Generally, this goal is achieved if the stratification variables are correlated with the survey variable of interest (such as literacy achievement and rural versus urban location).

The example of the three classes (mathematics, humanities, and potential early leavers) already given for cluster sampling can be extended for illustration. Suppose the provincial lists of classes could be organized into three strata, corresponding to the three types of classes. Random selection of classes from the first stratum would in general yield samples of students strong in mathematics, irrespective of the classes that were selected. Similarly, the second stratum would result in a selection of students who generally were relatively weak in mathematics. With stratified random sampling, the sample from each of the three strata should give a result that is closely representative of the strata as a whole and, when the results are combined, should give a precise estimate for the province as a whole.

Stratification can increase the precision of the estimates relative to SRS. According to Cochran (1977, 90),

> If each stratum is homogeneous, in that the measurements vary little from one unit to another, a precise estimate of any stratum mean can be obtained from a small sample in that stratum. These estimates can then be combined into a precise estimate for the whole population.

Stratification is particularly important in the case of skewed populations (that is, when the distribution of values of a variable of interest is not symmetric, but leans to the right or the left). For example, the first-stage sampling frame might simply be a list of schools containing approximate but out-of-date enrollment figures. In that case, more accurate estimation of total enrollment might in itself be a goal of the assessment survey. If SRS is used, a few schools can exert a large influence on the estimates of total enrollment. If the largest schools happen to be selected, they can cause serious overestimation of the total. Stratifying by size (a stratum for the largest schools, a stratum for midsize schools, and a stratum for small schools) can help ensure that schools selected in each stratum represent other schools of roughly the same size in the population.

Stratifying by school size appears reasonable if an estimate of the size of the enrolled population is desired. Stratifying by school size, however, may not be recommended if the variable of interest is, say, average age of mathematics teachers, because no reason exists to assume a correlation between teacher age and school size. Frequently, stratification variables are chosen on the basis of their expected correlation with the key variables being assessed (such as language or mathematics) in the national assessment. Note that a stratification approach that is statistically efficient for one survey variable may not work well for other variables.

Ensuring Coverage of the Domain of Interest

In a national assessment, policy makers may seek estimates of achievement for subgroups of the population, called *domains*, as well as for the total population. They may, for example, wish to compare achievement levels of students in different provinces or regions, or of girls and boys, or of students attending different types of schools (public or private). Creating estimates for subgroups is called *domain estimation*. If domain estimates are required, the sample design should ensure that the sample size for each domain is adequate. Ideally, the strata should correspond to the domains of interest.

Avoiding "Bad" Samples

Stratification helps guard against drawing a "bad" or unusual sample. In SRS, sample selection is left entirely to chance. Stratified sampling attempts to restrict potentially extreme samples by taking steps to ensure that certain categories of the student population are included in the sample. For example, if a national assessment focused on the effects of school size on learning achievement, the sample design could include stratification by school size.

The national assessment team in Sentz considered various stratification options. Limiting the frame to the two regions, Northeast and Southwest, was considered inadequate because it would not provide sufficiently informative data for policy makers. Instead, the team opted to stratify by province (three in the Northeast and two in the Southwest). Calculating regional estimates would be a simple summation process when provincial-level estimates were available.

Furthermore, if the files for each provincial stratum are sorted by town density (that is, urban or rural) before the selection of schools, systematic sampling (whether with equal probability or with probability proportional to the size of city) will guarantee that some urban and some rural schools are selected, yielding reasonably efficient domain estimates if urban compared with rural analysis is later thought to be important. The national assessment team felt that using the towns directly as strata was unnecessary (it would have yielded 33 strata, a number of which would have only two eligible schools).

ALLOCATION OF THE SAMPLE ACROSS STRATA

After the population has been divided into strata, the national assessment team, with guidance from its sampling adviser, should determine how many units should be sampled from each stratum. This step is referred to as *allocation of the sample*.

Inclusion probabilities (that is, the probability that the unit will be chosen in a sample) usually vary from stratum to stratum because they depend on how the sample is allocated to each stratum. To calculate the inclusion probabilities for most sample designs, one must consider the size of the sample and the size of the population in each stratum. To illustrate, consider a population of $N = 1,000$ schools stratified into two groups, rural and urban. The urban group or stratum has $N_1 = 250$ schools and the rural stratum has $N_2 = 750$ schools. If SRS is used to select $n_1 = 50$ schools from the first stratum and $n_2 = 50$ schools from the second, then the probability that a school is selected from the first stratum is $\pi_1 = 50/250 = 1/5$, and the probability that a school in the second stratum is selected is $\pi_2 = 50/750 = 1/15$. Schools thus have different probabilities of inclusion depending on their location or stratum. In this instance, an urban school is more likely to be selected than a rural school.

Allocating the national assessment sample to the strata can be a difficult task. With a fixed budget and limited (if any) knowledge of the characteristics of the units of interest, most of the theory on stratification and optimal sample allocation is of limited use. Frequently, resorting to practical considerations and seeking expert advice are necessary to devise a viable sample allocation strategy.

Two common sample allocation strategies are (a) equal allocation and (b) proportional allocation. With equal allocation, each stratum is allocated the same number of sample units; this method is recommended for well-balanced strata. In proportional allocation, each stratum receives a share of the sample that corresponds to its share of the population; this method is the preferred option when national estimates are of greatest interest. Equal allocation may not be as good as proportional allocation for national estimates, but it may be preferable if domain estimates are required and if strata and domains correspond. Equal allocation can also help ensure that enough units are sampled from each domain or stratum.

If proportional allocation is used, the sample of schools must be allocated so that the number of students in the sample in each stratum is proportional to the number of students in the population in each stratum. Some schools may have a measure of size (MOS) of zero for the target population. They should remain in the frame if they have some chance of acquiring eligible students during the testing period; they should be given a preliminary MOS value of one and be included in the relevant totals. If virtually no chance exists that these schools will acquire any eligible students in time for the assessment, they should be removed from the sampling frame.

In general, if separate estimates are required for strata, then equal levels of sampling precision will usually be required for each stratum. Such precision usually requires sampling an equal number of schools in each stratum regardless of the size of the stratum. Because each stratum should have a minimum of two participating schools to allow for estimation of sampling error (see annex IV.C), the number allocated for selection should be adjusted for the anticipated nonresponse.

The members of the national assessment team entrusted with sampling are responsible for ensuring that the school sample is allocated correctly. They should consult a sampling specialist. Often such specialists are found in ministries other than education (such as the national statistical office or the ministry responsible for national household surveys). A sampling specialist can provide assistance on issues such as how many schools to include per strata and what to do when a stratum has very few schools. Exercise 8.1 deals further with allocation to strata. Other sampling strategies that require much more detailed information about the individual units are beyond the scope of this chapter.

EXERCISE 8.1

Sample Size Calculation and Allocation to Strata

According to the most recent available information from the Ministry of Education of Sentz, the average class size is expected to be about 37 students. Suggestions from colleagues in neighboring countries with similar educational characteristics suggest that the intraclass correlation for the mathematics score, chosen as the key target variable, is likely to be between 0.25 and 0.30. This rate of homogeneity equates to a design effect somewhere between 10 and 12. In calculating the sample size, the sampling team opted for the midpoint of this range, 11. Thus, to obtain an effective sample size equivalent to 400 under SRS, it needed a sample of 4,400 students for the proposed design. Because the plan involves selecting a single class per selected school, the team must select 4,400/37 = 118.9 schools. For practical purposes, this figure can be rounded up to 120 schools.

The Ministry of Education had advised the national assessment team to optimize the precision of the national estimates. Hence, the team used a sample allocation proportional to the size of the strata (in this case, the five provinces), where MOS is the relevant size measure. Under this allocation approach, the percentage of students in the sample in each stratum should be about the same as the percentage of students in the population in each stratum.[a]

By completing the following SPSS steps, you will be able to

- Examine provincial-level information.

- Compute provincial totals.

- Compute a national total.

(continued)

EXERCISE 8.1 *(continued)*

- Compute the proportional allocation of a sample size of *n* = 120 schools to the strata (provinces).

- Store all of this information for later use.

First, open the **PROVINCES** file, using the following commands:

File – Open – Data – Look in[b]

    ...\BASE FILES\PROVINCES.SAV

Open

You will see a total MOS (*PROV_SIZE*) for rural and urban parts of each province. The national total will also be required; hence, a dummy **COUNTRY** variable will be created and set to **1** as follows:

Select **Transform – Compute Variable.** Type **COUNTRY** in **Target Variable.** Type **1** in **Numeric expression**, and click **OK.**

Select **Data – Aggregate.** Then move **COUNTRY PROVINCE** to **Break variables.** Next, move **PROV_SIZE** to **Summaries of variables.**

Click **Function** and select **Sum.** Click **Continue.**

Click **Name & Label.** Type **PROV_TOT** as a name, and click **Continue.**

Click **Create a new dataset...** and type in a name, **PROVTOT.** Click **OK.**

You should see **PROV_TOT** data for each of the five provinces; check the output windows because the results may appear in a different window **Untitled [PROVTOT]**. The **PROV_TOT** data for province 2 is 4,448.

Bring the **PROVTOT** data set you just created to the view screen and select **Data – Aggregate.** Next, move **COUNTRY** to **Break variables.** Then, move **PROV_TOT** to **Summaries of variables.**

Click **Function** and select **Sum.** Click **Continue.** Now, click **Name & Label.** Type **COUNTRY_TOT** as a name, and click **Continue.** Click **Add aggregated....** Finally, click **OK.**

You should see a national total of 27,654 in the **Data View** screen.

Now the data set **PROVTOT** contains both the national and the provincial totals. The provincial allocation of 120 schools can now be computed, and the results stored for later use. This exercise uses the **RND** function to obtain integer values.

Select **Transform – Compute Variable.** Then type **ALLOC** in **Target Variable.** Type **RND(120*PROV_TOT/COUNTRY_TOT)** in **Numeric expression.** Click **OK.**

EXERCISE 8.1 *(continued)*

The file that contains the sample allocation now looks as shown in exercise figure 8.1.A.

EXERCISE FIGURE 8.1.A   Sentz Sample Allocation

	COUNTRY	province	PROV_TOT	COUNTRY_TOT	ALLOC	var
1	1.00	1	5565.00	27654.00	24.00	
2	1.00	2	4448.00	27654.00	19.00	
3	1.00	3	9511.00	27654.00	41.00	
4	1.00	4	2222.00	27654.00	10.00	
5	1.00	5	5908.00	27654.00	26.00	

Title bar: *Untitled2 [PROVTOT] - PASW Statistics Data Editor
Menu: File Edit View Data Transform Analyze Graphs Utilities Add-ons Window Help
1 : COUNTRY 1.00

Source: Authors' example within SPSS software.

Store this file in the **MYSAMPLSOL** directory as follows:

Select **File – Save as – Look in**

...**MYSAMPLSOL**\

Type **SCHOOLALLOC** as the file name. Click **Save.** Then click **File – Close**. You can also close the **PROVINCES** data set without saving any changes you made to it.

a. If the ministry or the steering committee had specified that priority be given to certain subnational estimates (such as regions), some form of disproportional allocation might be more efficient, at the expense of slightly less precision for the national estimates. Such a situation should be discussed with an experienced statistician because it could also affect the decisions on stratification.

b. SPSS17 was used to prepare all the programs and examples. SPSS18 has some minor changes; details of some functions or menu items may have changed (for example, the "next" statement is no longer required to close some submenus). Depending on the options selected during installation, SPSS18 may compile automatically a very useful log of all the procedures and scripts executed.

SAMPLING WITH PROBABILITY PROPORTIONAL TO SIZE

Unequal probability sampling occurs when selection probabilities differ from one unit to the next. For example, larger cities or larger schools may have more diversified information because they have more students than smaller cities or schools; therefore, the national assessment sampling adviser may give priority, in the form of a higher probability of selection, to the larger units over the smaller ones. Smaller towns or schools may, in some instances, yield little additional information, and data collection costs may be almost as expensive as for larger units. In the interest of economy, the sampling team may be tempted to restrict sampling to the larger units, perhaps even to limit selection to the 5 or 10 largest towns or schools. If this happens, the smaller units have effectively no chance of being selected. The sample is *not* a probability sample from the defined population or from the available sampling frame because many schools have been excluded.

An alternative approach would be to adopt an unequal probability sampling plan that would give a higher probability to the larger units and a smaller probability to the smaller units. Under this plan, all units would have some chance of being selected, but the larger and more informative units would receive preferential treatment. Assuming an example of a population of 12 schools, 4 with 100 students and 8 with 50 students each, one could draw a sample of students by selecting the large schools with probability 1/4 (or 100/400) and the smaller schools with probability 1/8 (or 50/400). The larger schools would have twice as many chances of being selected as the smaller schools, but all schools would have *some* chance of being drawn.

In probability sampling, each sampled unit represents a certain number of units in the population in such a way that the sample as a whole represents the entire population. The number of population units represented by a given sampled unit is called its *sampling weight*. When the sample is drawn with equal probability (for example, two schools selected with probability 1/10 each), then each selected school represents the same number of schools in the population. Likewise, in unequal probability sampling, the number of schools in the population represented by a sampled school will vary according to the chances the school had of being selected: the more chances of being selected, the smaller the sampling weight and vice versa.

The major international studies of educational achievement (such as Programme for International Student Assessment, Progress in International Reading Literacy Study, and Trends in International Mathematics and Science Study) use unequal probability sampling. The samples are drawn with an unequal probability method known as

PPS, which stands for probability proportional to size. Typically, the school selection probabilities are based on their MOS (that is, the number of students in the target population in each school). For example, in a city with five schools having 400, 250, 200, 100, and 50 students for a total of 1,000 students, PPS sampling would result in school selection probabilities proportional to these sizes: 400/1,000, 250/1,000, 200/1,000, 150/1,000, and 50/1,000, respectively, if only one school is to be selected, or 800/1,000, 500/1,000, 400/1,000, 300/1,000, and 100/1,000 if two schools are to be selected. Note that if three schools are to be selected in this example, the first school cannot be given a probability of 1,200/1,000, which is greater than 1; it must be selected with certainty. The probability of selection with PPS for the two remaining schools selected is determined by reallocating the remaining size measures among the other four schools. The selection probabilities under PPS of these four schools would be 500/600, 400/600, 200/600, and 100/600.

This sampling approach can be applied to school-level sampling frames as well as to area-based sampling frames (such as lists of provinces or towns) if the appropriate MOS data are known.

MULTISTAGE SAMPLING

In many surveys of human populations, direct access to the individuals is not possible. A central up-to-date registry of persons may not exist, or if it does, its use may be strictly regulated, or it may be out of the reach of survey takers. This situation is almost always the case with educational assessments of students within classrooms, within schools, within cities, or within other jurisdictions. Indirect access to members of the target population may still be possible by using a technique called *multistage sampling*. In multistage sampling, a list of coarse units is prepared (such as geographic units or schools in education surveys), and some of those units are sampled. For each sampled unit, a list of smaller units is prepared (typically, addresses or houses or, in educational surveys, teachers or students). A sample of those smaller units is then selected within each unit selected earlier, and the process continues until the sampling team identifies the individuals to

FIGURE 8.5

Multistage Sampling

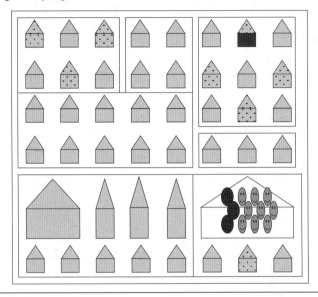

Source: Authors' representation.

be surveyed or tested. The units sampled at the first stage are called *primary sampling units* (PSUs); similarly, there are secondary sampling units and tertiary sampling units.

Many national assessments of educational achievement use a two-stage design with schools as PSUs and students as secondary sampling units. This design corresponds to one of the sampling plans considered for the Sentz case study. Some larger countries extend the design to three stages by first selecting geographic areas within which the two-stage design just described is implemented. Within schools, the selected unit is often the class, because school administrators of large schools tend to consider testing an entire target class less disruptive than testing selected individual students from different target classes in the school.

Figure 8.5 depicts a three-stage sample of students: three of seven neighborhoods are selected at stage 1; then, three, four, and two schools are selected at stage 2; finally, some students are selected from each selected school (stage 3).

DRAWING SAMPLES

The time has now come to select the samples for the two designs for Sentz: (a) the reference SRS of 400 students (see exercise 8.2) and (b) the sample of 4,400 students using the recommended two-stage design.

EXERCISE 8.2

Selection of SRS of 400 Students

The following instructions draw a simple random sample of size $n = 400$ students from the complete frame stored in the **SRS400** directory. If you want to reproduce this exact sample, you need to specify the seed[a] value that SPSS was given in creating this sample.

Choose **File – Open – Data – Look in...**

   ...\BASE FILES\STUDENTS.SAV.

Click **Open**.

Then use the following commands: **Analyze – Complex samples – Select a sample.** Select **Design a sample** and give a file name to save it (for example, **SRS400**).

Click **Next**. Skip **Design variables.** Click **Next** again.

In **Sampling Method**, choose **simple random sampling** and click **without replacement**. Then click **Next**.

In **Sample size**, choose **counts**, click **value**, and type **400**. Then click **Next**.

In **Output variables**, select at least **population size**, **sample size**, and **sample weight**. Click **Next**.

In **Summary**, click **No** because there are no further stages of sampling. Then click **Next**.

Now, the sample plan is detailed, and the sample selection can proceed.

In **Draw sample selection options**, click **Yes** and **All (1)** stages. Click **Custom value**,[b] and type **1234321** to obtain the sample that appears later in this section; otherwise, click **A randomly-chosen number** to obtain a fresh sample. Click **Next**.

In **Draw sample output files**, select **External file** and call it **...\MYSAMPLSOL\ STUDENTSRSAMPLE**. Click **Save** and then **Next**.

In **Completing the sampling wizard**, choose **Save the design to a plan file and draw the sample.** Click **Finish.**

The first few variables from the file **...\MYSAMPLSOL\STUDENTSRSAMPLE** should look as shown in exercise figure 8.2.A. In some instances, the order of the variables may differ from what is shown here.

(continued)

EXERCISE 8.2 *(continued)*

EXERCISE FIGURE 8.2.A   SRS Selection Variables

	schoolid	studentid	region	province	density	town	school	nbclass	class	classid
1	1101	1101103 NE		1	rural	1	1	2	1	11011
2	1101	1101203 NE		1	rural	1	1	2	2	11012
3	1103	1103218 NE		1	rural	1	3	4	2	11032
4	1103	1103236 NE		1	rural	1	3	4	2	11032

(continued)

	class_size	student	age	gender	InclusionProbability_1_	SampleWeightCumulative_1_	PopulationSize_1_	SampleSize_1_	SampleWeight_1_	SampleWeightht_Final_
1	41	3	13	1	.01	69.14	27654	400	69.14	69.14
2	48	3	15	1	.01	69.14	27654	400	69.14	69.14
3	52	18	13	1	.01	69.14	27654	400	69.14	69.14
4	52	36	15	0	.01	69.14	27654	400	69.14	69.14

Source: Authors' example within SPSS software.

a. A *seed* is a number used as a starting point by programs that compute "pseudo-random" numbers; each seed will give a unique sequence of pseudo-random numbers.
b. This is the seed value used for this example.

Various software packages, notably SPSS, SAS (Statistical Analysis Software), and Stata, have their own sample selection tools. SPSS offers a suite of procedures called Complex Sample. Stata offers a number of scripts, and SAS proposes five procedures specifically designed to handle complex sample designs. The Research Triangle Institute has created a large number of SAS-callable routines, named SUDAAN (for Survey Data Analysis), for processing and analyzing complex survey data. Westat Inc.'s estimation software WesVar can be downloaded free of charge from its Westat's Web site. Users should note, however, that WesVar does not draw random samples. Excel's sampling function has limitations; at the time of writing this document, its results appear to be biased under some conditions. A national assessment team should seek the advice of a sampling statistician before selecting a particular software package for sampling.

The recommended sample design for Sentz has two stages. The sample size calculation, stratification, and allocation of the first-stage sample to strata have already been done. The exercise now proceeds with the sample selection itself. The overall sampling process leading up to the selection of one randomly selected class per school from a

EXERCISE 8.3

Stratified PPS without Replacement, Selection of Schools: Reading School and School Allocation Files

The sample selection must be done independently in each stratum (in this case, within each province). Some answer files have been placed in the folder **2STG4400** to facilitate this task. A sample allocation has already been computed and stored that must be specified here. You have already completed the sample allocation task (exercise 8.1) and you will use these data in the following task. This allocation will be attached to the sampling frame before selection of schools can proceed. Start by sorting the files by province. Again, to reproduce the sampling result you will see later, you must use the seed given to SPSS. The sample is stored in a file named **...2STG4400\PPS_SAMPLE_OF_SCHOOLS**.

First, read and sort the school frame using the following commands:

File – Open – Data – Look in

    ...BASE FILES\SCHOOLS.SAV

Click **Open**, and select **Data – Sort cases**. Move **PROVINCE** to **Sort by** and click **OK**.

Next, read and sort the school allocation file using the following commands:

File – Open – Data – Look in

    ...\MYSAMPLSOL\SCHOOLALLOC.SAV

Click **Open**. Select **Data – Sort cases**. Move **PROVINCE** to **Sort by** and click **OK**.

randomly selected sample of schools is outlined in exercise 8.3. Because it involves several steps, for ease of reading, the exercise is divided into a number of steps (exercises 8.3 to 8.8).

The school frame and school allocation files are merged in exercise 8.4. Once merging the school and school allocation files is completed, the first stage of sample selection can begin. This requires selection of 120 schools (see exercise 8.1) from a total of 227 schools (exercise 8.5).

If the sample just selected does not readily appear on the screen, open the file **...\MYSAMPLSOL\PPS_SAMPLE_OF_SCHOOLS**. Figure 8.6 presents an excerpt from the first few lines of the data from **...\MYSAMPLSOL\PPS_SAMPLE_OF_SCHOOLS** that should be on your screen.

Now that the sample of schools is selected, the next step is to select one classroom per selected school. This step is similar to the simple random sample that was drawn earlier, selecting one secondary

EXERCISE 8.4

**Stratified PPS without Replacement, Selection of Schools:
Merging School and School Allocation Files**

In SPSS, the order in which the files are manipulated is important: the larger file (school frame) should be on the screen while the command menus are clicked.

Bring the **SCHOOLS** file to the screen; select the file as follows: **Data – Merge files – Add variables**. Choose **SCHOOLALLOC** from **Open dataset**, and click **Continue**.

Click **Match cases on key variables**. Move **PROVINCE** from the **Excluded variables** to the **Key variables**.

Move **COUNTRY, PROV_TOT**, and **COUNTRY_TOT** from the **New active dataset** to the **Excluded variables**.

Click **Non-active dataset is keyed table** and, finally, click **OK**. Click **OK** if the following warning message appears: **"Warning: Keyed match will fail if data are not sorted in ascending order of key variables."**

The variable **ALLOC** should now appear as the last variable of the **SCHOOLS** data set. For safety, at this point you may want to save this **SCHOOLS** file in your file **...\MYSAMPLSOL\SCHOOLS**.

EXERCISE 8.5

**Stratified PPS without Replacement, Selection of Schools:
Selecting Schools**

Verify that your **SCHOOLS** file is on the view screen. Then use the following commands:

Analyze – Complex samples – Select a sample

Select **Design sample** and give a file name to save it (for example, **2STAGE_1**). If SPSS will not readily accept a name, click **Browse** and select the **MYSAMPLSOL** subdirectory on your drive before you type in the file name. Click **Next**.

In **Design variables,** take the following actions: Move **PROVINCE** to **Stratify by**. Move **SCHOOLID** to **Clusters**. Type a name in **Stage Label**, for example, **STAGE1**. Click **Next**.

In **Sampling Method** take the following actions: Select **PPS Systematic**. Move **SCHOOL_SIZE** to **Measure of size – Read from variable**. Click **Next**.

In **Sample size** take the following actions: Choose **Read values from variable**. Move **ALLOC** to that selection box. Click **Next**.

In **Output variables**, select **population size, sample size**, and **sample weight**. Click **Next**.

EXERCISE 8.5 *(continued)*

In **Summary**, click **No** because there are no other stages of sampling for now, and then click **Next**.

Now, the sample plan is detailed and the sample selection can proceed.

In **Draw sample selection options**, click **Yes** and **All (1)** stages.

Click **Custom value**, and type **1234321** to obtain the sample that appears in this section of volume 3. Otherwise, click **A randomly-chosen number** to obtain a fresh sample. Click **Next**.

In **Draw sample output files**, select **External file** and call it ...\MYSAMPLSOL\PPS_SAMPLE_OF_SCHOOLS. Again, if SPSS will not readily accept the file name, click **Browse** first to select the subdirectory and type in the file name. Click **Save** and then **Next**.

In **Completing the sampling wizard**, choose **Save the design to a plan file and draw the sample**. Finally, click **Finish**.

FIGURE 8.6

Data Excerpt

*PPS_SCHOOL_SAMPLE_EX.sav [DataSet8] - PASW Statistics Data Editor

File Edit View Data Transform Analyze Graphs Utilities Add-ons Window Help

16 : town 4

	schoolid	region	province	density	town	school	nbclass	school_size	avgclass
1	1101	NE	1	rural	1	1	2	89	44.5
2	1103	NE	1	rural	1	3	4	221	55.3
3	1104	NE	1	rural	1	4	4	214	53.5
4	1202	NE	1	rural	2	2	3	153	51.0
5	1203	NE	1	rural	2	3	3	146	48.7

Source: Authors' example within SPSS software.

unit (one class) per selected primary unit (per school). The file **CLASSES** contains the relevant information about classes in all the schools, not just the selected ones. In real life, the national assessment coordinator from each school would create a list of eligible classrooms and either would send it to the survey coordinator or would be instructed to draw a sample of one eligible class at random, according to a prescribed series of national assessment procedures.

In the following steps, SPSS is used to select one class in each school. First the sample of 120 schools must be merged to the class file to get a list of all eligible classrooms for each selected school (exercise 8.6). The procedure is similar to that of attaching the sample allocation to the school frame that was carried out earlier (see exercise 8.4).

EXERCISE 8.6

Stratified PPS without Replacement, Selection of Schools: Identifying Eligible Classes

Read the school sample and sort by *SCHOOLID* using the following commands:

File – Open – Data – Look in

>...\MYSAMPLSOL\PPS_SAMPLE_OF_SCHOOLS.SAV

Then, click **Open**. Select **Data – Sort cases**. Move *SCHOOLID* to **Sort by**. Click **OK**. Read the list of classrooms and sort by *SCHOOLID* using the following commands:

File – Open – Data – Look in

>...\BASE FILES\CLASSES.SAV

Click **Open**. Note: School 1101 has two classes, one with 41 students and the second with 48 students.

Select **Data – Sort cases**. Move *SCHOOLID* to **Sort by**. Click **OK**.

Merge the school frame and the school allocation file; again, which file is visible on screen and which is the "keyed table" (see instructions below) are important to SPSS.

Bring the *PPS_SAMPLE_OF_SCHOOLS* file to the screen. Then use the following commands:

Data – Merge files – Add variables

Choose *CLASSES* from the **Open dataset**. Click **Continue**. Then click **Match cases on key variables**.

Move *SCHOOLID* from the **Excluded variables** to the **Key variables**. Click **Active dataset is keyed table**. Click **OK** and then click **OK** again.

These steps will modify the *PPS_SAMPLE_OF_SCHOOLS* and add classroom-level information, even for schools that were not selected. Those records must be removed.

To remove the unnecessary records, use the **Filter** and retain those cases where *PROVINCE* has a numerical value, as follows:

Data – Select Cases – Use filter variable

EXERCISE 8.6 *(continued)*

Move **PROVINCE** to **Use filter variable**. Click **Copy selected cases…**. Type in a name such as **CLASS_FRAME**, and click **OK**.

Close and *do not* save the modified **PPS_SAMPLE_OF_SCHOOLS**. Bring the **CLASS_FRAME** data set to the view screen and save it by using the following commands:

File – Save as – Look in

    …\MYSAMPLSOL

Type in **CLASS_FRAME** as the file name and click **Save**

With completion of exercise 8.6, the schools to be selected in each stratum have been identified and the list of eligible classrooms for each selected school has been constructed or obtained. The next step is to select one class per school for testing. This procedure is similar to the simple random sample drawn earlier, selecting one secondary unit (one class) per selected primary unit (per school). Figure 8.7 shows what that **CLASS_FRAME** looks like.

FIGURE 8.7

CLASS_FRAME

*class_frame.sav [CLASS_FRAME] – PASW Statistics Data Editor

File Edit View Data Transform Analyze Graphs Utilities Add-ons Window Help

1 : schoolid   1101

	schoolid	region	province	density	town	school	nbclass	school_size	avgclass	alloc	InclusionProbability_1_
1	1101	NE	1	rural	1	1	2	89	44.5	24	.38
2	1101	NE	1	rural	1	1	2	89	44.5	24	.38
3	1103	NE	1	rural	1	3	4	221	55.3	24	.95
4	1103	NE	1	rural	1	3	4	221	55.3	24	.95
5	1103	NE	1	rural	1	3	4	221	55.3	24	.95
6	1103	NE	1	rural	1	3	4	221	55.3	24	.95
7	1104	NE	1	rural	1	4	4	214	53.5	24	.92
8	1104	NE	1	rural	1	4	4	214	53.5	24	.92
9	1104	NE	1	rural	1	4	4	214	53.5	24	.92
10	1104	NE	1	rural	1	4	4	214	53.5	24	.92
11	1202	NE	1	rural	2	2	3	153	51.0	24	.66
12	1202	NE	1	rural	2	2	3	153	51.0	24	.66
13	1202	NE	1	rural	2	2	3	153	51.0	24	.66
14	1203	NE	1	rural	2	3	3	146	48.7	24	.63
15	1203	NE	1	rural	2	3	3	146	48.7	24	.63
16	1203	NE	1	rural	2	3	3	146	48.7	24	.63
17	1301	NE	1	rural	3	1	3	143	47.7	24	.62
18	1301	NE	1	rural	3	1	3	143	47.7	24	.62

Source: Authors' example within SPSS software.

Before drawing the sample, however, the class frame has to be cleaned. Some variables inherited from the school sampling step will interfere with the design variables that SPSS will automatically create as the sample of classrooms is created (exercise 8.7).

After data cleaning, the class frame can be submitted to the Complex Samples software to draw one class at random from each selected school (exercise 8.8).

In the case of Sentz, all students of the selected classes are surveyed because the classes are of moderate size. In a country where classes would be much larger (for example, more than 50 students), one might need to select a sample of students from each selected class (perhaps 25 to 30 per class). The sample design would then become a three-stage design. In Sentz, the third stage (sampling students from the sampled classes) is "invisible" for now. It will become apparent when student nonresponse arises (see part IV of this volume). The next steps in the assessment process are to contact schools and make the administrative and material arrangements with each participating school so that the assessment instruments can be administered to the selected students. Following administration of the survey, the national assessment data will be scored and cleaned (see part III of this volume).

EXERCISE 8.7

Stratified PPS without Replacement, Selection of Schools: Cleaning the Sampling Frame

Now the class frame can be submitted to the Complex Samples software to draw one class at random from each selected school by using the following commands:

   File – Open – Data – Look in

        ...\MYSAMPLSOL\CLASS_FRAME.SAV

Click **Open**.

To clean the class frame, first, click on the **Variable View** tab on the left lower corner of the SPSS screen.

Highlight the **avgclass** line and delete the variable (right click and **Clear**).

Highlight the **InclusionProbability_1_** line and delete the variable.

Highlight the **SampleWeightCumulative_1_** line and delete the variable.

EXERCISE 8.7 *(continued)*

Highlight **PopulationSize_1_** and rename it **PopulationSize1**.

Highlight **SampleSize_1_** and rename it **SampleSize1**.

Highlight **SampleWeight_1_** and rename it **Weight1**.

Highlight the **SampleWeight_Final_** line and delete the variable.

Save the file as **...\MYSAMPLSOL\CLASS_FRAME**, and click the **Data View** tab. The **CLASS_FRAME** should now look as shown in exercise figure 8.7.A.

EXERCISE FIGURE 8.7.A Clean Class Frame

File Edit View Data Transform Analyze Graphs Utilities Add-ons Window Help

1 : schoolid   1101

	schoolid	region	province	density	town	school	nbclass	school_size	ALLOC	Population Size1	Sample Size1	Weight1	classid	class_size
1	1101	NE	1	rural	1	1	2	89	24	47	24	2.61	11011	41
2	1101	NE	1	rural	1	1	2	89	24	47	24	2.61	11012	48
3	1103	NE	1	rural	1	3	4	221	24	47	24	1.05	11031	57
4	1103	NE	1	rural	1	3	4	221	24	47	24	1.05	11032	52
5	1103	NE	1	rural	1	3	4	221	24	47	24	1.05	11033	55
6	1103	NE	1	rural	1	3	4	221	24	47	24	1.05	11034	57
7	1104	NE	1	rural	1	4	4	214	24	47	24	1.08	11041	56
8	1104	NE	1	rural	1	4	4	214	24	47	24	1.08	11042	54
9	1104	NE	1	rural	1	4	4	214	24	47	24	1.08	11043	54
10	1104	NE	1	rural	1	4	4	214	24	47	24	1.08	11044	50
11	1202	NE	1	rural	2	2	3	153	24	47	24	1.52	12021	58
12	1202	NE	1	rural	2	2	3	153	24	47	24	1.52	12022	43
13	1202	NE	1	rural	2	2	3	153	24	47	24	1.52	12023	52
14	1203	NE	1	rural	2	3	3	146	24	47	24	1.59	12031	46
15	1203	NE	1	rural	2	3	3	146	24	47	24	1.59	12032	46
16	1203	NE	1	rural	2	3	3	146	24	47	24	1.59	12033	54
17	1301	NE	1	rural	3	1	3	143	24	47	24	1.62	13011	49

Source: Authors' example within SPSS software.

EXERCISE 8.8

Stratified PPS without Replacement, Selection of Schools: Selecting One Class per School

To select one class per school, use the following commands:

Data – Sort cases

Move **SCHOOLID CLASSID** to **Sort by**. Then click **OK**.

Open **Analyze – Complex samples – Select a sample**. Select **Design sample** and give a file name to save it (for example, **2STAGE_2**). Click **Next**.

(continued)

EXERCISE 8.8 *(continued)*

In **Design variables** take the following actions: Move *SCHOOLID* to **Stratify by**. Move *CLASSID* to **Clusters**. Type a name in **Stage Label**, for example, *STAGE2*. Click **Next**.

In **Sampling Method**, choose **Simple Random Sampling**, then click **without replacement**. Click **Next**.

In **Sample size**, choose **counts**, click **value**, and type *1*. Click **Next**.

In **Output variables**, select **population size, sample size**, and **sample weight**. Click **Next**.

In **Summary,** click **No**, because there are no other stages of sampling to execute on this frame, and then click **Next**. Now the sample plan is detailed, and the sample selection can proceed.

In **Draw sample selection options**, click **Yes** and **All (1)** stages.

Click **Custom value** and type *1234321* to obtain the sample that appears in this manual.[a] Otherwise, click **A randomly-chosen number** to obtain a fresh sample. Click **Next**.

In **Draw sample output files**, select **External file** and click **Browse** to ensure you will be using the correct directory. Name your file *...\MYSAMPLSOL\CLASS_SAMPLE*, and click **Save**. Click **Next**.

In **Completing the sampling wizard**, choose **Save the design to a plan file and draw the sample**. Click **Finish**.

Now, bring the sample of classes to the screen and clean the file using the following commands:

File – Open – Data – Look in

> *...\MYSAMPLSOL\CLASS_SAMPLE.SAV*

Click **Open**. Click on the **Variable View** tab on the left lower corner of the SPSS screen.

Highlight the **InclusionProbability_1_** line and delete the variable.

Highlight the **SampleWeightCumulative_1_** line and delete the variable.

Highlight **PopulationSize_1_** and rename it *PopulationSize2*.

Highlight **SampleSize_1_** and rename it *SampleSize2*.

Highlight **SampleWeight_1_** and rename it *Weight2*.

Highlight the **SampleWeight_Final_** line and delete the variable.

Save the file as *...\MYSAMPLSOL\CLASS_SAMPLE*, and click the **Data View** tab. The *CLASS_SAMPLE* should now look as shown in exercise figure 8.8.A.

EXERCISE 8.8 (continued)

EXERCISE FIGURE 8.8.A   A Selection of One Class per School

*CLASS_SAMPLE.sav [DataSet7] - PASW Statistics Data Editor

File   Edit   View   Data   Transform   Analyze   Graphs   Utilities   Add-ons   Window   Help

1 : schoolid   1101   Visible: 18 of 1

	schoolid	region	province	density	town	school	nbclass	school_size	ALLOC	Population Size1	Sample Size1	Weight1	classid	class_size	Population Size2	Sample Size2	Weight2
1	1101	NE	1	rural	1	1	2	89	24	47	24	2.61	11011	41	2	1	2.00
2	1103	NE	1	rural	1	3	4	221	24	47	24	1.05	11032	52	4	1	4.00
3	1104	NE	1	rural	1	4	4	214	24	47	24	1.08	11041	56	4	1	4.00
4	1202	NE	1	rural	2	2	3	153	24	47	24	1.52	12023	52	3	1	3.00
5	1203	NE	1	rural	2	3	3	146	24	47	24	1.59	12033	54	3	1	3.00
6	1301	NE	1	rural	3	1	3	143	24	47	24	1.62	13011	49	3	1	3.00
7	1403	NE	1	urban	4	3	4	144	24	47	24	1.61	14033	35	4	1	4.00
8	1404	NE	1	urban	4	4	4	130	24	47	24	1.78	14043	36	4	1	4.00
9	1407	NE	1	urban	4	7	4	146	24	47	24	1.59	14072	31	4	1	4.00
10	1409	NE	1	urban	4	9	3	107	24	47	24	2.17	14092	27	3	1	3.00
11	1411	NE	1	urban	4	11	3	112	24	47	24	2.07	14111	37	3	1	3.00
12	1413	NE	1	urban	4	13	4	152	24	47	24	1.53	14132	37	4	1	4.00
13	1415	NE	1	urban	4	15	4	142	24	47	24	1.63	14154	30	4	1	4.00
14	1417	NE	1	urban	4	17	4	155	24	47	24	1.50	14171	43	4	1	4.00
15	1502	NE	1	urban	5	2	3	113	24	47	24	2.05	15023	26	3	1	3.00
16	1504	NE	1	urban	5	4	3	84	24	47	24	2.76	15042	26	3	1	3.00
17	1506	NE	1	urban	5	6	4	165	24	47	24	1.41	15063	43	4	1	4.00

Source: Authors' example within SPSS software.

Selected classes in the selected schools are now stored in the permanent SPSS dataset named ...**MYSAMPLSOL\\CLASS_SAMPLE**.

a. In actual applications, it may be wise to change seeds at each draw and to record them for reference and debugging.

SAMPLING: FOLDERS AND FILES

The CD accompanying this manual contains a number of files with the necessary frame and sample data for the case study of Sentz. A summary description of the files can be found in table II.A.1. Figure II.A.1 shows the sampling file directory structure.

TABLE II.A.1

Description of Folder Contents

BASE files	Description or contents (all SPSS files)	Number of records
Provinces	Number of rural and urban towns and students in each province and region	9
Towns[a]	Number of schools and students by town, urbanization, province, and region	33
Schools	Number of classes, number of students, and average class size by school, town, urbanization, province, and region	227
Classes	Number of students per class, for each class, school, town, urbanization, province, and region	702
Students	Age and gender for each student in each class of each school, with all other geographic markers	27,654
Responses	Age, gender, achievement scores, socioeconomic status, and participation status for each student in each class, school, town, urbanization, province, and region	27,654
Census	Age, gender, achievement scores, socioeconomic status for each student in each class, as if everyone had participated	27,654

2STG4400 files	Description or contents (SPSS files)	Number of records
SCHOOLALLOC	Number of schools allocated to each province	5
ASSIGNJK	*SCHOOLID, JKZONE, JKREP,* and two temporary variables	120
PPS_SAMPLE_OF_ SCHOOLS	Selected schools, with first-stage weight	120
CLASS_FRAME	List of classes available for sampling for 120 selected schools	397
CLASS_SAMPLE	Selected classes from the selected schools, with first-stage weight, second-stage weight, and full design weight	120
PPSRESPONSES	Identifiers, background variables, scores, participation status, and design weight for each selected student, by class, school, province	4,896

TABLE II.A.1

Description of Folder Contents *(continued)*

2STG4400 files	Description or contents (SPSS files)	Number of records
RESP2STGFINAL WT[b]	Identifiers, background variables, scores, participation status, design weight, nonresponse adjustment, and final weight for each selected student, by class, school, province	4,896
RESP2STGWTJK[b]	Identifiers, background variables, scores, participation status, design weight, nonresponse adjustment, final weight, JK stratum, and JK replicate for each selected student, by class, school, province	4,896

SRS400 files	Description or contents (SPSS files)	Number of records
STUDENTSR SAMPLE	Identifiers, background variables, and design weight for each selected student	400
SRSRESPONSES	Identifiers, background variables, scores, participation status, and design weight for each selected student	400
RESPSRSFINALWT[b]	Identifiers, background variables, scores, participation status, design weight, nonresponse adjustment, and final weight for each selected student	400

NATASSESS files	Description or contents (SPSS and WesVar versions)	Number of records
NATASSESS	Identifiers, background variables, math scores, derived scores, estimation weight and normalized weight, JK stratum, and JK replicates	4,747

Source: Authors' compilation.
a. Town-level data were not analyzed in the exercise.
b. These files have WesVar versions.

FIGURE II.A.1

Sampling File Directory Structure

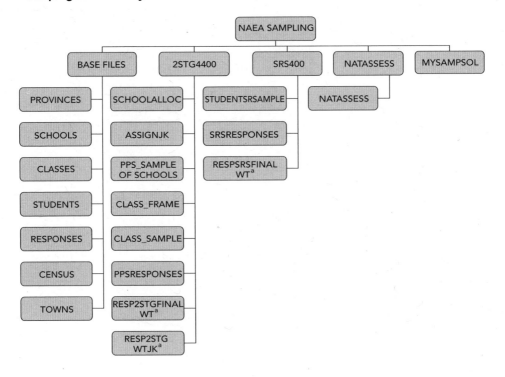

Source: Authors' representation.
a. Both SPSS and WesVar.

PART **III**

DATA PREPARATION, VALIDATION, AND MANAGEMENT

Chris Freeman and Kate O'Malley

Part III focuses on the typical tasks analysts involved in data cleaning perform in a national assessment, using examples and exercises to demonstrate the processes undertaken. The primary objective is to enable the national assessment team to develop and implement a systematic set of procedures that will help ensure that the assessment data are reliable and accurate. The accompanying CD contains examples of files containing typical data collection errors that allow the reader to practice the procedures described. Solutions for each of the exercise data, together with the cleaned files containing the test data, are provided to allow the reader to compare and verify the outcomes or results of the exercises.

The Microsoft application Access 2007 is used throughout this section for data entry and data validation, while SPSS (Statistical Package for the Social Sciences)[1] and to a lesser extent Excel 2007 are used for data verification. Alternatively, an SPSS Data Entry specialized module can be used to perform the data entry functions for which this section uses Access. Whichever approach is used, data, when captured, should be imported into SPSS for cleaning and verification procedures. The three applications referred to in this section are used to limit the dangers inherent in transposing data from program to program. Nevertheless, transposing the data inevitably introduces potential avenues for error, and the transfer of data between programs should be kept to a minimum. This point is elaborated on in later parts of this section.

The following checklist summarizes the topics covered in the chapters of this part. They list the recognized major potential sources of data error that, if not addressed, can undermine confidence in the integrity of the data.

Summary Checklist of Data Cleaning Processes

Component	Documents or processes	Key questions	Checked
Data formats	Test codebook	Data types defined?	
		Mandatory data defined?	
		Field lengths defined?	
		Test codebook matches test content?	
Data collection	Data entry software	Field data formats consistent with codebook definitions?	
		Validation routines in data entry software established?	
		Adjudication of capture errors?	
Data cleaning	Between-file checks	Merge data from different sources?	
		Routines to ensure accuracy and completeness of data? All records accounted for?	
	Data verification and within-file checks	Wild codes checked? Incorrect coding rectified?	
		Missing (mandatory) data checked?	
		Other missing data fields handled?	
		Routines to ensure integrity and completeness of data?	
	Unique identifiers	Assessment booklet matches one, and only one, entry on the sampling frames and tracking forms?	
		Duplicate records removed? Missing records checked?	
Documentation	File history, data cleaning history	Copies of data files before and after processing archived?	
	README. DOCX	Complete record of processes and outputs maintained?	

The routines described in this section are supported by practical exercises, presented in files in the folder **Exercises** in the accompanying CD. The solutions or corrected files can be examined in the folder **Exercise Solutions**. To help master the key data cleaning skills, the reader must set up the following easy-to-follow filing system.

Important Step: Saving the CD Files to Your Hard Drive or Server

On your local hard drive or server, create a folder called *NAEA DATA CLEANING* (or similar) and copy the files from the accompanying CD into this folder.
Create a new subfolder called *MY SOLUTIONS,* which you will use to save all of your exercise solutions for comparison with the files located in the **EXERCISE SOLUTIONS** folders.
You should now have three folders within the *NAEA Data Cleaning* folder: *EXERCISES, EXERCISE SOLUTIONS,* and *MY SOLUTIONS.*
From this point on, you should be working from the files located on your hard drive or server.

Annex III.A contains a brief summary of the various files and a diagram of the structure of the file used in part III. Note that Microsoft Office 2007 was used to prepare the files. The files can be run in Microsoft Office 2010. Although the ribbons at the top of some pages will appear to be slightly different from those in the 2007 version, the working sections of each program are virtually identical.

The following four admonitions, if heeded, will help ensure the accuracy of the data used in analyses.

1. Be suspicious. Even the most sophisticated assessment systems are likely to have wild codes and duplicate records after the data have been first entered. Assume some of the data are incorrect and must be changed.

2. Be systematic. Have a plan (a checklist) to work through the most probable sources of error. Check for duplicate records and out-of-range responses. These will often provide indicators of potential problem areas and also give insights into the quality of the data collection and data entry processes.

3. Be active in the data collection process. One of the best ways of ensuring that the national assessment data are clean is to insist that effective practices are implemented at the collection phase. The person in charge of data entry should be a member of the group that designs the codebook because it will have a major impact on the quality of the data entry processes. Checking that correct procedures and processes are implemented at the data entry stage can greatly reduce the time and cost needed to correct faulty data.

4. **Document all changes and versions**. Be absolutely thorough in recording all the changes that are made in the data during the data cleaning process, and keep an accurate record of the versions that are created and which version contains the final clean data files for analysis.

NOTE

1. This version 17 of SPSS is also referred to as Predictive Analytic Software, or PASW 17, during 2009 and 2010.

CHAPTER 9 | CODEBOOKS

In undertaking data cleaning and analysis, one must be sensitive to—and guided by—the information needs of the national assessment team members who will draft the final reports. People involved in data preparation have a specific responsibility to ensure that the data formats will provide the necessary level of detail the analysts require. Those involved in data preparation should also be very familiar with the contents of the test and questionnaire booklets and codebooks.

The starting point for any analysis of an assessment instrument is planning. The national assessment team should plan to ensure that the way in which data are collected produces the required information and that data are available in an accessible format. The test codebook defines the way the data collected in the assessment are recorded for analysis. The codebook defines the information about each component of the test and helps data entry personnel and analysts understand what they should expect in each data field. The codebook should be prepared jointly by the test developers and the person with overall responsibility for data entry.

Similarly, the student questionnaire codebook defines how the questionnaire data are recorded. Typically, questionnaire data refer to demographic items (such as gender, language background, or parental occupations) and are usually stored separately from the student achievement data because questionnaire data will usually contain a substantial number of qualitative responses that may need to be coded or analyzed differently. A sample student questionnaire instrument ***STUDENTQUESTIONNAIRE.DOCX*** has been placed in the ***EXERCISES*** folder for background information. For the purposes of the following exercises, however, only a small number of demographic items relating to gender, age, grade, and language background are included. Because of the small number of questionnaire items, these data are recorded in the same file as the student achievement data.

Figure 9.1, the cover page of a test booklet, shows the student-related information that was collected as part of the administration of

FIGURE 9.1

Example of a Test Cover Page

2007
MATHS
3A

Student ID: 1894305

Name: ______________________________
Given Name Family Name

School: ______________________________

Year level ***(e.g. Year 3):*** ____________________

Are you a boy or a girl?

☐ Boy ☐ Girl

How old are you turning this year?

☐ less than 8 ☐ 8 ☐ 9 ☐ more than 9

Do you usually speak a language other than <test language> at home?

☐ Yes ☐ No

Source: Authors' representation.

a mathematics test. It shows the unique student identifier (Student ID) that was created in exercise 7.1 and includes details of gender, age, and language. The ability to provide information about students depends on the information collected from test papers and questionnaires. For example, the information collected from the cover page of the test (figure 9.1) does not allow reporting on the student's home language because a question about the particular language spoken at home was not asked. Therefore, only the percentage of students who speak a language other than the language the test was printed in can be reported on.

Another limitation in the collection of data is exemplified in the way the field *Name* is treated. The data in the *Name* field can be collected as a single set of data that includes the given name and family name (for example, Juan Gonzalez) or as two separate fields: *Given Name* (Juan) and another field *Family Name* (Gonzalez). As a general rule, collecting specific information is better. If, for example, the assessment collects only one field called *Name*, sorting by name would be based on the student's given name only and would likely lead to unnecessary duplication. In this case, information for the name field should be collected as two separate fields, *Given Name* and *Family Name*. Note that the family name is listed first in some cultures.

Figure 9.2 shows the way in which the demographic information provided by students on the cover page of the test booklet shown in figure 9.1 was documented in the codebook. (See *EXERCISES-MATHS 3A CODEBOOK TEMPLATE.XLSX*) Excel was used to prepare the codebook in this instance, although Microsoft Word could also be used for this purpose. Note that if data were captured directly into SPSS (Statistical Package for the Social Sciences) software, the codebook would be created automatically by SPSS and would be available through a simple menu request: **Analyze – Reports – Codebook**. Each column of the questionnaire codebook is described in table 9.1.

Figure 9.3 presents the test codebook, which shows how the first six items of the test may be coded. Note the addition of the columns for *Item Name* and *Key*. The former provides a short reference to the item content for easy recognition, and the latter refers to the term used for the correct answer, as determined by the test developers or subject specialists.

FIGURE 9.2

Questionnaire Codebook for the Student Demographic (Background) Information

Field	Type	Data Type	Valid responses	Width	Missing	Comment
						Student Questionnaire
StudID	given	N		7		key as per paper
Given Name	CR	T		12	9	key as per paper
Family Name	CR	T		12	9	key as per paper
School Name	CR	T		20	9	key as per paper
Year level	CR	N		1	9	key one digit
Gender	MC	N	1,2,8,9	1	8,9	1 = boy, 2 = girl, 8 = multiple, 9 = missing
Age this year	MC	N	1,2,3,4,8,9	1	8,9	1 = age < 8, 2 = 8yo, 3 = 9yo, 4= age >9, 8 = multiple, 9 = missing
Test Language Spoken at home	MC	N	1,2,8,9	1	8,9	1 = yes, 2 =no, 8 = multiple, 9 = missing

Source: Authors' example within Excel software.

TABLE 9.1

Explanation of the Column Headings in the Codebook

Term	Explanation	Comment
Field	This is the name that identifies the information held in the data cell (for example, *Given Name*).	The field name must be unique and should be meaningful.
Question type	Three question types are possible: MC: Multiple choice CR: Constructed response or short answer TM: Response that requires teacher judgment	Numeric CRs can be marked by analysis programs such as SPSS.
Data type	This identifies format of the data in the field; usually data are numeric (N) or text (T).	Some programs refer to text data types as "string" or "alpha." SPSS numeric variables are further broken down into nominal, ordinal, and scale categories.
Valid responses	The complete list of expected and acceptable responses that can be found in the data for this field.	Other values are invalid and should be investigated.
Width	The maximum number of characters that are allowed to be collected in this field is specified here. (For example, this codebook permits a maximum of 20 letters in the school name.)	Note that values that include decimal places require a space for the decimal point.
Missing	This is the code that is given for duplicate (typically 8) and missing (typically 9) values.	
Comment	Additional information that will assist the data entry personnel, the data manager, and the analyst in interpreting the data can be included here.	

Source: Authors' compilation.

FIGURE 9.3

Test Codebook for the Item Fields of Maths 3a

Field	Item Name	Type	Data Type	Valid responses	Key	Width	Missing	Value Labels
Q3Aq01	4 + 11	CR	N	00 - 99		15	2	99 99 = missing data
Q3Aq02	tallest	MC	N	1,2,3,4,8,9		3	1	8,9 1 = "Leah", 2 = "Marie", 3 = "Sarah", 4 = "Kari", 8 = multiple, 9 = missing data
Q3Aq03	chair	MC	N	1,2,3,4,8,9		4	1	8,9 1 = 1 , 2 =2 , 3 = 3 , 4 = 4 , 8 = multiple, 9 = missing
Q3Aq04	number pattern	CR	N	00 - 99		28	2	99 99 = missing data
Q3Aq05	ruler	CR	N	000 - 99.9		14	4	99.9 accept 13.5 <key<14.5, 99.9 is missing
Q3Aq06	sequence	CR	N	00 - 99		24	2	99.9 99 = missing data
Q3Aq07	stickers	MC	N	1,2,3,4,8,9		3	1	8,9 1 = 1 , 2 =2 , 3 = 3 , 4 = 4 , 8 = multiple, 9 = missing

Source: Authors' example within Excel software.

Exercise 9.1 demonstrates how to enter national assessment data into a codebook.

EXERCISE 9.1

Entering National Assessment Data into a Codebook

If you have not done so already, follow the instructions in exercise 7.1 for saving the files of the accompanying CD to your local hard drive or server. Then follow these steps:

1. Open **\NAEA DATA CLEANING\EXERCISES\SAMPLE TEST PAPER 3A.DOCX**.

2. Open **\NAEA DATA CLEANING\EXERCISES\MATHS 3A CODEBOOK TEMPLATE. XLSX**. The demographic information on the **STUDENT QUESTIONNAIRE** tab and first seven items (Q3Aq01 to Q3Aq07) on the **MATHS_3A_ITEM_CODEBOOK** tab have already been filled in. (Click on the second tab at the bottom of the Excel screen.)

3. Using these first seven items as a guide, fill in the field information for the remaining seven items (Q3Aq08 to Q3Aq14), and save this file as **MATHS 3A CODEBOOK** in your **MY SOLUTIONS** folder.

The complete codebook for the Maths 3a paper is located in a file called **MATHS 3A CODEBOOK SOLUTION.XLSX** in the **EXERCISE SOLUTIONS** folder. Use this file to check your answers. (Click on the second tab to check item information.)

CHAPTER 10 DATA
MANAGEMENT

DATA ENTRY

Budget and expertise will dictate the method used to collect and record test item data. Available methods include online data collection, scanning of optical mark reader sheets, and manual key punching. Most national assessment systems, especially those with limited resources, use the key-punching approach to enter data. A well-designed template (figure 10.1) can enable key punchers to enter data accurately and quickly. This data entry template has been prepared in Access 2007, and the procedure is described in exercise 10.1. Although setting up the data entry procedure takes time, it is generally time well spent because poor procedures are the most common sources of data error.

Single Punching

Single punching involves a keyboard operator transcribing student responses into an electronic database in preparation for analysis. This method is generally the least expensive, but it is also the most risky in terms of data accuracy unless there are sound validation procedures within the program as well as close supervision of operators.

FIGURE 10.1

Data Entry Template (Access 2007)

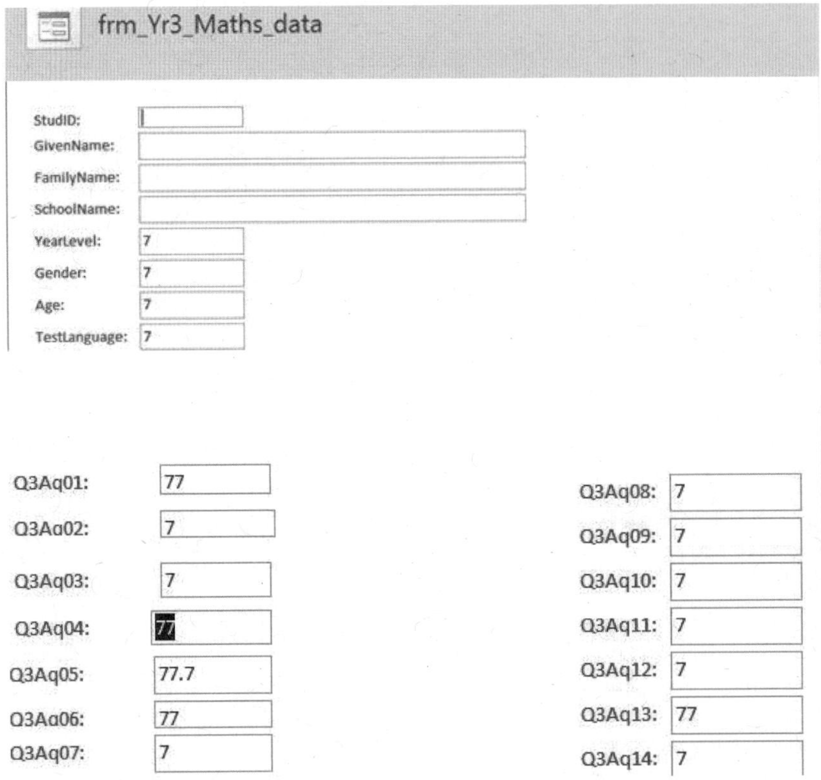

frm_Yr3_Maths_data

StudID:	
GivenName:	
FamilyName:	
SchoolName:	
YearLevel:	7
Gender:	7
Age:	7
TestLanguage:	7

Q3Aq01:	77	Q3Aq08:	7
Q3Aq02:	7	Q3Aq09:	7
Q3Aq03:	7	Q3Aq10:	7
Q3Aq04:	77	Q3Aq11:	7
Q3Aq05:	77.7	Q3Aq12:	7
Q3Aq06:	77	Q3Aq13:	77
Q3Aq07:	7	Q3Aq14:	7

Source: Authors' example within Access software.

Some data cleaning programs support a single data entry method with validation checks or routines to detect punching errors. These checks or routines greatly reduce the amount of incorrect data entry. Data, for instance, can be checked as they are being entered for wild codes—that is, codes that are incorrect—or miskeyed entries that are invalid or out of range of the expected response in a particular field. For example, if a data entry operator punched a "$" instead of "4" (which are on the same computer key), the program would immediately send a warning to the operator that the value is not valid for that particular cell. These validation routines are demonstrated later in this chapter.

EXERCISE 10.1

Creating a Database

The following steps will show you how to create a database:

1. Open Access 2007, and then click the **Blank Database** icon.

2. On the right-hand side of the window, click the folder icon next to the **File Name** box (see exercise figure 10.1.A). The program then opens a **File New Database** window. Save the file as **MATHS_3A_DATA.ACCDB** in your **MY SOLUTIONS** folder. Click **OK**, and then click **Create**.

EXERCISE FIGURE 10.1.A   Creating a New Access Database

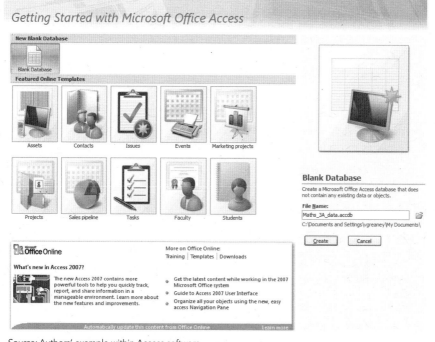

Source: Authors' example within Access software.

3. A new table has automatically been opened after creating the database. Click **View – Design View** in the top left-hand corner of the Access window. Access will automatically prompt you to save the table. The convention is that tables are saved with the prefix **tbl_** followed by a meaningful name for the table. Save the table as *TBL_YR3_ MATHS_DATA* and click **OK**. Exercise figure 10.1.B shows the table format (with the first field name *ID* automatically inserted) that is used to define the fields and data formats

(continued)

EXERCISE 10.1 *(continued)*

EXERCISE FIGURE 10.1.B The Database Table Design Layout

Source: Authors' example within Access software.

consistent with those described in the codebook. This format will be used to define the information for each field.

The **Field Name** column is used to list the variable names in the codebook. Each variable should be entered on a separate line. The field name should not include any spaces or other "illegal characters" such as exclamation marks, question marks, full stops, or commas.

The **Data Type** column typically uses **Text** for alpha variables (variables that have words as responses) or **Number** for numeric variables. In the event that you collect **Date of Birth** in your data, **Date/Time** would be entered as the data type.

The **Description** column is used to describe (or document) a variable to help other users understand the meaning of the variable. In addition, any form that is based on the table will use the contents of this description field as an instruction for data entry personnel, with the text being displayed at the bottom of the form when each particular data entry cell is selected.

Double Punching

Although double punching is both expensive and time consuming, it is often recommended as a method of minimizing data entry errors. The technique involves having two independent operators enter all the data and then comparing their outputs to identify inconsistencies. The rationale for this methodology is to account for keying errors. The most difficult of these errors to control is miskeying. If the data entry operator of a single-key methodology has typed, say, a "2" instead of a "3" when both are valid responses, there is no simple way to detect this error. If neither operator makes a mistake, the files will be identical. However, if one operator miskeys a response, a discrepancy will exist between the data. Between-file data verification can be undertaken using software programs such as SPSS (Data Entry module), UltraEdit (with UltraCompare capabilities), WinDem, and Excel. The first three of these programs present easy-to-use, reliable solutions to the issue of between-file consistency, but they are all expensive additions to the suite of software already used in this volume. For this reason, the section on verifying data in chapter 11 describes how to use Excel to detect punching errors.

Data Validation

Data validation is a process that helps prevent errors occurring as the data are entered into the national assessment database. Most common data entry applications (including WinDem, Access, and Excel) attach validation routines to each data entry cell to help minimize errors. These routines automatically warn the data entry person when they detect a problem with a particular value that is being entered. SPSS basic modules do not seem to offer quite this level of control over data entry.

Common errors in data punching include omission (missing a response), "sliding" the responses by missing one response and then entering the data from all the other responses in the wrong columns, miskeying (typing in a different response from the one indicated by the student), and duplicating a student's records by error or because the student has completed multiple test booklets. Error identification methods are described in chapter 11.

PREPARING A DATA ENTRY TEMPLATE USING MICROSOFT ACCESS

This section demonstrates the use of Access as a tool to minimize data entry errors and shows how to prepare a template to enter data. It covers validation rules to minimize incorrect coding and data entry.

TABLE 10.1

Typical Variables Collected or Captured in National Assessments

Variable (field) name	Data type	Description or use
Student ID	Numeric	The student's individual and unique identifier is created prior to test administration and used to locate records, match files, and so on.
Given name	Text	The student's given name is entered.
Family name	Text	The student's family name is used for sorting and reporting.
School name	Text	The school name is entered.
School national ID	Alphanumeric	The school identifier is entered as used on national administrative files.
School ID	Numeric	The school's individual and unique identifier, created at sampling, is used to locate records, match files, merge student records to their respective schools, and so on.
Teacher name	Text	Class or grade identification is used.
Class ID	Text or numeric	Class or grade identification is used.
Student's gender	Text or numeric	Gender may be coded as text (M or F) or number (1 = Male, 2 = Female).
Student's date of birth	Date	The data of birth is used to identify students in longitudinal data.
Student's age (in years)	Numeric	Age may be coded, grouped, or entered as discrete data.
Student's spoken language	Numeric	Usually language is coded as follows: 1 = native language, 2 = foreign language.

Source: Authors' compilation.

Table 10.1 presents a list of the typical variables (field names) that are common in national assessments. These variables enable analysis of the data by groups (for example, performance of five-year-olds compared with performance of six-year-olds or performance of boys compared with that of girls). The list is not exhaustive; in some national and international studies (such as the National Assessment of Educational Progress, the Programme for International Student Assessment, and Trends in International Mathematics and Science Study), the list of variables is extensive.

Entering Field Information into the Blank Table

Access and other databases usually require a sequence number to which data can be related. Link tables can be created using the assessment student identifier (ID).

For the purposes of exercise 10.2, the student ID has the field name **StudID**. It is used as a sequencing value to enable a quick

---

EXERCISE 10.2

Creating Database Variables

To create database variables, follow these steps:

1. Open ...*NAEA DATA CLEANING\MY SOLUTIONS\MATHS_3A_DATA.ACCDB*.

2. Open **TBL_YR3_MATHS_DATA**, which was created in exercise 10.1, by double-clicking on it in the left-hand side **Table** menu. Tables will automatically open in **Datasheet View** mode. To view the table in **Design View** mode, select **View – Design View** from the **Home** ribbon.

3. Change the default value (**ID**) to **StudID** in the first cell underneath **Field Name** (see exercise figure 10.2.A). Note that this first variable has been automatically defined as the primary key (denoted by the highlighted **Primary Key** button on the **Design** ribbon, and the small **Primary Key** icon next to the **Field Name**). This designation means that each record must contain a unique value (no duplicates) for this field so that each record can be identified and verified and so that other tables can be linked to this table at a later stage.

EXERCISE FIGURE 10.2.A Entering Variable Formats into the Table

Source: Authors' example within Access software.

(continued)

EXERCISE 10.2 *(continued)*

4. Tab across to the **Data Type** field. This should bring up the **Field Properties** dialogue box below the table. (*Note:* Some of the items listed under **Field Properties** have drop-down arrows. Click the right side of the box associated with each item to get the drop-down arrow.)

5. Click the drop-down arrow ▼ at the right of the **Data Type** cell in the *StudID* row. The data type options available in Access are now revealed.

6. Select *Text* from the drop-down menu using either the mouse or the arrow keys on the keyboard. Note that although the actual ID is in numeric format, it should really act like text so that the cell contents appear exactly as entered. Thus, for instance, an ID number with an initial digit of *0* will remain as such. The format shown in the **Field Properties** area is the default assigned by Access for an automatically assigned primary key of this data type (exercise figure 10.2.A).

7. Tab across to the **Description Column** and type *Student ID* in the cell.

8. As stated in step 6, Access will have defaulted to a set of values in the **Field Properties** area once *Text* was selected from the **Data Type** menu. In the **Field Size** field, enter the digit *7*, which is the length of the student ID in this instance. Set the **Required** field to **Yes**, and the **Allow Zero Length** field to **No**. The remaining fields can be left unchanged.

9. Select **Office button – Save**.

10. At any time, you can close the table using the ✕ icon in the top right-hand corner of the table, just above the vertical scroll bar. (*Note:* This icon is distinct from the close button in the top right-hand corner of the entire window. Clicking that icon will close the entire database.) Click the table's close button now to close the table. The table now appears as an icon in the **Tables** menu on the left-hand side of the window (exercise figure 10.2.B).

EXERCISE FIGURE 10.2.B Table Menu with Saved Table, *tbl_Yr3_Maths_Data*

Source: Authors' example within Access software.

reference for searching the database in some of the cleaning routines. **StudID** is a numeric variable that will identify a student in the Access database. The student ID was created on the sampling frames before the assessment was administered.

Entering Additional Fields

To create additional fields in the database, first reopen the table created in exercise 10.1 in **Design View** mode. Exercise 10.3 takes the reader through entering student demographic data.

EXERCISE 10.3

Creating Additional Database Fields

This exercise describes the steps for creating additional database fields:

1. Open ...*NAEA DATA CLEANING\\MY SOLUTIONS\\MATHS_3A_DATA.ACCDB*.
2. Open *TBL_YR3_MATHS_DATA* in **Design View** mode.
3. Enter the variables *GivenName* and *FamilyName* in the second and third rows in the **Field Name** column. The program will default to data type **Text**, and the **Field Properties** dialogue box will open automatically so that you can enter the data entry rules. You can move between all areas on this screen either by using the **Tab** key (moves cursor to the next cell) or by using the mouse to select the relevant field.
4. Enter information about the field name in the **Description** area to inform other users about the contents of the field, including those who carry out data entry (see exercise figure 10.3.A).

EXERCISE FIGURE 10.3.A   Adding the Student Data Field

Source: Authors' example within Access software.

(continued)

EXERCISE 10.3 *(continued)*

5. Change the **Field Size** in **Field Properties** to 20 characters for both variables (see exercise figure 10.3.A). The field length will be defined by the **Width** field used in the data capture program and the codebook. (*Note:* You may want to increase the field width and variable length if names longer than 20 characters are common in the country of administration.)

6. For the *GivenName* variable, leave all remaining field properties with their default values.

7. For the *FamilyName* variable, change the **Required** property to *Yes* in the drop-down box to indicate that a family name must be recorded.

8. For the **Allow Zero Length** field, if the data are optional, the default of *Yes* is allowed. However, some fields should have this property set to *No* to indicate that having no entry recorded is not allowable. In this case, set the value to *No*. The last five properties—**Indexed**, **Unicode Compression**, **IME Mode**, **IME Sentences,** and **Smart Tags**—can be left untouched with default values.

9. Enter the *SchoolName* variable using the same procedures. Consider the field properties that are required, and make sure they are consistent with the information in your codebook. All data fields have been set to text data types. The section titled "Default Values" deals with entering and defining numeric data types. The next variable is *YearLevel*. This is numeric data with a valid value of 3.

10. Enter the field name *YearLevel*; then tab to the **Data Type** field and select *Number* from the drop-down menu. The variable *YearLevel* is an indicator of the year level of the student taking the assessment. Sometimes classes are "mixed" when not all students are in Year 3 (that is, classes comprise both Years 2 and 3 or both Years 3 and 4), and you want to be able to filter for these data. We will address how to treat field properties for *YearLevel* in Exercise 10.5

11. Select **Office Button – Save** or (**CTRL+S**) to save the table.

Default Values

Including a default value is advisable to indicate when the data entry operator has not made a change. The default could be the expected value when the test is restricted to a particular group (such as Year 3, in this case). For example, one might have a field to indicate that the student has a textbook. If most of the students have a science textbook, the default value could be set to 1 to indicate "has a science textbook." In this case, one would enter data in this field only if the

---

EXERCISE 10.4

Setting Default Values

Follow these steps to set default values:

1. Open *...\NAEA DATA CLEANING\MY SOLUTIONS\MATHS_3A_DATA.ACCDB*.

2. Open *TBL_YR3_MATHS_DATA* in **Design View** mode.

3. Enter the variable *Gender* after the *YearLevel* variable, and set **Data Type** to *Number*.

4. In the **Description** column, enter *Gender: 1 = Boy; 2 = Girl; 8 = multiple response; 9 = missing*.

5. In the **Field Properties** area, set **Default value** to *7* (exercise figure 10.5.B in the next exercise).

By setting the default value outside the valid response range, an entry for the *Gender* variable becomes mandatory, meaning that the data entry operator cannot skip this variable. If the test booklet gives no datum, the data entry operator will be required to enter a *9* to represent missing data. Setting the valid response range is outlined in the "Validation" section.

---

student does not have a science textbook. Alternatively, one could set the default to be an invalid code (outside the range of responses) to ensure that an entry is forced. In such a case, the default value is automatically entered for all new records, and the value is then replaced as the data are entered. If, however, a student or respondent did not provide an answer, this is considered "missing data," and the value for missing data is inserted. In exercise 10.4, the default value is set to 7, which is outside the valid range of responses, to indicate where the data entry operator has made a change and where he or she has not. If an entry for a certain field is required, the data entry operator will need to enter a code that is within the valid response range (for example, 1 = A; 2 = B; 3 = C; 4 = D; 8 = duplicate; 9 = missing).

Validation

Validation is the process of ensuring that only plausible data can be entered into a field. In the interests of efficiency, setting up validation rules for this data source is advisable to minimize the amount of corrections to be done in the verification stage.

A four-option multiple-choice question should have only the values 1, 2, 3, or 4; 8 (for multiple responses); or 9 (for no response). These values make up the valid response range. There should be no value of 6, for example, because it does not represent a possible response.

Validation rules involve inserting codes into the data entry application to ensure that only valid responses are entered. If a key operator miskeys and attempts to enter an out-of-range value (a wild code), the program will not accept the value; it will prompt the key operator to enter a value within the valid range. In Access, validation rules are set within the field properties. Exercise 10.5 shows how to use these properties.

EXERCISE 10.5

Using the Validation Rule and Validation Text Properties

The following exercise describes how to use the validation rule:

1. Open ...\NAEA DATA CLEANING\MY SOLUTIONS\MATHS_3A_DATA.ACCDB.

2. Open tbl_Yr3_Maths_Data in Design View mode.

3. For the YearLevel variable, set the Default Value to 7. Click on the Validation Rule field, and in the Field Properties area enter the following: > 1 AND < 5. This value allows for mixed-level classes. If classes have students in multiple grades (for example, one class with Year 2 and Year 3 students being taught concurrently), you may want all students to take the same test to compare performance of the two cohorts. Setting the validation rule to values between 1 and 5 will enable you to do so. Validation Text is the next field in the Field Properties window. It allows the database creator to alert the data entry operator to any incidence of invalid codes or values being entered at the time of data entry.

4. Click on the Validation Text field and enter the following: Must be in Year 3 or mixed Year 3 class (see exercise figure 10.5.A). This is the error message that will appear if the data entry operator attempts to enter a value outside the valid range.

5. Complete the Validation Rule and the Validation Text for the Gender variable. Here, gender is coded as 1 for Boy, 2 for Girl, 8 for multiple response, and 9 for missing (see exercise figure 10.5.B). The test booklet records Age in four categories. Code 1 represents "Age is less than 8"; code 2 represents "Age is 8"; code 3 represents "Age is 9"; and code 4 represents "Age is greater than 9." Exercise figure 10.5.C shows how these data will be entered.

EXERCISE 10.5 *(continued)*

The next field is the indicator of whether a language other than that of the text (for example, English) is regularly spoken at home. The text used for responses (code frame) is often written in the **Description** column. Note that for the ***TestLanguage*** variable, the student responses are coded *1* for ***Yes*** (other language is regularly spoken) or *2* for ***No*** (other language is not regularly spoken) (see exercise figure 10.5.D).

EXERCISE FIGURE 10.5.A   Example of the Validation Rule

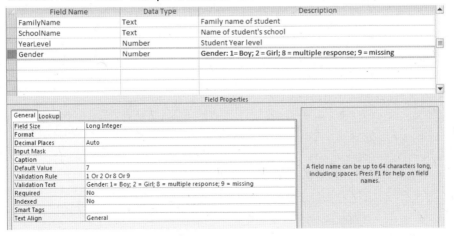

Field Name	Data Type	Description
StudID	Text	Student ID
GivenName	Text	Given name of student
FamilyName	Text	Family name of student
SchoolName	Text	Name of student's school
YearLevel	Number	Student Year level
Gender	Number	⚥nder: 1= Boy; 2 = Girl; 8 = multiple response; 9 = missing

Field Properties

General | Lookup

Field Size	Long Integer
Format	
Decimal Places	Auto
Input Mask	
Caption	
Default Value	0
Validation Rule	>1 And <5
Validation Text	Must be in Year 3 or in Year 3 class
Required	Yes
Indexed	No
Smart Tags	
Text Align	General

A field name can be up to 64 characters long, including spaces. Press F1 for help on field names.

Source: Authors' example within Access software.

EXERCISE FIGURE 10.5.B   Example of Validation Text: Gender

Field Name	Data Type	Description
FamilyName	Text	Family name of student
SchoolName	Text	Name of student's school
YearLevel	Number	Student Year level
Gender	Number	Gender: 1= Boy; 2 = Girl; 8 = multiple response; 9 = missing

Field Properties

General | Lookup

Field Size	Long Integer
Format	
Decimal Places	Auto
Input Mask	
Caption	
Default Value	7
Validation Rule	1 Or 2 Or 8 Or 9
Validation Text	Gender: 1= Boy; 2 = Girl; 8 = multiple response; 9 = missing
Required	No
Indexed	No
Smart Tags	
Text Align	General

A field name can be up to 64 characters long, including spaces. Press F1 for help on field names.

Source: Authors' example within Access software.

(continued)

EXERCISE 10.5 *(continued)*

EXERCISE FIGURE 10.5.C   Validation for Coded Values: Age

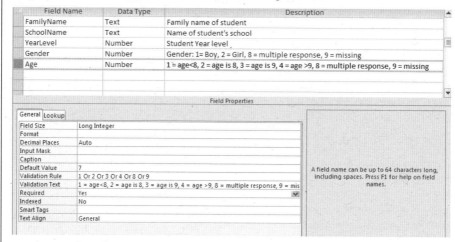

Field Name	Data Type	Description
FamilyName	Text	Family name of student
SchoolName	Text	Name of student's school
YearLevel	Number	Student Year level
Gender	Number	Gender: 1= Boy, 2 = Girl, 8 = multiple response, 9 = missing
Age	Number	1 = age<8, 2 = age is 8, 3 = age is 9, 4 = age >9, 8 = multiple response, 9 = missing

Field Properties

General | Lookup

Field Size	Long Integer
Format	
Decimal Places	Auto
Input Mask	
Caption	
Default Value	7
Validation Rule	1 Or 2 Or 3 Or 4 Or 8 Or 9
Validation Text	1 = age<8, 2 = age is 8, 3 = age is 9, 4 = age >9, 8 = multiple response, 9 = mis
Required	Yes
Indexed	No
Smart Tags	
Text Align	General

A field name can be up to 64 characters long, including spaces. Press F1 for help on field names.

Source: Authors' example within Access software.

EXERCISE FIGURE 10.5.D   Validation for Text Values: TestLanguage

Field Name	Data Type	Description
YearLevel	Number	Student Year level
Gender	Number	Gender: 1= Boy, 2 = Girl, 8 = multiple response, 9 = missing
Age	Number	1 = age<8, 2 = age is 8, 3 = age is 9, 4 = age >9, 8 = multiple response, 9 = missing
TestLanguage	Number	1 = Yes, 2 = No, 8 = multiple, 9 = missing

Field Properties

General | Lookup

Field Size	Long Integer
Format	
Decimal Places	Auto
Input Mask	
Caption	
Default Value	
Validation Rule	1 Or 2 Or 8 Or 8 Or 9
Validation Text	1 = Yes, 2 = No, 8 = multiple, 9 = missing
Required	No
Indexed	No
Smart Tags	
Text Align	General

A field name can be up to 64 characters long, including spaces. Press F1 for help on field names.

Source: Authors' example within Access software.

6. Complete the **Default Rule**, **Validation Rule,** and **Validation Text** fields for the *Age* and *TestLanguage* variables, and save the table (**CTRL+S**).

Preparing a Table to Receive Item Data

Most of the time spent recording data involves entering responses to test items (and questionnaires) administered in the national assessment. The process for preparing the table for item data is similar to that used for student demographic information. The field type for each response is generally numeric. Text-type data are used to record responses involving words, sentences, and longer passages.

Entering Data

At this stage, the table in which data from the student test forms will be recorded has been created, but no data have been entered. Now a data entry template must be prepared for the table to help ensure consistent and accurate data entry. In Access, this template is called a *form*. Exercises 10.6, 10.7, 10.8, and 10.9 deal with various aspects of entering data and preparing forms.

EXERCISE 10.6

Entering Item Field Data into a Database

This exercise teaches you how to enter item field data into a database:

1. Open ...*My Solutions\Maths_3a_data.accdb* (with changes saved from previous exercises).

2. Open *tbl_Yr3_Maths_Data* in **Design View** mode.

3. Enter the relevant field information for the first item: **Q3Aq01**. Again, you will need to refer to your completed codebook or the codebook solution provided in the *EXERCISE SOLUTIONS* folder. *Hint:* This item is a constructed-response question. Set **Field Properties** for response data to *Required*, set a **Default Value** of *77*, and include a **Validation Rule** and **Validation Text**. Compare your responses to those given in exercise figure 10.6.A.

   Note: For numeric data types, the **Field Size** will default to *Double* or *Long Integer*. This is an internal setting that enables mathematical operations to be computed on these data. Allow the default to be applied.

4. Enter the field properties for the second item on the mathematics test. It is also a four-option multiple-choice mathematics question (exercise figure 10.6.B).

(continued)

EXERCISE 10.6 *(continued)*

EXERCISE FIGURE 10.6.A   Item Field Data: Question 1

Field Name	Data Type	Description
StudID	Text	Student ID
GivenName	Text	Given name of student
FamilyName	Text	Family name of student
SchoolName	Text	Name of student's school
YearLevel	Number	Student Year Level
Gender	Number	1 = Boy, 2 = Girl, 8 = multiple response, 9 = missing
Age	Number	1 = age<8, 2 = age is 8, 3 = age is 9, 4 = age >9, 8 = multiple response, 9 = missing
TestLanguage	Number	1 = Yes, 2 = No, 8 = multiple, 9 = missing
Q3Aq01	Number	Question 1: 2 digits, 99 = missing

Field Properties

General | Lookup

Field Size	Long Integer
Format	
Decimal Places	Auto
Input Mask	
Caption	
Default Value	77
Validation Rule	<100
Validation Text	2 digits, 99 = missing
Required	Yes
Indexed	No
Smart Tags	
Text Align	General

A field name can be up to 64 characters long, including spaces. Press F1 for help on field names.

Source: Authors' example within Access software.

EXERCISE FIGURE 10.6.B   Item Field Data: Question 2

TABLE_YR_3_MATHS_DATA

Field Name	Data Type	Description
Gender	Number	1 = Boy, 2 = Girl, 8 = multiple response, 9 = missing
Age	Number	1 = age<8, 2 = age is 8, 3 = age is 9, 4 = age>9, 8 = multiple response, 9 = missing
TestLanguage	Text	1 = Yes, 2 = No, 8 = multiple, 9 = missing
Q3Aq01	Number	Question 1: 2 digits, 99 = missing
Q3Aq02	Number	Question 2: MC, 1-4 or 8 = multiple or 9 = missing

Field Properties

General | Lookup

Field Size	Long Integer
Format	
Decimal Places	Auto
Input Mask	
Caption	
Default Value	7
Validation Rule	1 Or 2 Or 3 Or 4 Or 8 Or 9
Validation Text	Question 2: MC, 1-4 or 8 = multiple or 9 = missing
Required	Yes
Indexed	No
Smart Tags	
Text Align	General

A field name can be up to 64 characters long, including spaces. Press F1 for help on field names.

Source: Authors' example within Access software.

The copy-and-paste procedure can be used to copy the information from item 2 to other multiple-choice items (such as **Q3Aq07**, **Q3Aq08**, **Q3Aq09**, and so on) where the response options are identical (for example, the text in the **Validation Rule** and **Validation Text** fields for these items).

Similarly, you can copy and paste information from one **Field Property** screen to another. For example, you can copy the validation rule and validation text material for

EXERCISE 10.6 *(continued)*

each multiple-choice question to every other multiple-choice question by copying the field **Q3Aq02 (CTRL+C),** which is highlighted in exercise figure 10.6.B, and pasting it **(CTRL+V)** into the correct position (for example, **Q3Aq07**). Change the **Field Name** (for example, to **Q3Aq07**), and repeat the process for each multiple-choice question in the test.

5. Enter the field properties for the remaining items, up to item 14.

Exercise figure 10.6.C shows the table format for all 14 questions as well as for the demographic data. It highlights the structure of question 11.

Q3Aq04 is a constructed-response item. The data entry operator will enter the student's actual response or **99** if the student has not attempted the question.

The test item data will be scored later when all the data have been checked and validated.

EXERCISE FIGURE 10.6.C Field Structure for All Demographic and Item Data

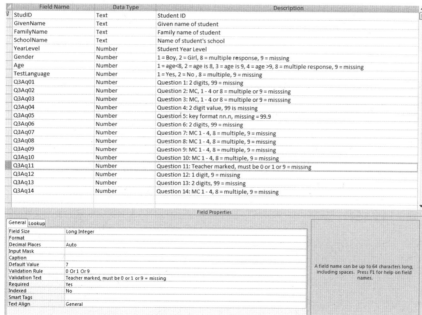

Field Name	Data Type	Description
StudID	Text	Student ID
GivenName	Text	Given name of student
FamilyName	Text	Family name of student
SchoolName	Text	Name of student's school
YearLevel	Number	Student Year Level
Gender	Number	1 = Boy, 2 = Girl, 8 = multiple response, 9 = missing
Age	Number	1 = age<8, 2 = age is 8, 3 = age is 9, 4 = age >9, 8 = multiple response, 9 = missing
TestLanguage	Number	1 = Yes, 2 = No , 8 = multiple, 9 = missing
Q3Aq01	Number	Question 1: 2 digits, 99 = missing
Q3Aq02	Number	Question 2: MC, 1 - 4 or 8 = multiple or 9 = misssing
Q3Aq03	Number	Question 3: MC, 1 - 4 or 8 = multiple or 9 = misssing
Q3Aq04	Number	Question 4: 2 digit value, 99 is missing
Q3Aq05	Number	Question 5: key format nn.n, missing = 99.9
Q3Aq06	Number	Question 6: 2 digits, 99 = missing
Q3Aq07	Number	Question 7: MC 1 - 4, 8 = multiple, 9 = missing
Q3Aq08	Number	Question 8: MC 1 - 4, 8 = multiple, 9 = missing
Q3Aq09	Number	Question 9: MC 1 - 4, 8 = multiple, 9 = missing
Q3Aq10	Number	Question 10: MC 1 - 4, 8 = multiple, 9 = missing
Q3Aq11	Number	Question 11: Teacher marked, must be 0 or 1 or 9 = missing
Q3Aq12	Number	Question 12: 1 digit, 9 = missing
Q3Aq13	Number	Question 13: 2 digits, 99 = missing
Q3Aq14	Number	Question 14: MC 1 - 4, 8 = multiple, 9 = missing

Field Properties

General | Lookup

Field Size	Long Integer
Format	
Decimal Places	Auto
Input Mask	
Caption	
Default Value	7
Validation Rule	0 Or 1 Or 9
Validation Text	Teacher marked, must be 0 or 1 or 9 = missing
Required	Yes
Indexed	No
Smart Tags	
Text Align	General

A field name can be up to 64 characters long, including spaces. Press F1 for help on field names.

Source: Authors' example within Access software.

6. Save (**CTRL+S**) the table.

7. Open ...*EXERCISE SOLUTIONS\\MATHS_3A_DATA_SOLUTION1.ACCDB* and compare the *TBL_YR3_MATHS_DATA_SOLUTION1* table with your *TBL_YR3_ MATHS_DATA* table. If the two tables differ significantly, copy the format and field data from *TBL_YR3_MATHS_DATA_ SOLUTION1* to your table.

EXERCISE 10.7

Creating a Form

In this exercise, you will learn how to create a form:

1. Open **...\MY SOLUTIONS\MATHS_3A_DATA.ACCDB** with changes saved from previous exercises.

2. Highlight the table **TBL_YR3_MATHS_DATA** in the left-hand menu. Then from the **Create** ribbon, click **Form** (see exercise figure 10.7.A).

EXERCISE FIGURE 10.7.A   Creating a Data Entry Form

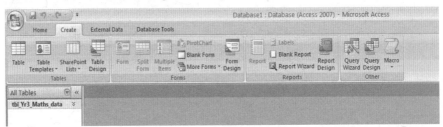

Source: Authors' example within Access software.

The program will automatically draft a form with fields corresponding to those in the original table, as shown in exercise figure 10.7.B.

EXERCISE FIGURE 10.7.B   Automatically Generated Form Fields

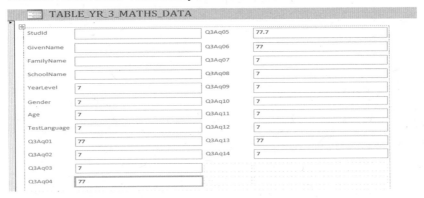

Source: Authors' example within Access software.

3. Save the form by clicking **Office button – Save** (or **CTRL+S**). Change the prefix from **tbl_** (indicating a table) to **frm_** (to indicate that this is the form for **TBL_YR3_MATHS_DATA**), and click **OK**.

The form layout shown in exercise figure 10.7.B may not be appropriate for rapid data entry. In some instances, arranging the form cells to accept the item data similarly to the layout of the test booklet or the answer sheet may make data entry easier.

EXERCISE 10.8

Changing the Form Layout

To change the form layout, follow these steps:

1. Open **...\MY SOLUTIONS\MATHS_3A_DATA.ACCDB** with changes saved from previous exercises.

2. From the **All Access Objects** menu on the left-hand side of the window, open **FRM_ YR3_MATH**S_DATA in **Design View** mode. Form fields can now be edited, added, or deleted.

3. Right click on the form on the left panel. Select all the fields on the form by using the click-and-drag function of the mouse to "lasso" all the text boxes on the form. You can select all the text boxes by pressing **CTRL+A** ('Select All'). From the **Form Design Tools – Arrange** section of the ribbon, click **Remove** on the **Control Layout** area. This will remove the previous layout applied to the controls and form fields can now be moved around the form.

4. Select the fields that you want to move to a different place on the form, and use either the mouse (click-and-drag function) or the arrow keys on the keyboard to move the field to the desired location (exercise figure 10.8.A). By clicking on the first field (for example, **StudID**) and then holding down the shift key while clicking on other fields, you can select multiple fields. Remember to release the shift key and place the cursor within any of the selected boxes before moving the highlighted fields (or you can release the shift

EXERCISE FIGURE 10.8.A   Moving Form Fields

Source: Authors' example within Access software.

(continued)

EXERCISE 10.8 *(continued)*

EXERCISE FIGURE 10.8.B   Resizing Fields

Source: Authors' example within Access software.

key and move the boxes with the arrow keys). You can also select multiple fields by using the click-and-drag function of the mouse to "lasso" the desired fields.

Note that you can drag down the **Form Footer** bar by placing the cursor on the top of the Form Footer box and using the click-and-drag function to drag it down to the desired location.

5. Fields can also be resized by clicking and changing their shape. Highlight the boxes you wish to resize, then drag the arrows on the corners or the sides of the highlighted small black boxes to get the desired shape (exercise figure 10.8.B).

6. Save any changes (**CTRL+S**) before exiting the form.

EXERCISE 10.9

Entering Data into the Form

Follow these steps to enter data into the form:

1. Open **...\MY SOLUTIONS\MATHS_3A_DATA.ACCDB** (with changes saved from previous exercises).

2. Open **FRM_YR3_MATHS_DATA** in the **All Access Objects** menu in **Form View** (the default view).

3. Enter the student demographic data (exercise figure 10.9.A) from the first student's test booklet into the form, together with the student's responses, which can be gleaned from the summary of this student's item responses presented in exercise figure 10.9.B. (*Note:* This information would ordinarily be taken directly from the student's booklet, but to conserve space, a summary of the student's responses has been created.)

4. The data (exercise figure 10.9.C) will be automatically saved in the table that you created for the form, in this case **TBL_YR3_MATHS_3A_DATA**. As the data are entered, the table expands to accept more and more records.

EXERCISE FIGURE 10.9.A   Student Data to Be Entered into the Form

2007
MATHS
3A

Student ID: **1294302**

Name: _Aaron_   _Anama_
       (Given Name)   (Family Name)

School: _Eaglehawk School_

Year: _3_

Are you a boy or a girl?
☑ Boy   ☐ Girl

How old are you turning this year?
☐ less than 8   ☑ 8   ☐ 9   ☐ more than 9

Do you usually speak a language other than *English* at home?
☑ Yes   ☐ No

Source: Authors' representation.

(continued)

EXERCISE 10.9 *(continued)*

EXERCISE FIGURE 10.9.B   Student Item Response Summary

Field	Type	Student Response
Q3Aq01	CR	15
Q3Aq02	MC	3
Q3Aq03	MC	4
Q3Aq04	CR	28
Q3Aq05	CR	1
Q3Aq06	CR	24
Q3Aq07	MC	2
Q3Aq08	MC	1
Q3Aq09	MC	3
Q3Aq10	MC	2
Q3Aq11	TM	1
Q3Aq12	CR	1
Q3Aq13	MC	
Q3Aq14	MC	1

Source: Authors' example within SPSS software.

EXERCISE FIGURE 10.9.C   Record 1 with Data Entered

frm_Yr3_Maths_data

StudID: 1294302

GivenName: Aaron

FamilyName: Anama

SchoolName: Eaglehawk School

YearLevel: 3

Gender: 1

Age: 2

TestLanguage: 1

Q3Aq01:	15	Q3Aq08:	1
Q3Aq02:	3	Q3Aq09:	3
Q3Aq03:	4	Q3Aq10:	2
Q3Aq04:	28	Q3Aq11:	1
Q3Aq05:	1.	Q3Aq12:	1
Q3Aq06:	24	Q3Aq13:	99
Q3Aq07:	1	Q3Aq14:	1

Source: Authors' example within Access software.

Any time an invalid entry is made, a dialogue box alerts the operator to the error. In exercise figure 10.9.D, for example, the data entry operator has attempted to enter **6** in the **YearLevel** field when the only valid values are ˆ2, 3, and 4.

If incorrect validation criteria have been specified in the original table design (for example, only values of 1, 2, 3, or 9 are defined as valid when 4 should also be a valid response) and are preventing the data entry operator from entering a valid value, you can amend the validation criteria by adding this valid value to the table properties in the design view of the table the form is updating (see exercise 10.6 for instructions on setting validation rules).

Make sure to test your table and form before you start entering data. Errors can easily be fixed at this stage but are more difficult to detect later.

If several persons are entering data, assign each one a separate copy of the Access form so that you can control each independently. Sometimes an individual data entry operator may be careless.

Tabbing between cells causes the next field to be automatically selected in **Edit** mode so that the data entered overwrite the default value. Tabbing past the final field in a record brings up the next record for entry.

EXERCISE FIGURE 10.9.D   Example of Attempt to Enter Invalid Data

Source: Authors' example within Access software.

Inserting New Fields or Adding Fields to the Template

More fields must sometimes be created (for example, if the template was created with 12 items and the test has 30 items). New fields can be added in one of two ways. The first involves clicking on the **ab|** icon on the toolbar on the **Form Design Tools – Design** ribbon and clicking on the area of the form where the field is to be added. (*Note:* If the icon is not visible, depress the hammer and wrench button on the toolbar, and it will appear.) The size and shape of the label and text box (as well as the properties of the fields) will be set to default values. They must be resized (or changed) manually if they are to be identical to the labels and text boxes already on the form. Then, set the control source for the text box by right-clicking on the text box (the box on the right), selecting **Property Sheet** from the **Design** ribbon, selecting the **Data** tab, and then choosing the relevant source from the **Control Source** drop-down menu. These steps will change the text box contents from **Unbound** to the relevant source.

The second (and faster) way to add another field involves copying (**CTRL+C**) a label and text box, and then pasting (**CTRL+V**) them onto the form. This copy will be identical in all respects to the original data and can be added by selecting and pasting groups (rather than just single sets) of labels and text boxes. Then, the text name and the variable data can be changed to the required values. The labels and text boxes will automatically be pasted into the top right-hand corner of the page and can be moved by clicking and dragging or by using the arrow keys.

Exporting Data

When all the data have been entered, you can review the completed data entry in the original table that is now linked to the form. The data entered into an Access form or table can be exported as an .xls or .txt file by opening the table to be exported and then clicking on either the **Excel** or **Text file** icon from the **Export** section of the **External Data** ribbon. The destination of the file can be edited by clicking on the **Browse** button and navigating to the desired location; the file name can be changed by editing the text in the **FileName** text box. Note that none of the exercises uses Excel export as a data source; it is used as a checking mechanism as described in exercise 11.1. Data cannot be directly exported to SPSS from Access, but they can be imported to SPSS following the instructions given in exercise 10.10. Transferring data from one application to another has the potential for error, however, and for this reason should be kept to an absolute minimum.

EXERCISE 10.10

Importing Data into SPSS

The following steps will allow you to import data from an Access form into SPSS:

1. Open SPSS (**Start – Programs – SPSS**).

2. Select **File – Open database – New Query**.

3. The **Database Wizard** window will now appear. Select **MS Access Database** from the **ODBC Data Sources** list. Then click **Next**.

4. The **ODBC Driver Login** window will now appear. Click the **Browse** button and navigate to where your Access database is stored (**...NAEA DATA CLEANING\MY SOLUTIONS**). Highlight your database (**MATHS_3A_DATA.ACCDB**), click **Open**, and then click **OK**.

5. The **tbl_Yr3_Maths_Data** table will appear in the **Available Tables** box. Either double-clicking on this icon or clicking the arrow to the right of this box will retrieve all fields from this table (exercise figure 10.10.A). Click **Next**.

EXERCISE FIGURE 10.10.A   Importing the Data File

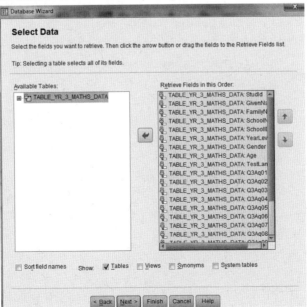

Source: Authors' example within Access software.

(continued)

EXERCISE 10.10 *(continued)*

6. The next screen allows you to limit the number of cases retrieved by specifying selection criteria. You want to import all cases, so simply click **Next**.

7. The next screen allows you to edit variable names and properties. For the purposes of this exercise, you will leave the default values in place and click **Next**.

8. The final screen shows the SPSS syntax that can be used to perform this particular import. If identical imports (or similar imports with small amendments made) will be performed in the future, you will want to paste the syntax for future use or modification. For now, leave the **Retrieve the data I have selected** option selected. Click **Finish**. (Note that in the **Variable View**, the **Label**, **Values**, and **Missing** columns are blank. These columns should ideally be filled out before analysis of the data is undertaken.)

The Access table imported into SPSS in exercise 10.10 will contain only the data manually entered in the previous exercises. To save time, a data set has been created and imported into SPSS. It is called *DATA_SET_1.SAV* in the *EXERCISES* folder. This SPSS file contains 297 records and contains some deliberate errors that have been added and that will be addressed in the exercises that follow. Data for the Label, Values, and Missing columns in *Variable View* have been added as well. Note also that a *SchoolID* column has been added for this data set. Parts 1 and 2 of this volume have covered how to create and use school identification numbers when conducting national assessments (see pp 22 and 67). Instructions on how to create derived variables are provided in parts II and IV of this volume.

CHAPTER 11 DATA VERIFICATION

Data verification is the process of ensuring that the data received from the various sources are free from error. Data entry processes that are well planned, documented, and supervised help reduce errors when student test and questionnaire responses are transferred to electronic data formats. However, sources of error remain, including miskeyed responses, omitted data, and errors in manipulating and merging data from different sources.

DOCUMENTATION

Given that national assessments involve teams working on different aspects of data, sometimes over a considerable time period, the national assessment agency must have a record of all changes made to data. This record will be especially helpful to those who carry out follow-up national assessments and to those who conduct secondary analyses of data.

For this reason, a ReadMe file should be created to record any changes made to the data file by the key operators during data entry. The file should also document the source and the file name of the cleaned data file. This record should help prevent confusion over the version of the data that should be analyzed. Although some programs, such as SPSS (Statistical Package for the Social Sciences), automatically record changes made to the data while using the program, keeping a ReadMe file throughout the duration of the project is still important so that a record of all changes from all programs and operations is stored in one place.

The ReadMe file called **README.DOCX** in the **EXERCISE SOLUTIONS** folder is an example of the documentation that supports the data cleaning processes (see annex III.A).

CONSISTENCY BETWEEN FILES

Many national assessments enter each data record twice. The purpose of double punching is to have two data sets that can be checked against each other to find miskeyed cases. If the national assessment requires a double-punch methodology, the accuracy of each file has to be checked and the original data corrected.

Exercise 11.1 contains the responses of six students taken from a much larger data set that were punched twice and compared for accuracy. For the sake of economy and practicality, Excel was used to compare responses for this exercise. Ordinarily, less readily available programs, such as WinDem, or more expensive programs, such as SPSS Data Entry module, would be used for between-file consistency checks. Crucially, using Excel in this way does not require that the data imported into Excel be used for any further analysis. Excel is merely used as a tool to highlight possible errors in the Access data, and these data are then updated manually in the Access database. This method, therefore, limits the potential avenues for error that exist when transferring data from one application to another. *Note:* During a real-life national assessment, a backup copy of the original (preedited) database should be created. This initial record can serve as an invaluable resource, especially if questions about possible erroneous changes arise.

WITHIN-FILE CONSISTENCY

Within-file consistency pertains to the checking processes to determine whether data are as accurate as possible. Even with a comprehensive

EXERCISE 11.1

Verifying Data Using Excel

The following steps will allow you to verify data through Excel:

1. Open ...\NAEA Data Cleaning\Exercises\Data Verification Exercise.xlsx. Note that the data from the two sources are placed in two individual sheets that are called **Final data** and **Punch 2**. Sheet 3 (**Verification**) will be used to verify the data.

2. Select **Office button – Save As** and save the file as **MY_DATA_VERIFICATION.XLSX** in your **MY SOLUTIONS** folder.

3. On the **Verification** sheet, type the formula into cell A4 with the following syntax: **='Final data'!A4='Punch 2'!A4**. This formula will compare the datum in cell A4 of the **Final data** data sheet to the datum in cell A4 of the **Punch 2** data sheet. Clicking and dragging this formula over all cells will create similar formulas for the entire data set.

4. Excel conducts a logical comparison to check if the cells are identical. This process returns **TRUE** if the corresponding values are identical and **FALSE** if the values differ. The outcome of the verification routines in **Verification** is shown in exercise figure 11.1.A.

EXERCISE FIGURE 11.1.A Outcome of Verification

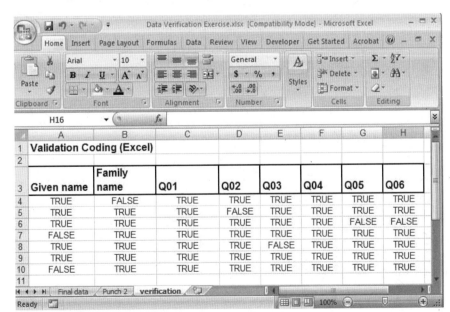

Source: Authors' example within Excel software.

(continued)

EXERCISE 11.1 *(continued)*

5. Save the spreadsheet (**CTRL+S**). The worked solution for this exercise is located here:
   ...*NAEA DATA CLEANING\\EXERCISE SOLUTIONS\\DATA_VERIFICATION_
   EXERCISE_SOLUTION.XLXS*.

The validation output in exercise figure 11.1.A shows two **FALSE** comparisons in the
Given name field, indicating keying errors in the given names. Five more errors in the
other data fields have to be checked by referring back to the original test booklets.

   Corrections to the data should be made to the relevant table in the Access database,
with all corrections recorded in the **README.DOCX** file as outlined in the "Documentation"
section of this chapter.

data entry template, errors or incomplete data are still possible. For
example, a national assessment may have been implemented in grades
3 and 7, but classes mixed with these year levels may have also participated. The valid responses to the field *Year level* should be only 2, 3, 4,
6, 7, and 8. If the validation rule specified that only numeric values
between 2 and 8 (inclusive) are valid, an incorrect value of 5 could be
miskeyed and would not be trapped by the validation rule.

   Typically, when data inconsistencies are found, the only option is
to extract the original source document (the student's test paper) and
correct the error. This need for cross-checking is the main reason for
ensuring that data entry personnel have easy access to the original
tests and questionnaires.

   SPSS is widely available and has therefore been used in the following section to verify within-file consistency. Other programs that can
carry out this task efficiently include WinDem, STATISTICA, and
SAS (Statistical Analysis Software).

Demographic Data (School Name) Consistency

Spelling mistakes on test booklets and questionnaires are not unusual
and can cause data management problems. A common source of error
is when a student misspells or abbreviates a school name and the data
entry operator copies this error exactly from the student test booklet.
(This type of error is not an issue when student identifiers, or IDs, that
include a school code are assigned before tests and questionnaires are
sent to schools.) Not uncommonly, the student booklets may have

several variations of the same school name. For this reason, matching and merging files are best done by using the school ID (kept from the sampling frame) rather than the name (provided by the responding students).

For reporting purposes, it is best to create a separate table in the Access database that contains all the correctly spelled school names with their corresponding school IDs. This table can then be linked to the student data table and used for all official reporting purposes (for example, printing the school name on a student's test certificate in rare cases in which students get results). Linking a school name table with the student response data table in this way is demonstrated in chapter 16.

The Frequency Command

The **Frequency** command in SPSS allows one to observe all the values that are present in each selected variable. If out-of-range values (invalid values) are present, they can be corrected after cross-checking with the original test booklet. The frequency output table can also be used to highlight the occurrence of implausible values. For example, if the national assessment was administered in all schools across the country at a particular year level, one may reasonably expect a relatively even 50:50 split of males and females in the gender variable. If the frequency table shows a 70:30 split, one would need to investigate why this might be the case and rectify the problem, if warranted.

The **Frequency** procedure is suitable for most noncontinuous variables in a data set. Checking all fields for anomalies is advisable as a matter of course, regardless of the data validation rules that may have been in place at the time of data entry. *Note:* The invalid value of 13 for the **Q3Aq02** field presented in exercise 11.2 theoretically should not be possible with the data validation rules set up in Access at the data entry stage; nonetheless, it is presented as an example of an invalid value for the sake of the exercise.

System-Missing Cells

As a general rule, the data set should have no blank spaces. The code frame and validation procedures should allow for all possible responses, including a nonresponse (usually a 9, 99, or 999, depending

EXERCISE 11.2

Using the Frequency Command in SPSS

This exercise teaches you how to use the **Frequency** command in SPSS:

1. Open *...\NAEA DATA CLEANING\EXERCISES\DATA_SET_1.SAV*.

2. Select **File – Save As**, and save the file as *MY_DATA_SET_1.SAV* in your *MY SOLUTIONS* folder.

3. From the **Analyze** menu, select **Descriptive Statistics – Frequencies**.

4. From the variable list in the **Frequencies** window that has appeared, select the *Q3Aq02* variable and click on the arrow (or just double-click the variable name) to bring it across to the variable list on the right-hand side (exercise figure 11.2.A). *Note:* You can select more than one variable at a time.

EXERCISE FIGURE 11.2.A Running a Frequency Command to Find Invalid Values

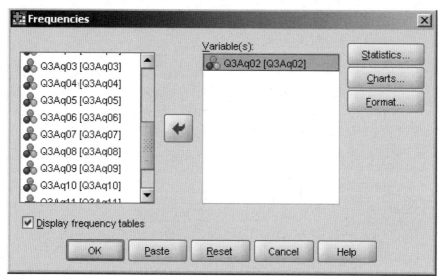

Source: Authors' example within SPSS software.

5. Click **OK**.

6. The following results should now be displayed in the SPSS output window (exercise figure 11.2.B). The number of responses (frequency) for each item value, including user-missing and system-missing values, is presented in the **Frequency** column. The respective percentages, valid percentages, and cumulative percentages for these responses are also given. The example shows a value of *13*, which is not a valid response for this item.

EXERCISE 11.2 *(continued)*

EXERCISE FIGURE 11.2.B   Drop-Down Values for the Variable Q3Aq02

Statistics

Q3Aq02

N	Valid	291
	Missing	6

Q3Aq02

		Frequency	Percent	Valid Percent	Cumulative Percent
Valid	A: Leah	1	.3	.3	3
	B: Marie	2	.7	.7	1.0
	C: Sarah	286	96.3	98.3	99.3
	D: Kari	1	.3	.3	99.7
	13	1	.3	.3	100.0
	Total	291	98.0	100.0	
Missing	8	2	.7		
	9	3	1.0		
	System	1	.3		
	Total	6	2.0		
Total		297	100.0		

Source: Authors' example within SPSS software.

7. Return to the **Data View** window of the original SPSS data sheet, highlight the column containing the *Q3Aq02* variable data, and select **Edit – Find** (**CTRL+F**).

8. Type *13* into the **Find** field and click **Find Next**. This command locates the invalid value in the data set, which, in this case, belongs to student Anthony Jamap (StudID 2152410).

   In the context of a national assessment, the response for this item would be checked against the response given in the test booklet and the value changed accordingly. In this instance, change the value in this student's *Q3Aq02* cell to *3*, and save (**CTRL+S**) the change.

9. Make the appropriate change to the *README.DOCX* file, as shown in exercise figure 11.2.C.

EXERCISE FIGURE 11.2.C   Extract from the README.DOCX File

Stud ID	Variable	Data value	Repaired value
2152410	Q3aq02	13	3

Source: Authors' representation.

If you rerun the **Frequency** procedure (steps 3 to 5), you will see that now no listing appears for the value of 13 and that the instances of the third item response (C: Sarah) have increased from 286 to 287 in the data set.

on the length of the field). Blank spaces are subject to misinterpretation and can introduce uncertainty about the data. A blank space may be interpreted as meaning that data are missing or that the data entry operator made a mistake or forgot to enter the data for that cell or that no response was required or expected because of skip patterns.

The data entry examples in chapter 10 used 7 as a default value for multiple-choice items. Because 7 was an invalid value, a value of 7 for multiple-choice items would indicate that no value was recorded by the key operator.

The **Frequency** command outlined in exercise 11.2 can be used to locate system-missing values so that values can then be entered for these cells after referencing the original student test booklet (see exercise 11.3).

EXERCISE 11.3

Using the Frequency Command to Locate Missing Values

You can use the **Frequency** command to find missing values as follows:

1. Open *...\NAEA DATA CLEANING\MY SOLUTIONS\MY_DATA_SET_1.SAV* (with changes saved from previous exercises).

2. Run the **Frequency** command (as demonstrated in the previous exercise), this time transferring all variables from *Gender* to *Q3Aq14* into the variable list.

3. From the Gender Frequency Table (exercise figure 11.3.A), you can see that this variable has one system-missing value, represented by the *1* appearing to the right of *System*. It is one of two missing values specified in this table; another user-missing value is represented by the *1* to the right of the *9* in the first column.

EXERCISE FIGURE 11.3.A   Gender Missing Values

Gender

		Frequency	Percent	Valid Percent	Cumulative Percent
Valid	Male	147	49.5	49.8	49.8
	Female	148	49.8	50.2	100.0
	Total	295	99.3	100.0	
Missing	9	1	.3		
	System	1	.3		
	Total	2	.7		
Total		297	100.0		

Source: Authors' example within SPSS software.

4. To locate this missing value in the data sheet (in **Data View**), select **Data – Sort Cases**. In the **Sort Cases** window that now appears, select the *Gender* variable, and click on the arrow to move this variable into the **Sort by** box. Then click **OK**.

5. The record with the missing *Gender* variable will now appear as the first record. The blank value should correspond with *StudID 4106321* for *Simon Patchatt* (exercise figure 11.3.B). If the gender of the student cannot be confirmed, you must insert a value of *9*. In this case, assume you checked the original test booklet, which listed 1 for gender, and insert the value of *1* (for *Boy*) in this cell.

EXERCISE FIGURE 11.3.B   Entering Correct Value

	SchoolID	StudID	GivenName	FamilyName	SchoolName	YearLevel	Gender	Age
1	4106	4106321	Simon	Patchatt	Thornfield Primary School	3	1	1
2	1294	1294302	Aaron	Anama	Eaglehawk Primary School	3	1	2
3	1294	1294505	Ahley	Laptar	Eaglehawk Primary School	3	1	3
4	1294	1294808	Aimee	Nupbat	Eaglehawk Primary School	3	1	1

Source: Authors' example within SPSS software.

6. Save (**CTRL+S**) the changes made to the SPSS datasheet.

7. Note the update (figure 11.3.C) in *...\EXERCISE SOLUTIONS\READ ME.DOCX*.

EXERCISE FIGURE 11.3.C   Update of README.DOCX

Stud ID	Variable	Data value	Repaired value
4106321	Gender	Missing data	1

Source: Authors' representation.

8. For the remaining variables with missing values or values of *7*, insert the appropriate code for missing response (for example, 9 or 99), and make the updates to your *ReadMe* document. You can compare your changes to those documented in the *Data Modifications* section of *README.DOCX* in the *EXERCISE SOLUTIONS* folder.

Creating New Variables

National assessment studies can use information provided by sources other than students, teachers, or schools. Such information includes an official identification number, the school's administrative region, and if the school was in a specific pilot initiative. Some of this information could be provided by the ministry of education, notably by an education management information system. Other variables of interest to the assessment team may be derived variables, not directly collected from the students, their teachers, or their schools, but obtained as a combination of data elements readily available in the booklets.

Even if the data set is created with Access, the derived variables can be computed in SPSS. Parts II and IV of this volume give several examples of variable creation in SPSS, using the menu commands **Transform – Compute Variable ...**, that can easily be adapted to meet particular needs, such as creating a parental education level index that is based on the highest levels of education attained by the mother and father.

Creating new variables can lead to errors. It is best to avoid manipulating many files and records. When derived variables are created using SPSS, considerable time can be saved by applying one command (which can be reversed) to many records.

CHAPTER 12

IMPORTING AND MERGING DATA

In chapter 10, routines were addressed to minimize data entry errors using Access. Part II looked at the creation of derived variables using the menu commands **Transform – Compute Variable** in **SPSS (Statistical Package for the Social Sciences)**. With these routines completed, if the additional variables have been created outside Access, it is useful to import the files back into Access to enable efficient merging of data. This chapter describes the process for exporting data from SPSS into Access and provides some useful verification routines.

THE DANGERS OF TRANSFERRING DATA BETWEEN PROGRAMS

Care should always be taken when transferring data between files or joining data from different sources because errors can occur. Such errors can be implicit or explicit. Implicit errors arise because programs store or code data in different ways, which may result in some data being irrevocably lost or changed during the transfer process. A common error arises when the item type for a data field in one application differs from that in another application. For example, one may choose to store certain numeric data as text, so that the digits will be stored exactly as entered. This method is commonplace to maintain the integrity of an identifier (ID) number beginning with a 0. However, the application to which these data are exported may register the digits in the fields and store the ID numbers as numeric data. Consequently, the data are stored as numbers and the 0 digit from the beginning of the ID number is deleted.

Data may also be lost on transfer if the field length for data items differs between programs. For example, if the original application has a field width of 15 characters and the application receiving the data has a field width of only 5 characters, any data in excess of 5 characters will be lost. Issues relating to consistency of field names, applications not accepting certain characters in field names, and consistency of coding (such as how missing values are stored) are also possible avenues for an error to be introduced in the data.

Errors of an explicit nature typically result from human error. Accidentally deleting data, "slipping" records, and partially transferring data are all examples of explicit data errors, and the more times data are transferred between programs, the more likely such errors will occur. For these reasons, importing and exporting routines should be performed with caution and only when absolutely necessary.

EXPORTING DATA FROM SPSS INTO ACCESS

SPSS has a function that can export data to an Access database. For the purposes of exercise 12.1, an SPSS file has been created with all the necessary corrections made to the errors in the raw data that were discovered in chapter 11. This corrected file is located in *...\NAEA DATA CLEANING\EXERCISE SOLUTIONS\DATA_SET_1_SOLUTION. SAV*.

Note: If importing data into Access from another source, one should ensure that the field names do not contain any spaces or special characters (for example, *, &, $). If such spaces or special characters do exist, they should be replaced with the underscore character (_), which is allowed. Because SPSS does not allow these characters in its

EXERCISE 12.1

Exporting Data from SPSS into Access

The following exercise will demonstrate how to export data from SPSS into Access:

1. Open *...\NAEA DATA CLEANING\EXERCISE SOLUTIONS\DATA_SET_1_SOLUTION.SAV*.

2. From the toolbar, select **File – Export** to **Database**.

3. From the **ODBC Data Sources** box, highlight **MS Access Database**, and click **Next** (or simply double-click on MS Access Database).

4. From the **ODBC Driver Login** screen, browse for the database you created earlier (*...\MY SOLUTIONS\MATHS_3A_DATA.ACCDB*). Click **Open**, and then click **OK**.

5. From the **Choose how to export the data** screen, check the last box: **Create a new table**.

6. In the **Name** textbox, type in *TBL_MATHS_3A_DATA_CLEANED*. Then click **Next**.

7. From the **Select variables to store in new table** screen, highlight all variables in the left-hand box (**CTRL+A**). Then click one of the arrows in the right-hand table to bring all variables over to the *Table: TBL_MATHS_3A_DATA_CLEANED* box (exercise figure 12.1.A).

EXERCISE FIGURE 12.1.A Selecting Variables to Export

Source: Authors' example within SPSS software.

8. Click **Next** and then **Finish**.

SPSS has exported the data into Access and created the new table, *TBL_MATHS_3A_DATA_CLEANED*, as evidenced by this table being listed in the **All Access Objects** menu in your Access database.

field names either, you should not encounter this problem when exporting and importing data between SPSS and Access.

IMPORTING OTHER RELATED DATA

As already noted, some important information not collected on the student test paper about the school, the system, or the students may be held in an official central file. These data may facilitate state or regional performance comparisons or include other important group-related information. In some countries, for example, required information about parents or student background may be held in official central departmental databases.

Exercise 12.2 shows how such data can be imported into Access and demonstrates how queries can be used to link the data from different tables. In this example, the other data to be imported and

---

EXERCISE 12.2

Importing School Data into Access

The following steps show you how to import school data from Excel into Access:

1. Open *...\NAEA DATA CLEANING\MY SOLUTIONS\MATHS_3A_DATA.ACCDB* (with changes saved from the previous exercise).

2. From the **External Data** ribbon, select **Excel** from the **Import** section.

3. Click the **Browse** button and navigate to *...\NAEA DATA CLEANING\EXERCISES\SCHOOLS.XLSX*.

4. Highlight the *SCHOOLS.XLSX* spreadsheet and click **Open**. Then click **OK** to import the data into a new Access table.

5. Highlight *Sheet1* and then click **Next**.

6. Leave the box **First row contains column headings** checked and click **Next**.

7. The next screen allows you to specify information for the data that you are importing. For the purposes of this exercise, simply click **Next**.

8. This screen allows you to adjust the primary key settings for this data table. Click **Choose my own Primary Key**, and select *SchoolCode* from the drop-down menu. Then click **Next**.

9. Name the table *tbl_Schools*. Then click **Finish**. Your imported school data table will now appear in the **Tables** section of the **All Access Objects** menu.

linked relate to schools and are held in a central Excel file called **SCHOOLS.XLSX**. The **SchoolName** field from this file can also be used for all official reporting purposes that require the school name to be spelled correctly (for example, printing the school name on a student's test certificate), rather than the **SchoolName** field in the student response data table, which may often be misspelled by the student and should consequently be used for cross-referencing purposes only.

After all the data to be merged or interrogated are imported in table format to Access, queries can be created to search for information, to create new tables with specific information, or to perform other investigations of the data to check the contents and quality. The following section describes two key data cleaning processes. The first describes merging data from two files, which is a process that can be very time-consuming and error prone using other software programs such as Excel. Therefore, creating a single file to serve as the sole data source for all national assessment analyses is very important. The second section describes how to use Access to search for duplicate records. Key operators (and sometimes scanner operators) sometimes become distracted and accidentally enter the same information twice. Unless a specific routine is used to check for duplicates, this form of data cleaning problem is often hard to detect.

MERGING DATA FROM DIFFERENT TABLES USING THE ACCESS QUERIES

Because student test papers or answer sheets contain relatively little background information that could be of use to policy makers interested in the results of a national assessment, having recourse to other sources of information about schools and students may be necessary.

Previous exercises described the process for importing two tables into Access: (a) the modified data table of student responses following data cleaning (**TBL_MATHS_3A_DATA_CLEANED**) and (b) a table that includes school information (**tbl_Schools**). These tables share a common field: the unique school identifier, which is labeled **SchoolID** in the first table and **SchoolCode** in the second table. Exercise 12.3 now shows how to join these files.

EXERCISE 12.3

Creating a Simple Query in Access

The following steps will create a simple query in Access:

1. Open **...\NAEA DATA CLEANING\MY SOLUTIONS\MATHS_3A_DATA.ACCDB** (with changes saved from previous exercises).

2. From the **Create** ribbon, select **Query Design**. Access then delivers a dialogue box called **Show Table.** The function of this box is to allow you to select the tables you want to include in the query. (When you become more proficient in using Access you can have multiple tables and combinations of tables and queries in more complex designs.)

3. Select **TBL_MATHS_3A_DATA_CLEANED** and click **Add** (see exercise figure 12.3.A). Repeat the process to add the **tbl_Schools** to the query, and then **Close**. The query work area has two tables, each with a list of the variables that are present in the table. Scroll bars allow you to scroll down. The work area and the table sizes can be changed by placing the cursor on the edges of the tables and clicking and dragging.

EXERCISE FIGURE 12.3.A   Adding Tables to Query

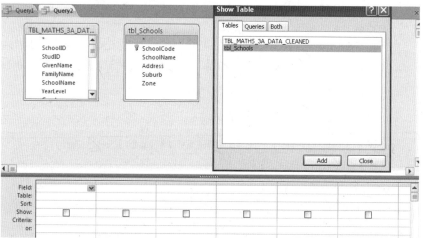

Source: Authors' example within Access software.

4. From the **TBL_MATHS_3A_DATA_CLEANED** table, select the variable **SchoolID**. Note that because the data in these two tables have come from different sources they do not have exactly the same variable name (**SchoolID** compared with **SchoolCode**). However, they do contain the same information in the same format. Both are numerical data. Although using common variable names is preferable, it is not always possible because data sets are sometimes maintained by different agencies.

EXERCISE 12.3 *(continued)*

5. Join the tables by clicking and dragging the variable **SchoolID** in **TBL_MATHS_3A_DATA_CLEANED** across to the variable **SchoolCode** in **tbl_Schools** and then releasing the mouse (see exercise figure 12.3.B).

EXERCISE FIGURE 12.3.B   Joining Tables

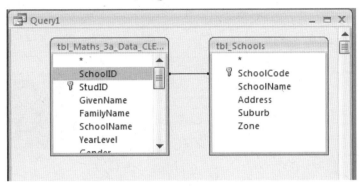

Source: Authors' example within Access software.

The line between **SchoolID** and **SchoolCode** indicates that these variables have been selected as the criterion that joins the two tables. Both tables have been linked, and any other data that are available in either data set can now be combined by selecting data from each table and either dragging them into the workspace below or double-clicking them.

6. Double-click the following variables from **TBL_MATHS_3A_DATA_CLEANED**: **StudID**, **GivenName**, **FamilyName**, and **Yearlevel**. *Note:* You can also select and drag multiple variables in one action by using the shift key while you select the multiple variable names and then dragging the highlighted names to the workspace. The usual drag-and-drop features of Microsoft apply to Access.

7. You want to include all the variables from **tbl_Schools**. Double-click the asterisk above the **SchoolCode** variable in **tbl_Schools**, which will bring all the variables down into the query table. These variables should now appear in the fields below, with the row called **Table** indicating the source of the data (see exercise figure 12.3.C). School information comes from the **tbl_Schools** table, and student information comes from **TBL_MATHS_3A_DATA_CLEANED**. Select school information from **tbl_Schools** because it is a more trustworthy source for school information than **TBL_MATHS_3A_DATA_CLEANED**, which is taken from test booklet covers.

8. Highlight the **YearLevel** column from the fields in exercise figure 12.3.C by clicking the small gray box above the field name. Keeping the cursor on the small gray box so that the cursor turns into a white arrow, click and drag this column to the end position (after the **tbl_Schools*** variables). This action will ensure that the **YearLevel** variable is displayed at the end of the resulting data sheet.

(continued)

EXERCISE 12.3 *(continued)*

EXERCISE FIGURE 12.3.C   Query Variables

Source: Authors' example within Access software.

9. If necessary, click on an open space to remove the highlight.

10. Execute the query by clicking the red **!** icon on the Access toolbar. The resulting data sheet should look like that in exercise figure 12.3.D. The output of the query provides a record per row with all the known data about the student held in one file. This file can then be interrogated for final cleaning before being exported to the data analysts as a clean data set.

EXERCISE FIGURE 12.3.D   Query Result

StudID	GivenName	FamilyName	SchoolCo	SchoolName	Address	Suburb	Zone	YearL
4106101	Dylan	Boxall		4106 Thornfield Prin	Bourke Road	Thornfield	4	
4002410	Nathaniel	MacDonald		4002 St Margaret's P	1001 Day Stree	Ambervale	3	
4106716	Ellen	Knught		4106 Thornfield Prin	Bourke Road	Thornfield	4	
4002309	Nathan	Kummuhp		4002 St Margaret's P	1001 Day Stree	Ambervale	3	
4106431	Taj	Trapp		4106 Thornfield Prin	Bourke Road	Thornfield	4	
4106909	Dylan	Davuap		4106 Thornfield Prin	Bourke Road	Thornfield	4	
4106936	Emma	Paponja		4106 Thornfield Prin	Bourke Road	Thornfield	4	
4106404	Sean	Caughy		4106 Thornfield Prin	Bourke Road	Thornfield	4	
4106303	Sara	Carpton		4106 Thornfield Prin	Bourke Road	Thornfield	4	
3965320	Max	Watt		3965 Southharbour I	1 Harbour Drive	South Harbou	3	
4002107	Nakeya	Hoppman		4002 St Margaret's P	1001 Day Stree	Ambervale	3	
3965219	Makyla	Upaac		3965 Southharbour I	1 Harbour Drive	South Harbou	3	

Source: Authors' example within Access software.

11. Select **Office Button – Save** and save the query as ***qry_student_&_school_data_combined*** and press **OK**.

12. Note that your newly created query now appears as an icon in the **All Access Objects** menu.

A limited number of variables were used in exercise 12.3 to describe the process of combining data sets. For a national assessment, one would typically use many more variables derived from student, parent, teacher, and school questionnaire data.

VERSION CONTROL

Each time a change to the data has been effected through data validation, verification, or management procedures, a new version of the data set has been created. Although intrinsic names have been used for each version of the modified data, only the final export file should be used for future analysis.

Therefore, a thorough record of the pathway that has been followed to develop the final data and a record of the intermediate steps and files that have been created in producing the final clean data set are important.

The *README.DOCX* file provides the vehicle for this documentation. This file is updated to record the path of the final data set, which is important because people need to be prevented from working on different versions of the data source and producing different results.

SECURING THE DATA

Issues of confidentiality and security are undoubtedly important in conducting a national assessment. Therefore, keeping the data from such assessments as secure as possible is crucial, both for reasons of confidentiality and to prevent the data from being altered (either inadvertently or intentionally) by those who may gain access to the data. When data are in electronic format, it is important to consider setting levels of access to the data at both a network and an individual computer level. In addition, the database in which the data are stored should be secured, which can be implemented in two distinct, though not mutually exclusive, ways: through applying a database password and through adding user-level security.

Applying a Database Password

When a password is applied to a database, users will be prompted to enter it before they can use the application. The password function simply restricts access to the system to those with knowledge of the password. In its most basic form, each database can have one password. Setting a password for an Access database requires that the database be opened in exclusive use mode. To open the database for exclusive use, close the database and then reopen it using the instructions provided in the warning message (figure 12.1).

Once the database is opened exclusively, the password can be set by clicking on **Set Database Password** from the **Database Tools** tab, entering the desired password in the requisite text boxes, and clicking **OK**. From that point on, Access will prompt the user for the password before allowing the database to be opened.

Adding User-Level Security to the Database

Adding different permission levels, or user-level security, to a database is an effective way of restricting the use and manipulation of data to certain users of the system. For instance, individuals whose sole task is to enter data into a data entry tool do not need to have access to any facilities that would allow them to modify the design of this, or any other, database object. Therefore, user-level security should be set to prevent these individuals from modifying the database in any way that is extraneous to the tasks they were employed to undertake.

FIGURE 12.1

Exclusive Use Warning Message

 You must have the database open for exclusive use to set or remove the database password.

To open the database exclusively, close the database, and then reopen it by clicking the Microsoft Office Button and using the Open command. In the Open dialog box, click the arrow next to the Open button, and then select Open Exclusive.

> OK

Source: Warning message within Access software.

Defining user-level security should be one of the last actions to take place when designing a database because, after it is applied, making further modifications to the system can be difficult, and users will need to be given access to the new objects created. Applying this type of security should be done in an ordered manner, because one can easily become locked out of the system while defining user levels. This problem may be avoided by creating an unsecured backup copy of the database before beginning this process. The backup should be stored separately until the addition of user-level security to the original database has been successfully applied. At that stage, the unsecured backup copy should be deleted.

In Access, user-level security can be added to a database by clicking **Users and Permissions – User Level Security Wizard** from the **Database Tools** tab and following the step-by-step process the Wizard sets out. As an extra measure, an effective way to keep track of the changes being made during the security setup process is to press **CTRL+Print Scrn** at each stage of the setup. This action will copy the current window, which can then be pasted into a Word document.

CHAPTER 13

DUPLICATE
DATA

This chapter addresses the issue of duplicate data—in particular, how to check for duplicate identifiers (IDs) and duplicate records.

USING ACCESS TO CHECK FOR DUPLICATE IDS

Entering a student's record twice in a data file can easily happen, and if undetected, the extra data will distort the results. Data that include a student ID should be checked to ensure that each student has only one record. This check applies even if the national assessment team created unique IDs, because data entry personnel may have inadvertently duplicated one or more records. Although the validation rules created in previous exercises for the **StudID** variable did not allow the creation of duplicate IDs, running through the following procedures as a double-checking mechanism is still prudent. Exercise 13.1 shows how to use Access routines to check for duplicate IDs.

INVESTIGATING DUPLICATE RECORDS

Performing a **Find duplicates** query on a table may return one or more duplicate entries when the data have been incorrectly entered on

167

EXERCISE 13.1

Creating a "Find Duplicates" Query in Access

The following steps allow you to use Access routines to check for duplicate IDs:

1. Open **...\NAEA DATA CLEANING\MY SOLUTIONS\ MATHS_3A_DATA.ACCDB** (with changes saved from previous exercises).

2. From the **Create** ribbon, select **Query Wizard** in the **Other** section. Access then delivers a dialogue box called **New Query**. Select **Find Duplicates Query Wizard**, then click **OK**.

3. Access will then prompt you to choose the table in which you want to search for duplicate values. In this case, highlight the table **TBL_MATHS_ 3A_DATA_CLEANED**, and then click **Next**.

4. From the list of available fields on the left (as shown in exercise figure 13.1.A), highlight the fields in which you suspect data may be duplicated, in this case **StudID**. Transfer it to the right-hand box by using the **>** sign between the boxes, and then click **Next**.

EXERCISE FIGURE 13.1.A Duplicate-Value Fields

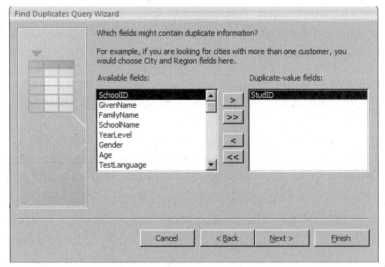

Source: Authors' example within Access software.

The Access dialogue box will request that you select the fields that you want to include in the report of values that are found by the query.

5. Select **SchoolID**, **GivenName**, **FamilyName**, and **SchoolName** (exercise figure 13.1.B), because these will enable easy identification of any record for correction, then click **Next**. Access will recommend a name for the query (in this case, **Find duplicates for TBL_MATHS_3A_DATA_CLEANED**).

EXERCISE 13.1 *(continued)*

EXERCISE FIGURE 13.1.B Additional Query Fields

Source: Authors' example within Access software.

6. Select **View the results** and then **Finish**.

multiple occasions. This situation can occur when an operator loses concentration and enters data from the same booklet twice or when completed booklets are accidentally put back in the pile of unscored test booklets and rekeyed. Note, the data referred to in figures 13.1, 13.2, 13.4, and 13.5 are from a fictional assessment. They are used to demonstrate the output from a duplicate data query in Access. Fictional data were used in these cases as the StudentID variable in our data would not allow duplicate values to occur (and thus a duplicate data query based on StudentID would have returned a null value).

Exercise 13.1 had no duplicate IDs because **StudID** was set as the primary key (and duplicate data are not allowed in the primary key field), so the exercise query returned no records that met the search criteria. For an example of how duplicates are displayed, see figure 13.1.

The results in figure 13.1 suggest that the data have been recorded in error. When a query returns a duplicate, the validity of both records must be checked. If the student response patterns are identical, a duplicate entry is highly likely. The records, however, must still be

FIGURE 13.1

Duplicate Records Identified

Find duplicates for tbl_National_Assessment_Example						_ ☐ X
UniqueID ▾	StudentID ▾	Given_Name ▾	Family_Name ▾	School_Cod ▾	School_Name ▾	
2	510	Paul	Nguyen	99	Park St School	
1	510	Paul	Nguyen	99	Park St School	
* (New)						

Record: I◄ ◄ 1 of 2 ► ►I ►☰ ⅩNo Filter Search

Source: Authors' example within Access software.

checked against the original data sources—the student test papers. A record of the error in the *README.DOCX* is shown in figure 13.2 with the subsequent amendment noted.

FIGURE 13.2

Documentation of Correction of Student ID Mistakes

Unique ID	Student ID	Variable	Data Value	Repaired Value
2	510	Entire Record	Duplicate Record	Record Deleted

Source: Authors' representation.

To delete a record, highlight it by clicking on the row that contains the data to be deleted. On the **Home** ribbon, select **Delete** from the **Records** section. Take great care in this process. Access will not allow an **Undo** of a deletion. To minimize accidental deletions, Access will ask if you want to delete the record (see figure 13.3). Clicking **Yes** will delete the record.

The **Find duplicates** query can also show if the same *StudID* has been entered for two students (see figure 13.4). This situation can occur when an analyst uses an incorrect copy-and-paste routine or when a value has been manually changed in error. Figure 13.5 shows the relevant *README.DOCX* entry for such a modification.

FIGURE 13.3

Deleting a Record

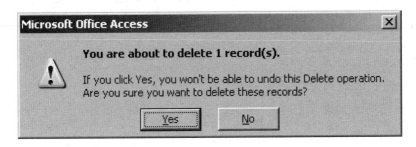

Source: Warning message within Access software.

FIGURE 13.4

Same Student ID for Two Students

UniqueID	StudentID	Given_Name	Family_Name	School_Code	School_Name
4	755	Lee	Pillar	85	Riverview Primary School
3	755	Lee	Papillo	85	Riverview Primary School
(New)					

Find duplicates for tbl_National_Assessment_Example

Record: 1 of 2   No Filter   Search

Source: Authors' example within Access software.

FIGURE 13.5

Documentation of Correction of Student ID Mistakes

Unique ID	Student ID	Variable	Data Value	Repaired Value
4	755	StudentID	755	756

Source: Authors' representation.

USING ACCESS TO CHECK FOR DUPLICATE NAMES

Access is also used to search for duplicate names in the same school (exercise 13.2). If it is established that two listings with the same name but different student IDs exist in the school, the original test

EXERCISE 13.2

Using a Find Duplicates Query to Locate Duplicate Student Names

This exercise demonstrates how to use a **Find duplicates** query in Access:

1. Open *...\MY SOLUTIONS\MATHS_3A_DATA.ACCDB* (with changes saved from previous exercises).

2. From the **Create** ribbon, select **Query Wizard** in the **Other** section. Access then delivers a dialogue box called **New Query**. Select **Find Duplicates Query Wizard** and click **OK**.

3. Select *TBL_MATHS_3A_DATA_CLEANED* and click **Next**.

4. Select *GivenName*, *FamilyName*, and *SchoolID* (exercise figure 13.2.A). Then click **Next**.

EXERCISE FIGURE 13.2.A   Duplicate-Value Fields

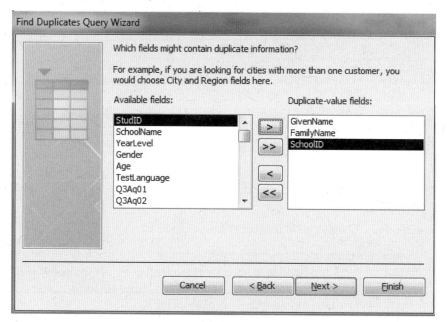

5. From the next screen, select *StudID* and *SchoolName* as the variables you want in the report (see exercise figure 13.2.B). This action will enable easy identification of any duplicate names. Then click **Next**.

6. Name this query *Find duplicates for TBL_MATHS_3A_DATA_CLEANED_names*. Then select **View the results** and click **Finish**. The Access report (see exercise figure 13.2.C) shows that this data file may have a duplicate record, because two students

EXERCISE 13.2 *(continued)*

EXERCISE FIGURE 13.2.B   Additional Query Fields

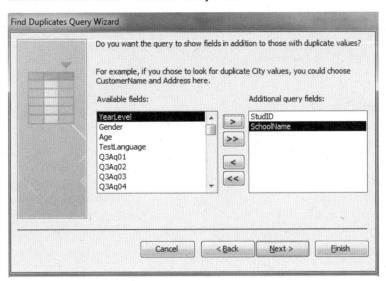

Source: Authors' example within Access software.

EXERCISE FIGURE 13.2.C   Query Results

GivenName ▾	FamilyNam ▾	SchoolID ▾	StudID ▾	SchoolName ▾
Jack	Crokar	3870	3870204	Oxenford State School
Jack	Crokar	3870	3870305	Oxenford State School
*				

Source: Authors' example within Access software.

from the same school have the same name and have been assigned different student IDs. The data operator should check the original test booklets or the list of students in the named school to see if, in fact, two students with the same name took the test or if one of the records is a duplication error. If the record has an error and the data have been duplicated, the data table in the Access database should be corrected.

7. Open ***TBL_MATHS_3A_DATA_CLEANED*** in your database.

8. To locate the records, select **Find** from the **Home** ribbon (**CTRL+F**) and type the number ***3870204*** into the **Find what** text box. Click **Find Next**.

   Access will locate this student ID in the data file, and the two entries with the same name will be visible (exercise figure 13.2.D). There are two possible reasons for two

(continued)

EXERCISE 13.2 *(continued)*

EXERCISE FIGURE 13.2.D Duplicate Names Observed

SchoolID	StudID	GivenName	FamilyNam	SchoolName	YearLevel
3870	3870204	Jack	Crokar	Oxenford State School	
3870	3870305	Jack	Crokar	Oxenford State School	

Source: Authors' example within Access software.

students with the same name at the same school: either two students in the national assessment sample have the same name, or a data entry error has occurred and the student's data have been entered twice.

The data operator must check the school records or the original test booklets. If two students are found to have the same name, each must be easily identifiable. You can distinguish between the two students by adding an initial corresponding to a student's second name (such as JohnC for John Charles) or by adding a number to each first name. The correction must be made in the table. It should not be made in the query.

9. In **TBL_MATHS_3A_DATA_CLEANED**, key in the number **1** after *k* in *Jack* for the first record. Do the same with **2** to the second record (see exercise figure 13.2.E).

EXERCISE FIGURE 13.2.E Making Duplicate Names Unique

SchoolID	StudID	GivenName	FamilyNam	SchoolName	YearLevel	Gender
3870	3870204	Jack1	Crokar	Oxenford State School	3	1
3870	3870305	Jack2	Crokar	Oxenford State School	3	2

Source: Authors' example within Access software.

10. Record the two changes in the **README.DOCX** (exercise figure 13.2.F).

EXERCISE FIGURE 13.2.F Duplicates in README.DOCX

Stud ID	Variable	Data value	Repaired value
3870204	GivenName	Jack	Jack1
3870305	GivenName	Jack	Jack2

Source: Authors' representation.

11. Rerun the query to check that Jack Crokar's error has been fixed. It should return no entries. (*Note:* To rerun the query, double-click on the **Find duplicates TBL_MATHS_3A_FINAL_NAMES** query in the **All Access Objects – Queries** menu.)

booklets should be checked to see if, in fact, the school has two identically named students. The need to perform such checks is the main reason test booklets should be carefully filed after scoring for easy retrieval in the event of a query.

The process is similar to that described in the previous section. A query must be created that uses the variables for the student name and the school ID and that checks to identify any other student in the school with identical names. Access joins the variables to create a search variable to find any match in the data. If, for example, one chooses **GivenName John**, **FamilyName Smith**, and **SchoolID 1294**, then the temporary search variable created within Access is **1294**. Access does not attempt to find all the students named John or all the students named Smith but limits its search to all the students in school 1294 who are named John Smith.

The reader can check his or her progress in exercises 13.1 and 13.2 against the database at *...\NAEA DATA CLEANING\EXERCISE SOLUTIONS\MATHS_3A_DATA_ SOLUTION2.ACCDB*.

To carry out analyses, the user will need access to a file that contains the test data results. In this case, a total score can be calculated for each student using SPSS, which can be exported into Access with the rest of the cleaned data as shown in exercise 12.1. Through the steps outlined in exercise 12.3, a query can be created from the imported table that isolates students' item responses and total score data, along with the student background and school data.

Many of the actions taken here when merging two files are aimed at ensuring that the correct number of records was retained, that the records from one file were matched to the correct record on the second file, and that duplicates were identified and removed if necessary. Those tasks were performed in part II of this volume when creating the sampling frames for the probability proportional to size sample of students. SPSS will routinely ask what to do with duplicates found during a file match. Please refer to those exercises and note how the match is set up and executed.

III.A

DATA CLEANING AND MANAGEMENT: FOLDERS AND FILES

This annex describes the files to be used to perform the exercises in part III. These files can be found on the CD that accompanies this manual. Annex table III.A.1 describes the contents of the *Exercises* folder. Annex figure III.A.2 shows the contents of the *Exercise Solutions* folder. The data cleaning and management file directory structure is shown in annex figure III.A.1.

TABLE III.A.1

Exercises

File Name	Program	Explanation
DATA VERIFICATION EXERCISE.XLSX	Excel 2007	Perform logical comparisons to check whether the cells are identical.
DATA_SET_1.SAV	SPSS	Run frequency commands and correct file records with errors.
MATHS 3A CODEBOOK TEMPLATE.XLSX	Excel 2007	Add all the codebook values for the last 7 items.
SAMPLE TEST PAPER 3A.DOCX	Word 2007	Use as a reference tool for codebook creation.
SCHOOLS.XLSX	Excel 2007	Import school list into Access database.
STUDENTQUESTIONNAIRE.DOCX	Word 2007	Use as an example of a student questionnaire for a national assessment.

Source: Authors' compilation.

TABLE III.A.2

Exercise Solutions

File Name	Program	Explanation
DATA VERIFICATION EXERCISE_SOLUTION.XLSX	Excel 2007	Solution to logical comparison check
DATA_SET_1_SOLUTION.SAV	SPSS	Solution to correction of data errors task
MATHS 3A CODEBOOK SOLUTION.XLSX	Excel 2007	Solution to codebook creation task
MATHS_3A_DATA_SOLUTION1.ACCDB	Access 2007	Solution to table and form creation task
MATHS_3A_DATA_SOLUTION2.ACCDB	Access 2007	Solution to data export and query creation tasks
README.DOCX	Word 2007	Record of corrections made to data files

Source: Authors' compilation.

FIGURE III.A.1

Data Cleaning and Management File Directory Structure

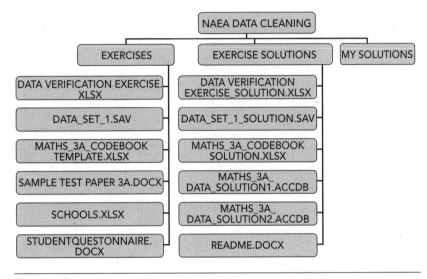

Source: Authors' representation.

PART IV

WEIGHTING, ESTIMATION, AND SAMPLING ERROR

Jean Dumais and J. Heward Gough

Part IV focuses on preparing data for analysis, which takes place after sampling, test administration, data entry, and cleaning. The exercises build on the earlier work that should have been carried out in part II on the Sentz data set. This part covers a series of important preanalysis steps, including computing and using survey weights and computing estimates and their sampling errors. Finally, a range of special topics, including nonresponse and issues relating to oversize and undersize schools, is addressed.

 14 COMPUTING SURVEY WEIGHTS

This chapter describes estimation weights, including how to compute them, how to adjust for nonresponses, and how to use auxiliary up-to-date information to adjust estimation weights to compute national totals.

DESIGN WEIGHTS

Estimation is a technique for producing information about a population of interest based on data gathered from a sample of that population. The first step in estimation is to assign a weight to each sampled unit or to each of the responding sampled units. The *design weight* can be thought of as the average number of units in the survey population that each sampled unit represents and is determined by the sample design. The design weight, w_d (where d stands for design), for a unit in the sample is the inverse of its inclusion probability π. It was noted earlier that in probability sampling, each unit has a known probability, π, of being sampled. If the inclusion probability is, for example, 1 in 50, then each selected unit represents, on average, 50 units of the survey population; hence, the design weight is $w_d = 50$.

Note that for a multistage design (which is frequently used in a national assessment of educational achievement), a unit's probability of selection is the combined probability of selection at each stage.

Simple random samples and systematic random samples are equal probability designs because each unit has an equal chance of being included in the sample. Stated in statistical terms, in the case of simple random sampling (SRS), the inclusion probability is $\pi = n/N$ for each unit, and the design weight is $w_d = 1/\pi = N/n$. In the case of systematic random sampling, the inclusion probability, $\pi = 1/k$, where the integer $k = [n/N]$, is the sampling step; thus, for each unit, the design weight is $w_d = 1/\pi = k$.

Exercise 14.1 shows how to calculate the design weight for a simple random sample (SRS).

When stratification is a feature of the sample design, the strata are considered as distinct populations, each providing its own part of the full sample. Hence, the design weights are computed independently for each stratum according to the sampling design used in each stratum.

Suppose that a population of $N = 1,000$ schools is divided into two strata, urban and rural, on the survey frame. The urban stratum is composed of $N_1 = 400$ schools and the rural one of $N_2 = 600$ schools. Table 14.1 shows that the total sample of size $n = 200$, across both strata, was allocated equally to each stratum. The inclusion probability, or

---

EXERCISE 14.1

Design Weight for a Simple Random Sample of 400 Students

Recall that the first sample selected for Sentz assumed a perfect list frame of all 27,654 eligible students, from which a simple random sample of 400 students was drawn. Thus, the inclusion probability for each student is $\pi = n/N = 400/27,654$, and the design weight is $w_d = 1/\pi = 27,654/400 = 69.135$. This weight was added to the sample file by SPSS (Statistical Package for the Social Sciences) as the sample was selected. You can see this by accessing the folder **SRS400** and opening the file **STUDENTSRSAMPLE** using the following commands:

File – Open – Data – Look in

   ...\MYSAMPLSOL\STUDENTSRSAMPLE.SAV

Open

The result should look like the data in exercise figure 14.1.A, after (a) removing the automatic variables that will not be needed (namely, **Inclusion Probability_1_**, **SampleWeightCumulative_1_**, and **SampleWeight_Final_**); (b) renaming those variables that will be useful later in the survey process (namely, **PopulationSize**, **SampleSize**, and **SampleWeight**); and (c) saving the file. This cleaning step is identical to what was done to the school and the class samples earlier (see exercise 8.3).

You may want to save the file **STUDENTSRSAMPLE** under **...\MYSAMPLSOL** for later.

EXERCISE FIGURE 14.1.A   Data in Student Sample File

	schoolid	studentid	region	province	density	town	school	nbclass	class	classid	class_size	student	age	gender	Population Size	Sample Size	Sample Weight
1	1101	1101103	NE	1	rural	1	1	2	1	11011	41	3	13	1	27654	400	69.14
2	1101	1101203	NE	1	rural	1	1	2	2	11012	48	3	15	1	27654	400	69.14
3	1103	1103218	NE	1	rural	1	3	4	2	11032	52	18	13	1	27654	400	69.14
4	1103	1103236	NE	1	rural	1	3	4	2	11032	52	36	15	0	27654	400	69.14
5	1104	1104249	NE	1	rural	1	4	4	2	11042	54	49	13	0	27654	400	69.14
6	1104	1104337	NE	1	rural	1	4	4	3	11043	54	37	15	1	27654	400	69.14
7	1201	1201103	NE	1	rural	2	1	2	1	12011	57	3	13	1	27654	400	69.14
8	1201	1201211	NE	1	rural	2	1	2	2	12012	52	11	13	1	27654	400	69.14
9	1202	1202322	NE	1	rural	2	2	3	3	12023	52	22	14	1	27654	400	69.14
10	1203	1203145	NE	1	rural	2	3	3	1	12031	46	45	13	0	27654	400	69.14
11	1203	1203325	NE	1	rural	2	3	3	3	12033	54	25	15	0	27654	400	69.14
12	1204	1204130	NE	1	rural	2	4	2	1	12041	57	30	13	0	27654	400	69.14
13	1204	1204223	NE	1	rural	2	4	2	2	12042	48	23	15	0	27654	400	69.14
14	1301	1301204	NE	1	rural	3	1	3	2	13012	52	4	13	0	27654	400	69.14
15	1301	1301206	NE	1	rural	3	1	3	2	13012	52	6	14	0	27654	400	69.14
16	1301	1301242	NE	1	rural	3	1	3	2	13012	52	42	14	1	27654	400	69.14

Source: Authors' example within SPSS software.

TABLE 14.1

Stratified Simple Random Sample with Equal Allocation

Stratum	Population size	Sample size	Sampling fraction/inclusion probability
Urban	$N_1 = 400$	$n_1 = 100$	$\pi_1 = 1/4$
Rural	$N_2 = 600$	$n_2 = 100$	$\pi_2 = 1/6$
Total	$N = 1{,}000$	$n = 200$	

Source: Authors' compilation.

sampling fraction in this case, for the urban stratum is thus equal to $n/N = 100/400 = 1/4 = 0.25$. The sampling fraction for the rural stratum is equal to $n/N = 100/600 = 1/6 = 0.167$. On the sample file, each school in the urban stratum has a design weight of $w_{d,1} = 4$, and each school in the rural stratum has a design weight of $w_{d,2} = 6$.

For multistage sampling, the overall design weight is calculated by taking the inverse of the probability of selection at each stage or phase and then multiplying them. Suppose a two-stage cluster sample selects a simple random sample of $n_1 = 10$ out of $N_1 = 100$ schools at the first stage and a simple random sample of $n_2 = 30$ students within each school (cluster) at the second stage, where the number of units within each cluster is $N_2 = 60$. The probability of selection at the first stage is

$$\pi_1 = \frac{n_1}{N_1} = \frac{10}{100} = \frac{1}{10},$$

and the probability of selection at the second stage is

$$\pi_2 = \frac{n_2}{N_2} = \frac{30}{60} = \frac{1}{2}.$$

So the design weight for each selected student is

$$w_d = \frac{1}{\pi_1} \times \frac{1}{\pi_2} = 10 \times 2 = 20.$$

For the three-stage sampling design used in the Sentz case study (schools, classes, and eventually students by virtue of nonresponse), where the probability of selection for student i is π_{ki} at the kth stage, the design weight for that student is

$$w_{di} = \frac{1}{\pi_{1i}} \times \frac{1}{\pi_{2i}} \times \frac{1}{\pi_{3i}}$$

$$= \text{school\_weight} \times \text{class\_weight} \times \text{student\_weight}$$

$$= \text{school\_weight} \times \text{class\_weight} \times 1.$$

Note that the sample, as initially designed for Sentz, selected all students in selected classes, so that student_weight = 1. Thus, the design appears to have only two stages. However, the importance of the third stage becomes evident later, when one establishes that not all selected students actually participated in the national assessment. In this instance, the third-stage weights have to be adjusted for nonresponse (see the next section).

Exercise 14.2 shows how to calculate the design weight for a probability proportional to size (PPS) sample. Exercises 14.3 and 14.4 show how to add test results.

EXERCISE 14.2

Design Weight for a PPS Sample of Schools and Classes

Under the two-stage design, in each stratum several schools were selected with probability proportional to their measure of size (MOS) so that each selected school has its own probability of selection. To calculate these probabilities, you need three quantities: n_h, the number of schools selected in stratum h; z_{hi}, the size of school i in stratum h; and Z_h, the total size measure (*cumMOS*) for stratum h.

The selection probability for the school is then

$$\pi_{1hi} = n_h \times \frac{z_{hi}}{Z_h}.$$

For example, the total number of students in Province 1 is $Z_1 = 5{,}565$, and the sample allocated to that province is of size $n_1 = 24$. If the MOS for school 1101 is $z_{1,1101} = 89$ (see lines 1 and 2 of exercise figure 14.1.A), the probability of selection for that school would be

$$\pi_{1,1,1101} = n_1 \times \frac{z_{1,1101}}{Z_1} = 24 \times \frac{89}{5565} = 0.384.$$

Then one class was selected with equal probability from the list of eligible classes for each selected school; if there are M_{hi} classes in school i in stratum h, the second-stage probability of selection is

$$\pi_{2hi} = \frac{1}{M_{hi}}.$$

SPSS Complex Samples computes both the selection probabilities and the design weights (called by SPSS *sample weights*) as it selects the samples. Because two nested samples were selected, the overall school and class design weight must be computed as the product of the two components.

(continued)

EXERCISE 14.2 *(continued)*

Open the file with the following commands:

File – Open – Data – Look in

...\MYSAMPLSOL\CLASS_SAMPLE.SAV

Open

Then select **Transform – Compute Variable**. Type *DesignWeight* in **Target Variable**. Type *Weight1*Weight2* in **Numeric expression**. Click **OK**.

To adjust the format of the *DesignWeight* variable, switch the display to **Variable View** (lower left tab) and ensure that the format is two or three decimal places. Return to **Data View** and save the **CLASS_SAMPLE** file. The data from the **CLASS_SAMPLE** file, which include the design weight in a two-decimal format, are displayed in exercise figure 14.2.A.

You may want to save the file **CLASS_SAMPLE** under ...\MYSAMPLSOL\ for later.

EXERCISE FIGURE 14.2.A   Data from the Class Sample File

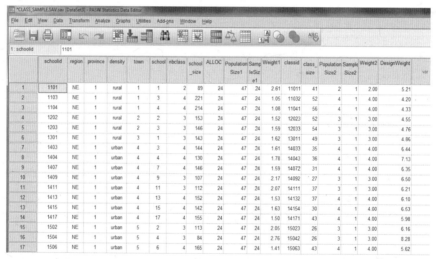

Source: Authors' example within SPSS software.

EXERCISE 14.3

Adding Test Results for a Simple Random Sample of 400 Students

The fictitious test results for all the eighth-grade students are stored in ...\BASE FILES\ **RESPONSES**. (In real life, they would have been entered after test administration and data cleaning, sometime after the calculation of the initial design weights.) In this next step, you will match the file containing the 400 selected students with the file of test results for these students. Again, you will be sorting and merging files.

1. Read and sort the **RESPONSES** file using the following commands:

    File – Open – Data – Look in

    > ...*BASE FILES\RESPONSES.SAV*

    Open

    Select **Data – Sort cases** and move **STUDENTID** to **Sort by**. Click **OK**.

2. Read and sort the file containing the simple random sample of students in the same way:

    File – Open – Data – Look in

    > ...*MYSAMPLSOI\STUDENTSRSAMPLE.SAV*

    Open

    Select **Data – Sort cases** and move **STUDENTID** to **Sort by**. Click **OK**.

3. Merge the responses and the sample of students. Drop some extraneous variables and retain only the sample records. (In real life, these actions would correspond to the phases of data collection and data capture.)

    Bring the **RESPONSES** file to the screen. Select **Data – Merge files – Add variables**. Choose **STUDENTSRSAMPLE** from the **Open dataset** and click **Continue**. Click **Match cases on key variables...**, and move **STUDENTID** from the **Excluded variables** to the **Key variables**.

    Click **Non-active dataset is keyed table**. Then click **OK** and click **OK** again.

    The variables **PopulationSize**, **SampleSize**, and **SampleWeight** should now appear as variables of the **RESPONSES** data set. Most of the records have empty cells. You will retain the records for the 400 SRS students, not for all the students.

    Use the following commands: **Data – Select Cases – Use filter variable**.

    Move **PopulationSize** to **Use filter variable**. Click **Copy selected cases...**. Type **SRSResponses** in the **Dataset name** box and click **OK**.

    Close **RESPONSES** and *do not* save it. Bring **SRSResponses** to the screen, and save the file under ...*MYSAMPLSOL\SRSRESPONSES.SAV*.

    Exercise figure 14.3.A contains the saved data file for three students, which includes an excerpt of the test results for the sample of 400 students, ready for weighting and estimation. The order of variables on your screen may be different. Notice the *status* variable, which indicates the student's status at the time of testing. Scroll down the file and observe that some students were absent from school on the day of testing and others had dropped out of (or changed) schools since the date on which the school had created the student lists. Absenteeism, dropout, and transfers are typical problems in national assessment surveys.

(continued)

EXERCISE 14.3 (continued)

EXERCISE FIGURE 14.3.A   Excerpt of Test Results for Sample of Students

	schoolid	studentid	region	province	density	town	school	nbclass	class	nbelev	student	age	gender	socec	geog	math
1	1101	1101103	NE	1	rural	1	1	2	1	41	3	13	1	2	106	221
2	1101	1101203	NE	1	rural	1	1	2	2	48	3	15	1	3	108	228
3	1103	1103218	NE	1	rural	1	3	4	2	52	18	13	1	1	103	216

(Continued)

	civics	lang	status	CLASSID	Population Size	Sample Size	Sample Weight
1	58	195	participant	11011	27654	400	69.14
2	134	214	participant	11012	27654	400	69.14
3	131	212	participant	11032	27654	400	69.14

Source: Authors' example within SPSS software.

EXERCISE 14.4

Adding Test Results for a PPS Design

The process of adding test results for a PPS design is similar to adding test results for the SRS400 students. However, in this instance the sampling sequences are important: schools were sampled first, then classes, and finally students. This structure influences how files are sorted and merged. This exercise corresponds to the data capture activities of a real-life national assessment. To begin, you have to open the full response file containing the data on all 27,654 grade 8 students. These responses will then be matched to the (sampled) students of the sampled classes and the matching records will be retained.

1. Read and sort the **RESPONSES** file as follows:

   File – Open – Data – Look in

   ...\BASE FILES\RESPONSES.SAV

   Open

   Select **Data – Sort cases** and move **SCHOOLID CLASSID** to **Sort by**. Click **OK.**

2. Read and sort the file containing the sample of 120 classes as follows:

   File – Open – Data – Look in

   ...\MYSAMPLSOL\CLASS_SAMPLE.SAV

   Open

EXERCISE 14.4 *(continued)*

Select **Data – Sort** cases and move *SCHOOLID CLASSID* to **Sort by**. Click **OK**.

3. Merge the responses and the sample of classes. Drop some extraneous variables and retain only the sample records.

Bring the *RESPONSES* file to the screen. Select **Data – Merge files – Add variables**. Choose *CLASS_SAMPLE* from the **Open dataset**, and click **Continue**.

Click **Match cases on key variables.**

Move *SCHOOLID* and *CLASSID* from the **Excluded variables** to the **Key variables**. Click **Non-active dataset is keyed table**. Click **OK** and click **OK** again.

The variables population sizes, sample sizes, and weights should now appear on the response file. Retain the sampled records by selecting **Data – Select Cases**.

Move *DesignWeight* to **Use filter variable**. Click **Copy selected cases...** and type *PPSResponses* in the **Dataset name** box, and then click **OK**.

Bring *PPSResponses* to the screen, and click the **Variable View** tab. The following variables will not be needed and can be dropped: *nbclass, class_size, school_size, alloc*.

Save the file under *...\MYSAMPLSOL\PPSRESPONSES.SAV*.

Exercise figure 14.4.A presents an excerpt of the test results based on two-stage random sampling with PPS.

EXERCISE FIGURE 14.4.A   Excerpt of Test Results Based on Two-Stage Random Sampling

Source: Authors' example within SPSS software.

Close all open data files without saving them.

WEIGHT ADJUSTMENT FOR NONRESPONSE

All surveys suffer from nonresponse, which occurs when all or some of the information requested from sampled units is unavailable for some reason. Nonresponse can occur when the school or student refuses to participate, when the school cannot be located, when students are absent, or when the information obtained is unusable. The easiest way to deal with such nonresponse is to ignore it. However, not compensating for the nonresponding units leads to bias. It could, for example, result in underestimating or overestimating the mean achievement levels of students, the size of the national enrollment, or the size of the teaching workforce.

The most common way of dealing with total nonresponse is to adjust the design weights on the assumption that the responding units represent both responding and nonresponding units. This adjustment is reasonable under the assumption that, for the characteristics measured in the survey, the nonrespondents are like the respondents. The design weights of the nonrespondents are then redistributed among the respondents. This step is often done using a nonresponse adjustment; the factor is multiplied by the design weight to produce a nonresponse-adjusted weight, as illustrated in the following example.

The nonresponse adjustment factor is usually defined as the ratio of the sum of the weights in the original sample to the sum of the weights of the responding units.

The sampling team should consult with those responsible for test administration and establish the number of nonrespondents in each school. Data on nonrespondents should be available in a record such as a student tracking form (see box 4.1). The sampling team can use this information to compute the appropriate adjustment factors.

Suppose a simple random sample of $n = 20$ students was selected from a class of $N = 40$ students. The number of respondent units is denoted by n_r. Of the original target sample of 20 students, only $n_r = 16$ students completed the assessment. To determine the design weight and the weight adjusted for nonresponse for the responding units, one must take the following steps:

- First, calculate the inclusion probabilities for a simple random sample:

$$\pi = \frac{n}{N} = \frac{20}{40} = \frac{1}{2}.$$

Therefore, the design weight for every sampled unit is $w_d = 2$.

- Second, calculate the nonresponse adjustment factor. Because only $n_r = 16$ persons of the $n = 20$ selected provided the information required, the final sample size is 16. If one assumes that the responding units can be used to represent both responding and nonresponding units, the nonresponse adjustment factor is

$$A = \frac{\sum_{sample} w_d}{\sum_{response} w_d} = \frac{20 \times 2}{16 \times 2} = 1.25.$$

- The last step is to compute the nonresponse-adjusted weight. The nonresponse-adjusted design weight, w_{nr}, is the product of the design weight and the nonresponse adjustment factor:

$$w_{nr} = w_d A = 2 \times 1.25 = 2.5.$$

Each respondent now represents 2.5 students in the national assessment (compared to 2.0 students had all students responded). Therefore, a final weight of 2.5 is assigned to each unit on the data file.

Exercise 14.5 is presented for pedagogical purposes. This example shows how to handle the issue of weighting students who, although sampled, did not participate in the national assessment.

If one assumes that all nonrespondents in a national assessment are alike in terms of the characteristics measured in the assessment, then the same nonresponse adjustment factor can be applied to all responding groups. However, there is often good reason to assume that subgroups differ in their response propensities and in their characteristics. For example, students in rural schools may be absent from school more often than students in urban schools, or boys and girls may display different response rates. One adjustment applied to all respondents would likely bias the results. In such cases, separate nonresponse adjustments should be performed within each stratum.

EXERCISE 14.5

Nonresponse Weight Adjustment for Simple Random Sample of 400 Students

Some students in the sample of 400 selected from the frame according to the design were not tested. The sampling team must make allowance for nonresponses. It must consider two distinct types of nonparticipants.

First, some students may be unavailable for testing, having left the class (and school) permanently. They will be assigned the status *dropout* or *no longer at school* on the data files. In this case, some may argue to leave them in the frame, without changing their weights, but to give them scores of *0* on the tests. This may be considered a rather severe penalty for using an out-of-date frame. In effect, the students belonged to the population at the time the frame was created but were no longer members of the population at the time of assessment, which is the population to which the estimates will really refer. A common practice, however, is to set the weight of the dropouts to *0* and eventually to remove them from the database. This strategy assumes that the student simply moved to another school and still has a chance of being part of the assessment or of being represented by someone in the sample. No adjustment is made to the weights of the participating students.

Second, some students may have been temporarily absent, through illness or having to help their parents or for some other reason. These students, recorded as status *absent*, can be considered as "true" nonrespondents. They are still in the population, and on another day, they would have been tested. They can be thought of as "missing at random." Thus, the weights of the remaining members of the sample (including those who have left permanently, the dropouts, because they are on the frame and were members of the population at the time the design weights were determined) should be assigned a nonresponse weight adjustment. Later on, when the estimates for the survey population are computed, nonresponding elements of the sample (absentees, dropouts, and the like) will be filtered out.

The sampling team should obtain information on the participation status of each sampled student (participant, absent, dropout, or any other status as required) from the data collection team for each participating school and student. This information will have to be recorded and attached to the sample file in a manner similar to what is described here.

The students' responses and their design weight for the SRS design are stored in ...*MYSAMPLSOL\SRSRESPONSES*. The variable **STATUS** indicates who is a nonrespondent. The variable **RESP** is created as a marker for response or nonresponse. Because SRS does not use information about schools or classes, only the cases on file need to be counted and compared to the intended sample size. The weights of the sampled students are adjusted according to their participation status, and the final weights are stored in ...*MySamplSol\SRSResponses* for future use.

1. Read the *SRSResponses* file by using the following commands:

   File – Open – Data – Look in

   ...*MYSAMPLSOL\\SRSRESPONSES.SAV*

   Open

2. Create a marker for response and count the number of responding cases. Use the following commands: **Transform – Recode into Different Variables...**. Then move *STATUS* to **Input Variable**. Type in *RESP* in **Output Variable Name**.

If you wish, you can type in an explanatory title in the **Label** box. Click **Change**. Click **Old and New Values**. Under **Old Value**, click **Value** and type *absent*, respecting the uppercase and lowercase.

In **New Value**, type the number *0*. Click **Add**. In **Old Value**, click **All other values** at the bottom of the screen. In **New Value**, type the number *1* and click **Add**. Now click **Continue** and then **OK**.

Select **Data – Aggregate** from the menu. Move *RESP* to **Break variable**. Under **Aggregated variables**, click **Number of cases**. Type in *EFFSAM* for "effective sample" instead of keeping the default **N_BREAK**.

In **Save**, click **Add aggregated variables to active dataset**. In **Options**, click **Sort file before aggregating**, then click **OK**.

Note the number 19 under the heading *EFFSAM* where *RESP* is *0*. This number indicates that 19 sample members were nonrespondents among the 400 selected students.

3. Compute the nonresponse adjustment factor (*NRESADJ*) and the estimation weight. Select from the menu commands **Transform – Compute Variable**. Type *NRESADJ* in **Target Variable**. Type *SampleSize/EFFSAM* in **Numeric expression**.

Click **If...**. Click **Include if case satisfies condition**. Type in *RESP=1*, click **Continue**, and then click **OK**.

Select from the menu commands **Transform – Compute Variable** again. Type *NRESADJ* in **Target Variable**. Type *0* in **Numeric expression**.

Click **If...**. Click **Include if case satisfies condition**. Type in *RESP=0*. Click **Continue**, then click **OK** and click **OK** again.

Select from the menu commands **Transform – Compute Variable** again to check the estimation weight. Type in *FINALWEIGHT* in **Target Variable**. Type in *SampleWeight* NRESADJ* in **Numeric expression**.

Click **If...**. Click **Include all cases**. Click **Continue**. Click **OK**.

You should see that the final estimation weight is 0 for the absent students and about 72.6 (depending on the number of nonrespondents in the sample) for the participants and dropouts.

(continued)

EXERCISE 14.5 *(continued)*

If the nonresponse adjustment and final weight are displayed as integers, you can change the number of visible decimal places by going to the **Variable View** tab and changing the format there. Each respondent now represents 72.6 students.

Save the file as *...\MYSAMPLSOL\RESPSRSFINALWT.SAV*. This file will be used to compute estimates later on. Close without saving all other open data files.

The following example examines a situation in which a difference exists in the response rate between urban and rural students (in, for example, taking a mathematics test), resulting in the need for differential nonresponse adjustments to be applied to both sets of data. During the national assessment, although samples of size 100 were drawn to represent the urban and rural populations, only $n_{r,1} = 85$ students in the urban stratum and $n_{r,2} = 70$ students in the rural stratum took the mathematics test (table 14.2).

The results of the steps taken to calculate the nonresponse adjustment rates follow:

- The design weight in each stratum is $w_{d,1} = 4$ for the urban stratum and $w_{d,2} = 6$ for the rural stratum.

- The nonresponse adjustment factors for each stratum were calculated as follows:

$$\text{Stratum 1, urban:} \quad A_1 = \frac{100 \times 4}{85 \times 4} = 1.177.$$

$$\text{Stratum 2, rural:} \quad A_2 = \frac{100 \times 6}{70 \times 6} = 1.428.$$

- The nonresponse-adjusted weights for each stratum, the product of the design weight and the nonresponse adjustment factor, were

$$\text{Stratum 1, urban:} \quad w_{nr,1} = w_{d,1}A_1 = 4 \times 1.177 = 4.706.$$

$$\text{Stratum 2, rural:} \quad w_{nr,2} = w_{d,2}A_2 = 6 \times 1.428 = 8.571.$$

Thus, each respondent in the urban stratum in the sample file is given a final weight of 4.706, and each respondent in the rural stratum a final weight of 8.571 (see table 14.3). In other words, each urban

TABLE 14.2

Stratified Simple Random Sample: Urban and Rural Population and Sample Sizes and Response Rates

Stratum	Population size	Sample size	Number of respondents
Urban	$N_1 = 400$	$n_1 = 100$	$n_{r,1} = 85$
Rural	$N_2 = 600$	$n_2 = 100$	$n_{r,2} = 70$

Source: Authors' compilation.

TABLE 14.3

Stratified Simple Random Sample: Urban and Rural Population and Sample Sizes, Response Rates and Nonresponse-Adjusted Weights

Stratum	Population size	Sample size	Number of respondents	Design weight	Adjusted weight
Urban	$N_1 = 400$	$n_1 = 100$	$n_{r,1} = 85$	4	4.706
Rural	$N_2 = 600$	$N_2 = 100$	$n_{r,2} = 70$	6	8.571

Source: Authors' compilation.

student represented about 4.7 urban students, whereas each rural student represented about 8.6 students.

In some instances, adjustment for nonresponse may be possible or necessary in classes defined by variables other than those used for stratification; for example, if boys tend to respond much less than girls, adjusting for nonresponse on the basis of urbanization may not be as effective as adjusting by gender. Of course, such an adjustment requires that gender be available on class rosters of student lists for each sampled class. Consulting a survey statistician may be wise because such adjustments may be more delicate than they seem and may affect how the replication weights are to be computed (see chapter 16).

When calculating the nonresponse adjustment factor, one may find that the fact that some sampled units (students) may turn out to be out of scope (that is, not part of the target population) is an important consideration. For example, a boy with a learning disability may attend a regular class because of a national policy on school integration. This child, however, should have been excluded from the national assessment because he followed a reduced or adapted curriculum and was not part of the target population. The calculation of the nonresponse adjustment should be based on in-scope units because out-of-scope units in the sample typically represent other out-of-scope units in the frame. The preceding example assumes that all nonrespondents are in scope.

Nonresponse adjustment should be performed separately for groups of similar respondents, where each group of respondents represents the nonrespondents in that group. The sampling team might be advised to consult with a sampling specialist to help identify the response groups most appropriate for a specific assessment.

Exercise 14.6 shows how to calculate weight adjustment for a PPS sample.

EXERCISE 14.6

Nonresponse Weight Adjustment for a PPS Sample

In calculating the weights for the Sentz national assessment under the two-stage PPS design, assume that all selected schools and classes responded. In practice, this will likely not be the case, and additional weight adjustments will be required so that the participating schools account for the nonresponding schools in the sample.

As in the case of the SRS example, allowance must be made for nonresponse within selected classes. Again, you must distinguish between the dropouts, who remain on the file with test scores of 0, and the temporary absentees, who are treated as nonrespondents.

The weights of the remaining members of the class must be adjusted in standard fashion. The adjustment is calculated in the same way as for the SRS case, except that classes must be considered in the computations.

1. Determine the most appropriate response groups for the adjustment. If, for example, test scores or response rates are expected to differ substantially for boys and girls, or for urban and rural areas, these categories might be considered in making the nonresponse adjustments. In the present case, a quick examination of the results did not suggest that these factors were particularly important. As a result, adjustments for nonresponse will be made within each class. If, for instance, a class originally had 42 students, of whom 1 left school and 3 were temporarily absent, the original weights are now multiplied by $42/(42 - 3) = 42/39 = 1.0769$; the student who left school would keep the original weight, accounting for other students who had left the school.

The file *...\MYSAMPLSOL\PPSRESPONSES.SAV* contains the responses and design weights for the two-stage sample of students. The process for computing the nonresponse adjustment factors is identical to that used earlier for the simple random sample. Responses have to be counted by class and school, so the instructions will convey the hierarchy of the sample. In the absence of any information indicating that nonresponse is completely uniform throughout the population, it may be advisable to make the adjustments at the local rather than the global level.

Carry out the following steps to (a) open the appropriate response file, (b) compute the sample size at the last stage of sampling (the size of the class) and the number of respondents, (c) compute a nonresponse adjustment factor at the class level, and (d) compute the final weights.

First, read the **PPSResponses** file:

File – Open – Data – Look in

...\MYSAMPLSOL\PPSRESPONSES.SAV

Open

2. Create a marker for response and count the number of responding cases.[a] Select **Transform – Recode into Different Variables....** Move **STATUS** to **Input Variable**. Type in **RESP** in **Output Variable Name**.

If you want you can type in a label. Click **Change**. Click **Old and New Values**. In **Old Value**, click **Value** and type *absent* respecting the upper- and lowercases. In **New Value**, type the number **0**. Click **Add**.

In **Old Value**, click **All other values** (at the bottom of the screen). In **New Value**, type the number *1*. Click **Add**. Click **Continue**. Click **OK**.

Select **Data – Aggregate**. Move **SCHOOLID CLASSID** to **Break variable**. In **Aggregated variables**, click **Number of cases**. Type in **CLASS_SIZE** instead of keeping the default **N_BREAK**.

In **Save**, click **Add aggregated variables to active dataset**.

In **Options**, click **Sort file before aggregating**. Click **OK**.

Select **Data – Aggregate** again. Move **RESP** to **Break variable** and add it to **SCHOOLID CLASSID**, which should still be in the dialogue box from the previous step.

Under **Aggregated variables**, click **Number of cases**. Type in **CLASS_RESP** for number of respondents instead of keeping the default **N_BREAK**.

In **Save**, click **Add aggregated variables to active dataset**.

In **Options**, click **Sort file before aggregating**. Click **OK**.

3. Compute the nonresponse adjustment factor. Select **Transform – Compute Variable**. Type **NRESADJ** in **Target Variable**. Type **CLASS_SIZE/ CLASS_RESP** in **Numeric expression**.

Click **If...**. Click **Include if case satisfies condition**. Type in **RESP=1**. Click **Continue**. Click **OK**.

Select **Transform – Compute Variable**. Type **NRESADJ** in **Target Variable**. Type *0* in **Numeric expression**.

Click **If...**. Click **Include if case satisfies condition**. Type in **RESP=0**. Click **Continue**. Click **OK**. Click **OK** again.

(continued)

EXERCISE 14.6 *(continued)*

4. Compute the final estimation weight. Select **Transform – Compute Variable** from the menu. Type **FINALWEIGHT** in **Target Variable**. Type **DesignWeight*NRESADJ** in **Numeric expression**.

Click **If…**. Click **Include all cases**. Click **Continue**. Click **OK**.

Save the results of the nonresponse adjustment to the design weight to the file **…\MYSAMPLSOL\RESP2STGFINALWT.SAV** for future use.

Exercise figure 14.6.A shows an excerpt from the PPS sample data file with the final weight adjustments and the final weights depicted in the last two columns.

EXERCISE FIGURE 14.6.A Excerpt from PPS Sample Data File

Source: Authors' example within SPSS software.

---

a. In this example the count is up-to-date. In some situations there may be a time lag between the creation of the frame (for instance, in Month 1 of the school year) and the completion of the tests (for instance, in Month 10). The number of students may change due to factors such as natural migration (new arrivals, departures). In such an event you need to have a fresh count.

EXPORTING AND IMPORTING CLEAN DATA

The final step in the data cleaning and weighting process is to export the cleaned data set in a format that is appropriate for analysis. SPSS (Statistical Package for the Social Sciences) will import Access and various text formats. SAS (Statistical Analysis Software) will import Access and SPSS formats as well as many other text formats. WesVar readily accepts files from Access, EpiData, Epi Info, SAS, SPSS, and Stata.

POSTSTRATIFICATION: USING AUXILIARY INFORMATION TO IMPROVE ESTIMATES BY ADJUSTING ESTIMATION WEIGHTS

The design weight multiplied by the nonresponse adjustment factor can be used to produce final weights and survey estimates of the desired characteristics. However, sometimes information about the survey population is available from other sources (for example, from the latest enrollment statistics). This information can also be incorporated in the weighting process.

Two main reasons exist for using auxiliary data at estimation. First, having the survey estimates match known population totals is often important. For example, having the estimated numbers of male and female students match the official numbers of boys and girls enrolled in school may be desirable.

Second, poststratification can improve the precision of the estimates. Recall that an estimator with small sampling variance—a measure of sampling error—is said to be precise. At the design stage, however, auxiliary information must be available for all units on the frame. At estimation, auxiliary data can be used to improve the precision of estimates as long as the values of the auxiliary variables are collected for the surveyed units, and population totals or estimates are available for these auxiliary variables from another reliable source.

Auxiliary information may also be used to further correct for different nonresponse rates in subgroups of the population. It may also help adjust for coverage inadequacies that result in the survey population differing from the target population.

Successful use of auxiliary data at the estimation stage has three basic requirements:

- The auxiliary data must be well correlated with the survey variables.
- The external sources of information concerning the population must be accurate.
- The auxiliary information must be collected for all responding sample units if only population totals are known.

Typically, auxiliary information used for poststratification (such as the number of persons by gender and age group or the number of students taking advanced mathematics or specialized language arts classes) is obtained from official sources (a national census, the ministry of education) but is known (or made available) to the sampling team only as population totals, not as individual values for each member of the population. In poststratification, these population totals are to be compared with their corresponding estimates from the sample, which means that the information should be collected for each sampled individual as part of the background section of the questionnaire or test booklet.

The gains in efficiency of estimates that use auxiliary data depend on how well the survey variables correlate with the available auxiliary data. Not only do the data have to be reliable, but also the external data source must pertain to the same target population and be based on comparable concepts, definitions, and reference periods as that of the survey.

Poststratification is used to adjust survey weights using variables that are suitable for stratification but that could not be used at the design stage because the data were not available or because more up-to-date, reliable stratification information for the population became available after sample selection. Poststratification is used when the auxiliary data are available in the form of counts (for example, the number of male and female students in the population). It is very effective at reducing sampling variance when the population averages of the variables of interest are very different across the poststrata (such as when achievement scores for boys and girls are markedly different). Nevertheless, being able to stratify at the design stage is preferable to poststratifying.

The following rather simple example shows how to use poststratification to improve the estimate of the number of female teachers in a school.

Suppose that an outside research group conducted a survey to get information on school staff. A simple random sample of $n = 25$ persons was selected from the anonymous list of $N = 78$ school employees. For the purpose of this example, assume that auxiliary information that could be used for stratification was not available at the design stage.

TABLE 14.4

School Survey: Poststratum Distribution of Staff by Gender

Group	Poststratum 1, men	Poststratum 2, women	Number of respondents
All staff members	3	12	15
Mathematics teachers	1	7	8

Source: Authors' compilation.

In addition to information on gender, information on the age and subject specialty of each respondent was collected. Of the original $n = 25$ persons, $n_r = 15$ responded. Table 14.4 presents gender-specific data on the staff sample and on mathematics teachers.

Note the following:

- The inclusion probability for each sampled unit was

$$\pi = \frac{n}{N} = \frac{25}{78} = 0.32;$$

therefore, design weight was $w_d = 1/\pi = 3.12$.

- The nonresponse adjustment factor, assuming that everyone in the survey had the same probability of responding to the survey (that is, there was one nonresponse group), was

$$A = \frac{25}{15} = 1.67.$$

- The nonresponse-adjusted weight was

$$w_{nr} = w_d A = 3.12 \times 1.67 = 5.2.$$

Thus, all respondents had the same nonresponse-adjusted weight, $w_r = 5.2$. These weights were used to produce the survey estimates shown in table 14.5.

TABLE 14.5

Survey Estimates Adjusted for Nonresponse

	Men	Women	Total
Number of staff members	(3 × 5.2 =) 15.6	62.4	78.0
Number of math teachers	5.2	36.4	41.6
Proportion of math teachers	0.33	0.58	0.53

Source: Authors' compilation.

The nonresponse-adjusted weights led to an estimate of about 16 men and 62 women working in the school, with an estimated 33 percent of men and 58 percent of women in the school who teach mathematics.

Suppose that after the survey was conducted the outside research agency found that 42 men and 36 women were working in the school at the time of the survey. The estimates produced by the survey were quite different from these true values.

The agency decided that its survey estimates should be consistent with the known number of men and women. It was also of the opinion that a teacher's subject specialty might be related to gender. If gender-specific information on teachers had been available at the time of the sample design, the agency would have stratified by gender. What can the agency do?

The sample can be stratified after the fact to create what are referred to as *poststratified weights* to be used during estimation. The poststratified weight, w_{pst}, is the product of the nonresponse-adjusted weight, w_{nr}, and the poststratification adjustment factor.

The poststratification adjustment factor is computed for each poststratum. This factor corresponds to the ratio of the number of population units in the poststratum, N, to the estimated number of population units in the poststratum, $\hat{N}$, which is estimated using the design weights adjusted for nonresponse. (Although this example applies to SRS, the same formula, $N/\hat{N}$ can be used for more complex design weights.) In this example, the poststratification adjustment factors are

Poststratum 1, men: $\qquad \dfrac{N_{men}}{\hat{N}_{men}} = \dfrac{42}{15.6} = 2.69.$

Poststratum 2, women: $\qquad \dfrac{N_{women}}{\hat{N}_{women}} = \dfrac{36}{62.4} = 0.58.$

When applied to the nonresponse-adjusted weight, the poststratification adjustment factors produce the following final poststratified weights:

Poststratum 1, men: $\qquad w_{pst,men} = w_{nr} \times \dfrac{N_{men}}{\hat{N}_{men}} = 5.2 \times 2.69 = 14.$

Poststratum 2, women: $v_{pst,women} = w_{nr} \times \dfrac{N_{women}}{\hat{N}_{women}} = 5.2 \times 0.58 = 3.$

Using the poststratified weights, the estimates of the number of men and women are now consistent with the known totals of men and women in the school, and to the extent that gender is related to the number and proportion of teaching specialty, considerable improvements in precision may be obtained. Note that the proportion of mathematics teachers within each poststratum has not changed but that the proportion of mathematics teachers in the total population, which involves more than one poststratum, has changed. The revised survey estimates are presented in table 14.6.

More complex weight adjustment methods exist, but they are beyond the scope of this treatment of sampling. For more complex issues, a national assessment sampling team may wish to consult with a sampling specialist to explore the most appropriate adjustment method for a given situation.

Finally, note that no attempt has been made to poststratify the Sentz data. Possibly, after some initial analysis of the weighted results, differences may have been detected that would have led to a decision, prompted by the availability of accurate up-to-date information, to carry out poststratification on one or more key variables.

TABLE 14.6

Survey Estimates Adjusted for Nonresponse, before and after Poststratification Adjustment

Poststratification	Staff	Men	Women	Total
Before adjustment	Number	(3 × 5.2 =) 15.6	62.4	78.0
	Number of math teachers	5.2	36.4	41.6
	Proportion of math teachers	0.33	0.58	0.53
After adjustment	Number	(3 × 5.2 × 2.69 =) 42	36	78
	Number of math teachers	14	21	35
	Proportion of math teachers	0.33	0.58	0.45

Source: Authors' compilation.

CHAPTER **15**

COMPUTING ESTIMATES AND THEIR SAMPLING ERRORS FROM SIMPLE RANDOM SAMPLES

The purpose of the examples and computations up to this point was to calculate design weights and adjust them where necessary for nonresponse and auxiliary data (poststratified weights). These computations have resulted in a set of final estimation weights, which will be used to compute population estimates for the national assessment.

Simple descriptive statistics such as totals, averages, and proportions are produced for virtually every survey. Different types of estimators are appropriate for these different types of variables. Proportions and total counts are typically produced for qualitative variables, whereas averages and totals are estimated for quantitative variables. Having shown how estimation weights are computed in chapter 14, we show how to use those estimation weights to obtain estimates for some basic population characteristics, such as totals, means, and proportions. It also shows how to obtain estimates of precision (often called *sampling error*) for those estimates. This chapter concentrates on simple random samples. How to obtain estimates of sampling error under complex sample designs is described in chapter 16.

A consideration during estimation, in addition to type of data, is the nature of the population for which the estimates are to be made. Estimates can be produced for the whole survey population or for a specific subgroup, or *domain*, of the population (for example, province, subject matter taught, or source of school funding), whether or not the information defining the domain was known at the time of sampling. When the original classification of sampling units has changed between the time of sample selection and estimation, the new classification should be used for domain estimation. Such a change might occur if a teacher was recorded in the administrative files as a math teacher but describes himself or herself as a teacher of language arts.

Answers to the following questions will help determine how the survey estimates are computed:

- What type of data is being used: qualitative or quantitative?
- What type of statistic is needed: a total, an average, or a proportion?
- What are the final weights?
- What are the domains of interest?

The procedures for estimating totals, averages, and proportions for the whole survey population and domains using weights are described in this chapter for qualitative and quantitative variables. The estimators can be used for any probability sample design, whether simple (for example, simple random sampling or systematic random sampling) or more complex. What is important is that each unit's final weight correctly accounts for the sample design.

ESTIMATING A POPULATION TOTAL

To get correct estimates for national assessment population data, one must apply the correct final weights to the data. The statistical notation for calculating estimates is presented in annex IV.A. Estimation procedures are illustrated in exercise 15.1.

EXERCISE 15.1

Estimation for SRS400

This exercise involves constructing three estimates of interest to policy makers for the entire population of a simple randomized sample, SRS400: (a) the total number of students, (b) their average age, and (c) the proportion scoring 230 or better in mathematics. Then three estimates will be made for the subpopulation "boys" (gender = 1): the total number of boys, their average age, and their average math score.

The required data have been stored in *...\MYSAMPLSOL\RESPSRSFINALWT.SAV*.

The estimates must refer to the population at the time of assessment. Consequently, although the dropouts remain in the file and have final weights because they belonged to the initial frame, they do not contribute to the estimates; at the time of assessment, all their characteristics have a value of zero, including a conceptual dummy variable, **belongs to the population being assessed**, which is equal to zero. Assigning their characteristics a value of zero is equivalent to thinking of the assessed population as an estimation domain within the population defined by the frame. Records of the dropouts should therefore be excluded from the final file that will be used to compute the final estimates.

The only direct contributors to the estimates are thus the students who were actually assessed, who also represent the absentees through the adjustments that led to their final weights. In compiling estimates, one must take into consideration the status (participant or absentee) of each student and use the variable **STATUS** as a filter. A dummy variable, **MAT230**, must also be created because policy makers are interested in getting information on students who scored at least 230 on the mathematics test.

1. To begin the exercise, open SPSS, retrieve the data set, and create **MAT230**. Details of how to create **MAT230** under **WesVar** are presented in steps 8 to 12 in annex IV.D. Follow these commands:

   File – Open – Data

       ...\MYSAMPLSOL\RESPSRSFINALWT

   Open

   Transform – Recode into Different Variables...

2. Move **MATH** to **Input Variable**. Type **MAT230** in **Output Variable Name**. If you choose, you can also type in a label. Click **Change**.

3. Click **Old and New Values**. In **Old Value**, click **Range, value through HIGHEST** and type **230**. In **New Value**, type the number **1**. Click **Add**. In **Old Value**, click **All Other Values** (at the bottom of the screen). In **New Value**, type the number **0**. Click **Add**, **Continue**, and **OK**.

Before you can produce estimates, you need to filter out nonparticipants and use the estimation weight. Use the following commands:

   Data – Select Cases[a] **– If condition is satisfied... – If...**

(continued)

EXERCISE 15.1 *(continued)*

4. Move **STATUS** to the box on the top right-hand side. Type **= "participant"** and click **Continue**.

Under **Output**, click **Filter out unselected cases**, followed by **OK**.

5. Now you will use the SPSS wizard to walk through the steps required for estimation, much like you did for sampling. Make sure that only the participants are filtered in. Follow these commands:

Analyze – Complex Samples – Prepare for Analysis…

Create a Plan File

6. Click **Browse** to locate **MYSAMPLSOL** (exercise figure 15.1.A). Type **SRS_plan** to name the file. Then click **Save** and **Next**.

7. Move **FinalWeight** from **Variables** to the **Sample Weight** box and click **Next**. Click **Equal WOR** followed by **Next**. At this point, the program might issue a warning that the section is incomplete; move on to complete the section.

EXERCISE FIGURE 15.1.A Preparing for Analysis Wizard

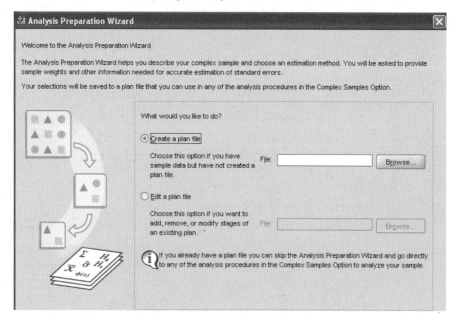

Source: Authors' example within SPSS software.

_____

a. This step might work differently under SPSS18; you might have to modify the instruction or format of the "condition" variable. (You could, for instance, convert **STATUS** to a numeric variable, using **TRANSFORM**.)

EXERCISE 15.1 *(continued)*

8. Click **Read values from variable**. Select **Population Sizes** from the **Units** box on the upper right-hand side. Move *PopulationSize* from **Variables** to **Read values…** and click **Next**.

In the **Summary** panel, click **No, do not add another stage** followed by **Next**. Then click **Finish**.

9. Now follow these commands:

   Analyze – Complex Samples – Descriptives

Select the plan file you just created, *…\MYSAMPLSOL\SRS_PLAN*. Select *…\MYSAMPLSOL\RESPSRSFINALWT* as the data set, and click **Continue** and **OK**.

Move *Age*, *Math*, and *MAT230* from **Variables** to **Measures**. Click **Statistics** and verify that **Means** and **Standard Error** are clicked on. Then click **Continue** followed by **OK**.

A small output table will be displayed in the **Output** window of SPSS (exercise figure 15.1.B).

EXERCISE FIGURE 15.1.B Descriptive Statistics for Age and Math

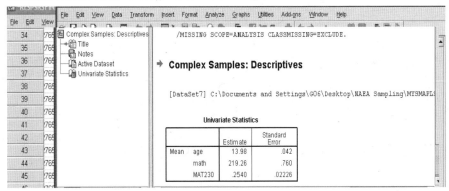

Source: Authors' example within SPSS software.

To compute the estimates for the domain "boys" rather than for the complete population, you can use the *SRS_plan* file that you just created and go directly to the **Descriptives** command and specify a subpopulation as follows:

   Analyze – Complex Samples – Descriptives

Select the plan file you just created *…\MYSAMPLSOL\SRS_PLAN*. Then select *…\MYSAMPLSOL\RESPSRSFINALWT* as the data set. Click **Continue** and **OK**.

Then move *Age*, *Math*, and *MAT230* from **Variables** to **Measures**. Move *Gender* from **Variables** to **Subpopulations**. Click **Statistics** and verify that **Means** and **Standard Error** are checked. Then click **Continue** followed by **OK**.

(continued)

EXERCISE 15.1 *(continued)*

The results for girls (**GENDER = 0**) and boys (**GENDER = 1**) are in the output table in exercise figure 15.1.C.

EXERCISE FIGURE 15.1.C **Descriptive Statistics for Age and Math, by Gender**

→ **Complex Samples: Descriptives**

```
[DataSet7] C:\Documents and Settings\G06\Desktop\NAEA Sampling\MYSMAPL
```

Univariate Statistics

		Estimate	Standard Error
Mean	age	13.98	.042
	math	219.26	.760
	MAT230	.2540	.02226

Subpopulation Descriptives

Univariate Statistics

gender			Estimate	Standard Error
0	Mean	age	13.92	.057
		math	215.85	1.069
		MAT230	.1800	.02702
1	Mean	age	14.05	.060
		math	223.10	1.006
		MAT230	.3371	.03523

Source: Authors' example within SPSS software.

ESTIMATING A POPULATION AVERAGE

For a quantitative variable, the estimate of an average value in the population (for example, the average age of students) is obtained by adding together the product of the sample value and the weight for each responding unit. This amount is then divided by the sum of the weights. In other words, the estimate of the average in the population is the estimate of the total value for a quantitative variable divided by the estimate of the total number of units in the population:

$$\hat{\bar{Y}} = \frac{\sum_{response} w_i y_i}{\sum_{response} w_i} = \frac{\hat{Y}}{\hat{N}}.$$

ESTIMATING A POPULATION PROPORTION

For qualitative data, the estimate of the proportion of units in the survey population having a given characteristic C is obtained by adding together the weights for the units having that characteristic and dividing that total by the sum of the weights for all respondents. A dummy variable, φ_i, can be used to indicate whether the ith unit has ($\varphi_i = 1$) or has not ($\varphi_i = 0$) the characteristic of interest. In other words, the estimate of the proportion in the population is the estimate of the total number of units possessing the given characteristic divided by the estimate of the total number of units in the population:

$$\hat{P}_c = \frac{\sum_{response} w_i \varphi_i}{\sum_{response} w_i} = \frac{\hat{N}_c}{\hat{N}}.$$

ESTIMATING FOR SUBGROUPS OF THE POPULATION

Estimates may be required for subgroups, which are often referred to as *domains* in the sampling literature. Such domains may include age group, source of school funding, and socioeconomic status of students. In such estimates, w_i indicates the final weights adjusted for nonresponse; the dummy variable δ_i indicates whether the ith unit is ($\delta_i = 1$) or is not ($\delta_i = 0$) in the subpopulation of interest; and the dummy variable φ_i indicates whether the ith unit has ($\varphi_i = 1$) or has not ($\varphi_I = 0$) the characteristic of interest. The size of the population for a subpopulation of interest for either qualitative or quantitative data is estimated as

$$\hat{N}_{subpopulation} = \sum_{response} w_i \delta_i.$$

The estimate of a subpopulation total for quantitative data is

$$\hat{Y}_{subpopulation} = \sum_{response} w_i \delta_i y_i.$$

The estimates of a subpopulation average for a quantitative or qualitative variable are, respectively,

$$\hat{\bar{Y}}_{subpopulation} = \frac{\sum\limits_{response} w_i \delta_i y_i}{\sum\limits_{response} w_i \delta_i} = \frac{\hat{Y}_{subpopulation}}{\hat{N}_{subpopulation}}$$

and

$$\hat{P}_{subpopulation} = \frac{\sum\limits_{response} w_i \delta_i \varphi_i}{\sum\limits_{response} w_i \delta_i} = \frac{\hat{N}_{subpopulation \cap C}}{\hat{N}_{subpopulation}}.$$

The appropriate final weight must be used to produce estimates. If the sampling weights are ignored (as has been the case in at least one national assessment), the estimates will be incorrect.

Having completed exercise 15.1, the interested reader may wish to see a comparison of SRS400 data and census data based on the entire population of 27,654 students. This comparison can be examined in annex IV.B.

CONCLUSION

This chapter was limited to estimation under simple random sampling. SPSS Complex Samples can be used to compute the estimates and their sampling errors under complex designs. However this software can be difficult to apply in this particular situation and would require a relatively deep understanding of survey sampling. An alternative approach and software are proposed in chapter 16 (see also annex IV.C).

CHAPTER **16** COMPUTING ESTIMATES AND THEIR SAMPLING ERRORS FROM COMPLEX SAMPLES

Estimates produced from a survey are subject to errors of two basic types: sampling errors and nonsampling errors. Nonsampling errors include measurement errors, trend errors, response errors, and the like. When these errors are systematic, they often cause bias and are difficult to measure. When they are random, they can be estimated with work and generous resources. In national assessments, nonsampling errors are caused by human factors, such as inadequate supervision during test administration, mistakes made during data cleaning and entry, lack of effort in answering tests or questionnaires, or false responses to questionnaire items. Sampling errors, in contrast, are not attributable to human factors. Sampling error is a measure of the extent to which an estimate from different possible samples of the same size and design, using the same estimator, differ from one another.

In a sample-based national assessment, sampling errors must be calculated. The purpose of this chapter is to illustrate how sampling variance (sampling error) is estimated in most assessment surveys and the importance of correctly incorporating the sample design into that estimation. The chapter explains how estimates of sampling error can be obtained rather easily using replication, in which, instead of selecting one sample of size n, k independent samples of the size n/k are selected. Variability among the k sample estimates is then used to estimate the sampling variance (see annex IV.C). Design-based sampling errors for the Sentz assessment are estimated using WesVar (exercise 16.1).

EXERCISE 16.1

Jackknife Variance Estimation for a PPS Sample

If you have not already installed WesVar on your computer, you should do it now; follow instructions given in annex IV.D, and resume the exercise here.

1. For Sentz, you first need to prepare the replicates, compute the jackknife weights, and assign them to the schools. Instructions to create 60 jackknife zones (two schools per zone) and compute the replication weights are given in annex IV.D. Those SPSS instructions can easily be modified to work with different sample sizes. The file *...\MYSAMPLSOL\RESP2STGWTJK* contains the responses, the final estimation weights, and the jackknife zones and jackknife units.

2. Obtain estimates for the average age, the average mathematics score, and the proportion of students with a mathematics score of at least 230 for the general student population and for boys. Statements are given so that jackknife estimates of variance are computed using WesVar.

3. Launch WesVar. Then, if necessary, see steps 8 to 17 in annex IV.D for instructions on how to create the derived variable *MAT230* and how to add some labels to *RESP2STGWTJK*. Save the dataset.

   Click **New WesVar Workbook** and select *...\MYSAMPLSOL\RESP2STGWTJK*. You can type in a name for that workbook for future reference. (Remember to save it!)

   Click **Table**, then click **Subset Detail** and type *STATUS = "participant"* in the **Subpop string** box.

   Click **Add Table Set (Single)**. Verify that **Missing**, **RS2**, and **RS3** are not clicked and that only **Value** is clicked.

   Move *GENDER* from **Source Variables** to **Selected**, and click **Add as New Entry**.

   Click **Computed Statistics** in the left pane and click *AGE* in the **Source Variables**. Then click **BlockMean**. *M_AGE* will be added to the list of **Computed Statistics**. Do the same with *MATH* and *MAT230*. You may want to change the labels as you did earlier. Now click the green arrow (or click **Requests – Run Workbook Requests**) to execute the request (exercise figure 16.1.A).

4. Click the **open book** icon, or click **Requests – View Output** and expand the display until you can click the *GENDER* button to see the results as displayed in exercise figure 16.1.B. Note that computing and displaying the statistics can take some time. The program has finished running when the **View Output** icon is present in the **Requests** icon.

EXERCISE 16.1 *(continued)*

EXERCISE FIGURE 16.1.A Executing a WesVar Request

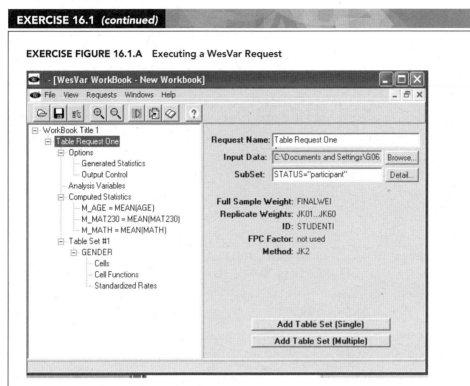

Source: Authors' example within WesVar software.

EXERCISE FIGURE 16.1.B Population Estimates for Age and Mathematics Variables by Gender

GENDER	STATISTIC	EST_TYPE	ESTIMATE	STDERROR	CV(%)	CELL_n	DEFF
0	SUM_WTS	VALUE	13888.12	233.733	1.683	2346	N/A
1	SUM_WTS	VALUE	13443.94	236.223	1.757	2285	N/A
MARGINAL	SUM_WTS	VALUE	27332.06	311.516	1.140	4631	N/A
0	M_AGE	VALUE	13.98	0.019	0.138	2346	1.319
1	M_AGE	VALUE	14.02	0.016	0.116	2285	0.907
MARGINAL	M_AGE	VALUE	14.00	0.012	0.086	4631	1.008
0	M_MAT230	VALUE	0.17	0.014	8.558	2346	3.459
1	M_MAT230	VALUE	0.35	0.022	6.240	2285	4.873
MARGINAL	M_MAT230	VALUE	0.26	0.018	6.756	4631	7.397
0	M_MATH	VALUE	214.59	0.668	0.311	2346	4.478
1	M_MATH	VALUE	224.15	0.752	0.335	2285	6.591
MARGINAL	M_MATH	VALUE	219.30	0.699	0.319	4631	9.521

TABLE : GENDER

Source: Authors' example within WesVar software.

The theory that supports the estimation of sampling error is beyond the scope of this chapter, but the interested reader can turn to textbooks on sampling theory (see, for example, Lohr 1999) for a detailed account of the exact design-based estimation methods or to textbooks devoted to the analysis of data from complex surveys (see, for example, Lehtonen and Pahkinen 1995). The procedure to calculate jackknife weights is described in annex IV.D. Other methods (such as bootstrapping and balanced repeated replication) exist but will not be covered here.

When the sample is large enough and the number of strata is moderate, alternative jackknifing strategies are available. In many international assessment programs, the estimates are computed by a central service in a standardized manner, and the method used may be different from what is described here. When participating countries are expected to produce their own estimates, the strategy described in exercise 16.1 is often adopted because of its appealing simplicity. There are limitations, however, to what jackknifing can accomplish. Jackknifing is quite efficient at estimating variances for totals and continuous functions of totals (for example, ratios, proportions, or correlation coefficients). It is not as good with respect to discontinuous nonlinear or order statistics (for example, Gini coefficients or medians). If such statistics are of interest, a sampling specialist should be consulted to determine the best replication approach.

The examples in exercise 16.2 were devised using the national assessment data file available as the SPSS file *...NATASSESS\ NATASSESS.SAV*. This data file is also the source of the data used in the first part of volume 4, *Analyzing Data from a National Assessment of Educational Achievement*.

A closing note of caution: The software market offers a wide array of personal computer data processing and statistical software products. A considerable number of these products, including ones that claim to specialize in survey processing, give inaccurate results if they fail to take into account that a survey was based on a complex sample design. The interested user is advised to consult professional reviews of statistical software (see, for example, http://www.fas.harvard. edu/~stats/survey-soft/survey-soft.html).

Calculating Gender Differences on a Mathematics Test

In this exercise, as you did with the demonstration file in exercise 16.1, you need to create a WesVar version of the file and compute jackknife replication weights for it before doing anything else.

Launch WesVar, click **New WesVar Data File**, and select **...\NATASSESS\ NATASSESS. SAV**. Scroll down the **Source Variables** to locate and move the design weight *WGTPOP* to the **Full Sample** box and *STUDID* to the **ID** box. Move all remaining variables to the **Variables** box. Save the file as **...\NATASSESS\NATASSESS.var**.

Click the **scale** button to create the replication weights. Because these assessment data were collected under a complex sampling plan, as described earlier, use two jackknife units per jackknife stratum. Click **JK2** as the **Method**; you may also want to change the prefix of the replicate weights to *JK*. Move *JKINDIC* to the **VarUnit** box (this is what *NATASSESS* calls the jackknife unit), and move *JKZONE* (that is, the jackknife stratum) to the **VarStrat** box. Click **OK** to create the weights and save the file. Neither recoding nor labeling is required at this stage. Close the screen and return to the WesVar file and WesVar workbook creation screen.

Alternatively you can open a **New WesVar Workbook** and select **...\NATASSESS\ NATASSESS.var** as the WesVar data file. Click **Open** and then click **Descriptive Statistics**. Click **Analysis Variables** in the left pane and move the three variables of interest (in this instance)—*MATHPC* (math percent correct), *MATHRS* (math raw score), and *MATHSS* (math scale score)—from **Source Variables** to **Selected**. Click the **green arrow** button to execute the request (exercise figure 16.2.A) and the **open book** icon (or click on **Requests – View Output**) to view the output. Expand by clicking the **+**. To get the data for *MATHPC*, click the **+** and **Statistics** (exercise figure 16.2.B).

This request produces a large number of univariate statistics for *MATHPC* (mean, percentile, population variance, and other basic weighted statistics) along with their estimated sampling errors, where appropriate, as displayed in exercise figure 16.2.C. Note that WesVar does not compute a mode.

Close the output window. Highlight **WorkBook Title 1** in the left pane, and click **Table** followed by **Add Table Set (Single)**. In the left pane, click **Computed Statistics**, highlight *MATHSS* under **Source Variables**, and click **Block Mean**; the mean math score will now be computed. Highlight **Table Set #1**, move *GENDER* from **Source Variables** to **Selected**, and click **Add as New Entry**. If needed, click **+** to expand **Table Set**. Click on the **Cells** node in the left pane. The right pane will display all cells that will be produced for that table under **Cell Definition**; highlight **1**, type *Boys* in the **Label** pane, and click **Add as New Entry**. Do the same for cell **2**, which will refer to the *Girls* (exercise figure 16.2.C).

Click **Cell Functions** (left pane), type *Diff = Boys – Girls* in the **Function Statistic** box, and

(continued)

EXERCISE 16.2 *(continued)*

EXERCISE FIGURE 16.2.A WesVar Workbook Prior to Analysis Stage

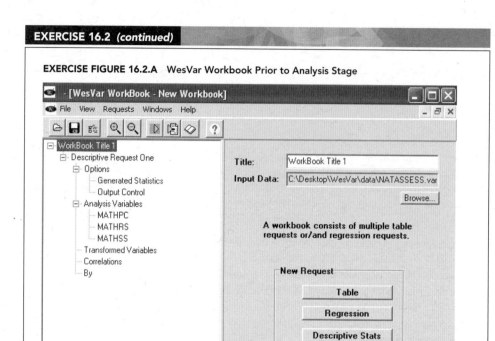

Source: Authors' example within WesVar software.

EXERCISE FIGURE 16.2.B WesVar Descriptive Statistics for MATHPC

Statistics	Unweighted	Weighted	SE Weighted
N	4747	51713.00	
Missing	N/A		
Minimum	0.07		
Maximum	0.99		
1	0.16	0.16	0.005
5	0.25	0.25	0.008
10	0.31	0.30	0.011
25	0.43	0.42	0.011
50	0.57	0.58	0.012
75	0.71	0.71	0.011
90	0.81	0.81	0.007
95	0.85	0.86	0.007
99	0.93	0.93	0.009
Mean	0.57	0.57	0.008
GeoMean	0.53	0.53	0.009
Sum	2705.44	29475.80	428.337
Variance	0.035	0.036	0.001
CV	0.326	0.332	N/A
Skewness	−0.133	−0.153	0.044
Kurtosis	−2519.933	−0.756	0.047

Source: Authors' example within WesVar software.

EXERCISE 16.2 *(continued)*

EXERCISE FIGURE 16.2.C   WesVar: Labeling Cells

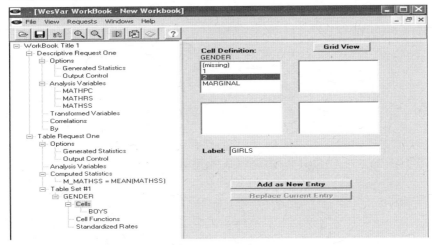

Source: Authors' example within WesVar software.

click **Add as New Entry**. Highlight the **For...** node in the left pane. Move *M_MATHSS* to the right-hand side, and move *SUM_WTS* back to the source **Variables** (exercise figure 16.2.D). Now execute the request by clicking the **green arrow** button. To view the statistics, click the **open book** icon (or **Requests – View Output**), and click *GENDER* in the

EXERCISE FIGURE 16.2.D   Computing Differences between Cell Entries

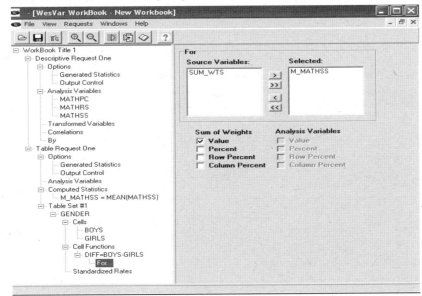

Source: Authors' example within WesVar software.

(continued)

EXERCISE 16.2 *(continued)*

expanded **Table Set**.

Finally, to see the results, click the **open book** icon (or **Requests – View Output**) and go to the relevant node.

The mean score for boys is estimated at 250.44 (sampling error = 2.88) and the mean score for girls at 249.55 (sampling error = 2.52) (exercise figure 16.2.E). To view the data on the difference between boys and girls, click **Functions** under *GENDER* (exercise figure 16.2.F).

Note that the set of statistics computed and displayed is controlled under the table

EXERCISE FIGURE 16.2.E   WesVar: Comparison of Mathematics Mean Scores by Gender

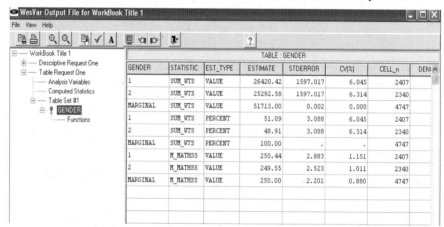

Source: Authors' example within WesVar software.

EXERCISE FIGURE 16.2.F   WesVar Mean Score Difference in Math

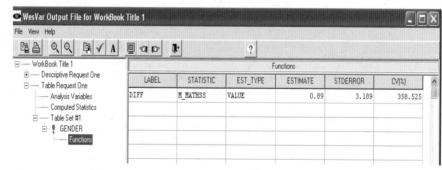

Source: Authors' example within WesVar software.

EXERCISE 16.2 *(continued)*

options node. The data displayed may differ from those presented in exercise figure 16.2.F because they will depend on the options selected.

The estimated difference is very small (diff = 0.89), and the associated *t*-value is 0.89/3.189 = 0.279, which makes the difference not statistically significant (*p*-value = 0.781 > 0.05).

CHAPTER 17 SPECIAL TOPICS

This chapter focuses on a number of additional sampling issues related to concerns, problems, and errors commonly encountered in national assessment studies. These topics include treatment of nonresponses, stratification, frame sorting, and sample selection; treatment of oversize and undersize schools; and standards for judging the adequacy of the response rates in a national assessment.

NONRESPONSE

There is no universal or uniform best way to deal with nonresponse. In a general social survey, reasons for nonresponse in one part of the country (for example, school closures on account of weather) may be different from those in another part of the country (for example, general dissatisfaction with local authorities). The magnitude, the source, and the impact of nonresponse are almost impossible to predict, making a global strategy to guard against it very difficult to devise. Over time, however, survey statisticians have developed a number of practices that are more or less accepted to deal with nonresponse.

One strategy is to augment the sample size to compensate for expected nonresponse. This method is valid as long as the reasons for nonresponse are not related to the survey subject matter. The augmentation can be over the complete sample, or it can be restricted to some strata or some groups of respondents for whom response has been low in the past. In the context of a national assessment of educational achievement, if a sample of 100 responding schools are needed, and 25 percent, for example, are expected to refuse to participate, 134 schools (75 percent of 134 = 100.5) should be selected and contacted. A better-than-expected response rate will add a little to data collection and processing costs. For this reason, allowing for potential additional costs in the initial budget is advisable.

A second strategy that is common among assessment studies is to use proxy responses, or replacement schools. Typically, for each sampled school, one replacement school is also selected. A replacement school should be as similar as possible to the selected school. If a sorted file exists (for implicit stratification), one technique is to use the school immediately after or immediately before the selected school on the sorted listing, assuming that school is available as a replacement. This strategy does not eliminate nonresponse bias but may keep it to a minimum, if the sorting is in fact related to outcomes. A school selected for the main sample can *never* be used as a replacement for another selected but nonresponding school. A replacement school may be tagged as a replacement for two consecutive selected schools (for example, when the sampling rate is very high in a stratum and the number of schools available for replacement is insufficient). In this situation, the replacement school can be used *only once*.

Replacement schools can be a reassuring fallback. However, national assessment teams can help limit the use of replacement schools by taking steps to encourage all originally selected schools to participate.

STRATIFICATION, FRAME SORTING, AND SAMPLE SELECTION

Most national assessment studies use a stratified multistage design. Such a design was illustrated in chapter 8. As indicated earlier, one may want to use strata to ensure that certain types of schools are selected in the sample (for example, by province) and that a given sample size is allocated to each group (for example, 75 schools per province). These strata are called *explicit*. One may also want to use other criteria for which the same level of precision is not required or for which proportional representation is sufficient (for example, towns within a province or funding within a province). These strata are called *implicit*. In practice, implicit strata are sorting variables within explicit strata. Finally, regardless of the sample selection technique used (such as simple random sampling, systematic random sampling, or probability proportional to size), the sampling frame should be sorted by school size before sample selection. Sorting by size will improve the selection of replacement schools.

One common feature of the selection process is the use of systematic random sampling. Some countries use it with equal probability, whereas others use it with probability proportional to school size.

Clearly, sorting of the frame should be done within each explicit stratum, because this corresponds to implicit stratification. One useful way to sort the sampling frame prior to sample selection is to alternate the order of sorting by size from one implicit stratum to the next. Table 17.1 shows how this type of sorting is accomplished.

TABLE 17.1

Sampling Frame with Different Measure of Size Order within Strata

Explicit stratum	Implicit stratum	Measure of size	School ID	Mailing address	Name of principal	Other frame variable
1	1	Small	1	...	...	...
1	...	...	...	...	...	...
1	1	LARGE	...	...	...	...
1	2	LARGE	...	...	...	...
1	...	...	...	...	...	...
1	2	Small	...	...	...	...
1	3	Small	...	...	...	...
1	...	...	...	...	...	...
1	3	LARGE	...	...	...	...
2	1	Small	...	...	...	...
...		...	...	...	...	...
H	3	...	N	...	...	...

Source: Authors' compilation.

Note: In column 3, all the schools in the country in the first stratum (the first three rows of data) are ranked in order of size from the smallest to the largest. It is not possible to list all the schools in each stratum in this figure; the symbol "..." represents the schools between the smallest and the largest.

Sorting the frame in this manner is not obligatory, but it improves the similarity of replacement and selected schools and should reduce nonresponse bias. This sorting by size also improves the chances of selecting schools of every size from each explicit stratum, minimizing stratum-to-stratum variation, and thus improving the precision of estimates.

OVERSIZE SCHOOLS

When using sampling with probability proportional to size, the design weight is directly affected by the size of the sampling unit. Very small units will have very large weights, and, conversely, very large units will have very small weights. Some units may even end up with weights of less than one. In this situation, the common practice is to choose the unit "with certainty" and redo the sampling for the rest of the sampling frame.

For example, consider the stratum of $N_h = 10$ schools in table 17.2, from which a sample of $n_h = 3$ schools is needed and the design weight each school would have if selected. If school 1 (which accounts for more than 50 percent of the students in the sampling frame) were selected, its design weight would be less than one. To address the

TABLE 17.2

Sampling Frame for 10 Schools and Associated Design Weights If Selected

School ID	School measure of size	Cumulative measure of size	Design weight
1	500	500	830/(3 × 500) = 0.5533
2	50	550	830/(3 × 50) = 5.5333
3	50	600	830/(3 × 50) = 5.5333
4	40	640	830/(3 × 40) = 6.9167
5	40	680	830/(3 × 40) = 6.9167
6	35	715	830/(3 × 35) = 7.9048
7	35	750	830/(3 × 35) = 7.9048
8	30	780	830/(3 × 30) = 9.2222
9	30	810	830/(3 × 30) = 9.2222
10	20	830	830/(3 × 20) = 13.8333

Source: Authors' compilation.

TABLE 17.3

Adjusted Sampling Frame

School ID	School measure of size	Cumulative measure of size	Design weight
1	500	500	500/500 = 1.0000
2	50	50	330/(2 × 50) = 3.3000
3	50	100	330/(2 × 50) = 3.3000
4	40	140	330/(2 × 40) = 4.1250
5	40	180	330/(2 × 40) = 4.1250
6	35	215	330/(2 × 35) = 4.7143
7	35	250	330/(2 × 35) = 4.7143
8	30	280	330/(2 × 30) = 5.5000
9	30	310	330/(2 × 30) = 5.5000
10	20	330	330/(2 × 20) = 8.2500

Source: Authors' compilation.

problem, one could decide that this school is selected and that it will represent only itself. School 1 is called a *self-representing unit*. Then, one would need to select two schools from the remaining nine, as shown in table 17.3.

If an expert on sampling suggests this strategy, he or she may also recommend that two classes be selected from school 1. Note that this selection will have the effect of bringing the weights for the remaining units closer to one another, which will result in smaller sampling error. If, after removing school 1, school 2 proved to cause a similar problem, it would also be removed, and the frame and sample would be amended in the manner illustrated previously. Of course, the sample would increase to four units (two self-representing units and two from the remaining eight).

UNDERSIZE SCHOOLS

Many countries with substantial rural populations have a relatively large number of small schools. Suppose that the smallest schools on the frame have so few in-scope students (say, fewer than 10 each) that they would not provide enough within-school information. (The minimum cluster size is decided by the psychometrics of the survey, the number of booklets used in the assessment, and other parameters outside the sampling process.)

Some assessment studies recommend that schools below some threshold (for example, five students per class) be excluded. This strategy will concentrate collection where the school and class sizes are sufficient to warrant economical assessment and reliable modeling and analyses. However, exclusion of the smallest schools may lead to some serious undercoverage issues in countries or in areas of countries that have many small rural schools. It can also tend to hide from analysts and policy makers problems or peculiarities specific to the smallest schools.

As an alternative, some sampling experts recommend that small schools that are geographically close be joined to form pseudo-schools, either through the union of many small schools or through the union of a large school and a small school.

Suppose that in an assessment policy makers are interested in statistics from all sizes of institutions, but the testing material is so voluminous that three booklets have to be rotated among the tested students. The researchers or investigators working on the assessment may have to run analyses that require having at least 15 children participate in each school, creating five rotation groups of the three booklets. In such a situation, small schools will create an additional problem. The ordered list of schools might look like that set out in table 17.4.

Schools 1012, 1013, 1014, and 1015 do not have enough students to comply with all of the assessment requirements. Moreover, those schools are not all from the same area. Now the frame can be sorted by area and measure of size, so that one can more easily see where the solutions lie and how best to create pseudo-schools if necessary. If schools 1011 and 1013 are rather close to each other and schools 1012 and 1014 are also in neighboring towns, the frame could be rearranged as set out in table 17.5.

Once joined, the various schools forming the pseudo-school are treated as a single sampling unit. For example, if pseudo-school 1111 were selected, then all students from original schools 1011 and 1013

TABLE 17.4

Sampling Frame

School ID	School measure of size	Geographic area	Cumulative measure of size
1001	75	1	75
1002	60	2	135
1003	50	2	185
1004	40	1	225
1005	40	2	265
1006	35	1	300
1007	15	1	315
1008	20	3	335
1009	30	2	365
1010	30	3	395
1011	15	2	410
1012	10	2	420
1013	5	2	425
1014	5	2	430
1015	2	3	432

Source: Authors' compilation.

would be invited to the assessment session. The response and partici-pation rates would be computed using pseudo-school 1111 rather than using original schools 1011 and 1013 separately. The estimation weight would be applied to the pseudo-school using its combined measure of size.

This strategy, while maintaining coverage to an optimum level, in-troduces noise in the within-school and between-school statistics that may be undesirable. Many psychometric analyses try to distinguish between the contribution of the school and the contribution of the student to the assessment score (in multilevel analyses) under the assumption that the school contribution is the same for all children attending the same school and may vary from school to school. Col-lapsing small schools into a larger pseudo-school may introduce a school-to-school variability in a model that expects that contribution to be fixed for all members of a single unit. Analysis should be per-

TABLE 17.5

Modified Sampling Frame

Original schools				Pseudo-schools		
School ID	School measure of size	Geographic area	Cumulative measure of size	Pseudo-School ID	Measure of size	Cumulative measure of size
1007	15	1	15	1007	15	15
1006	35	1	50	1006	35	65
1004	40	1	90	1004	40	90
1001	75	1	165	1001	75	165
1013	5	2	170	1111	20	185
1011	15	2	200	1111		
1014	5	2	175	1112	15	200
1012	10	2	185	1112		
1009	30	2	230	1009	30	230
1005	40	2	270	1005	40	270
1003	50	2	320	1003	50	320
1002	60	2	380	1002	60	380
1015	2	3	382	1115	22	402
1008	20	3	402	1115		
1010	30	3	432	1010	30	432

Source: Authors' compilation.

formed on the original school structure. This issue should be discussed by the survey managers, the survey statisticians, and the assessment analysts before the final sampling options are selected.

STANDARDS FOR JUDGING THE ADEQUACY OF RESPONSE RATES

As noted previously, exclusions (such as dropping schools on remote islands or very small schools) are often limited to 5 percent of the desired target population before some form of warning is issued in the publication of results. After schools have participated or have been replaced and sample data have been collected, one can compute various response and participation rates. Although no universal rule defines what is "good" and what is "bad," a certain standard has come to be recognized and is used in the most important international assessment studies.

The International Association for the Evaluation of Educational Achievement uses the following rule in many of its assessments:

- 85 percent (unweighted) of the original sample of schools (that is, before replacement)
  and
- 85 percent (unweighted) of the student sample from participating schools (whether original sample or replacements)
  or
- 75 percent (weighted) for the combined participation of schools and students (that is, school participation multiplied by student participation in participating schools)

Other rules could be devised; however, the lower the participation of either schools or students, the greater the likelihood of bias.

STATISTICAL NOTATION FOR CALCULATING ESTIMATES

For qualitative and quantitative data, the estimate of the *total number of units in the survey population* is calculated by adding together the final adjusted weights of the responding units:

$$\hat{N} = \sum_{response} w_i,$$

where i is the ith responding unit in the sample, w_i is its final adjusted weight, and this is summed over all responding units. For quantitative data, the estimate of a *total value* (such as total expenditure) is the product of the final weight, w_i, and the value, y_i, for each responding unit, summed over all responding units:

$$\hat{Y} = \sum_{response} w_i y_i.$$

One can define a dummy variable $y_i = \begin{cases} \delta_i = 1, \text{ for all responding units} \\ \delta_i = 0, \text{ for all nonresponding units,} \end{cases}$

and the sum of the estimation weights (adjusted for nonresponse) over all responding units is then

$$\hat{Y} = \sum_{sample} w_i y_i = \sum_{sample} w_i \delta_i = \sum_{response} (w_i \times 1) = \sum_{response} w_i = \hat{N},$$

which is an estimate of N, the size of the population.

A COMPARISON OF SRS400 DATA AND CENSUS DATA

The comparison of SRS400 data and census data uses a file called *...\BASE FILES\CENSUS.SAV*. This file contains data for each of the 27,654 students in Sentz. It is an ideal file that would not exist in real life. All students have assessment results except those who are considered dropouts, as indicated in the response status field. Thus, this file represents the results that would have been obtained by a perfect census. Using the **CENSUS** file and the **Data – Aggregate** menu, SPSS produced the results set out in table IV.B.1.

The estimates from the simple random sample and the census data will now be compared. Because this is a simple random sample, the unweighted estimates (right-most column in table IV.B.2) and the weighted estimates (middle column) of means and proportions

TABLE IV.B.1

Sentz Data Based on Census

Domain	Average age (years)	Average math score	Proportion over 230
Complete population	14.00	216.83	0.25
Girls	13.99	211.99	0.16
Boys	14.01	221.69	0.35

Source: Authors' compilation.

237

TABLE IV.B.2

Comparing Estimates Calculated with and without the Weights to Census Values, Beginning of School Year, Simple Random Sample

Variable of interest	"True" value (beginning of school year)	Correct estimate, using weights (± sampling error)	Incorrect estimate, ignoring weights (± sampling error)
N	27,654	27,437 ± 331	378
Average age (all)	14.00	13.98 ± 0.04	13.98 ± 0.04
Proportion ≥ 230 in math	0.25	0.25 ± 0.02	0.25 ± 0.02
N_{boys}	13,807	12,920 ± 722	178
Average age (boys)	14.01	14.05 ± 0.06	14.05 ± 0.06
Average math score (boys)	221.69	223.1 ± 1.0	223.1 ± 1.0

Source: Authors' compilation.

are equal; this result is expected for means and proportions but not for totals. The population that was created for this book contains nearly equal proportions of boys and girls. The data were arranged so that boys scored higher at mathematics than girls, girls scored higher on other topics, and urban dwellers scored higher than rural dwellers. This sample happens to have a rather large proportion of urban boys, which would help explain the difference between the census data and sample estimates for the relatively high proportion of boys scoring over 230 in math.

Moreover, the "true" value is computed for the population as it was known, say, at the beginning of the school year. Therefore, there are records on the "census" file for which no information is available (namely, the dropouts) and for which all the scores are zero. These null values bring the average score down.

If the statistics about the population could be updated to represent the population at the time of the assessment (which could be done by removing the students with a mathematics score of zero from the census file), the comparisons would show that the survey results come much closer to the "true" values, well within the margins of error. This result is shown in table IV.B.3.

Such a luxury of information is hardly ever available to survey planners, managers, or analysts.

TABLE IV.B.3

Comparing Estimates Calculated with and without the Weights to Census Values, Time of Assessment, Simple Random Sample

Variable of interest	"True" value (time of assessment)	Correct estimate, using weights (± sampling error)	Incorrect estimate, ignoring weights (± sampling error)
N	27,368	27,437 ± 331	378
Average age (all)	14.00	13.98 ± 0.04	13.98 ± 0.04
Proportion ≥ 230 in math	0.26	0.25 ± 0.02	0.25 ± 0.02
N_{boys}	13,665	12,920 ± 722	178
Average age (boys)	14.01	14.05 ± 0.06	14.05 ± 0.06
Average math score (boys)	224.00	223.1 ± 1.0	223.1 ± 1.0

Source: Authors' compilation.

ESTIMATING SAMPLING ERROR WITH RESAMPLING TECHNIQUES

In most complex designs (designs other than simple random sampling or systematic random sampling), the exact variance formula is difficult to derive, let alone program. In many instances, the practical implementation of the sampling design has created situations that render the use of the exact variance formula impossible. Approximate—yet sound and reliable—methods of estimating the sampling variance are needed. One class of such methods is called *replicated sampling*, or resampling. *Random groups, balanced repeated replication, jackknifing,* and *bootstrapping* are among the better known resampling variance estimation methods. A particularly clever variance approximation method was derived in the late 1950s (Keyfitz 1957) and later adapted to become jackknife estimation. Jackknife estimation is often used in large-scale international educational assessment surveys.

USING REPLICATED SAMPLING

In replicated sampling, the survey statistician selects k independent samples of size n/k, rather than one sample of size n. For each of these

k samples (or replicates), an estimate of the characteristic of interest is produced using the weights. The variability among the k sample estimates is then used to estimate the sampling variance. The estimate, t, of the characteristic of interest (such as a total, an average, a proportion, or a median) is given by the average of the estimates produced for each replicate j:

$$t = \sum_{j=1}^{k} \frac{t_j}{k}.$$

The estimated sampling variance of t, $Vâr(t)$ is given by the following expression:

$$Vâr(t) = \frac{1}{k} \sum_{j=1}^{k} \frac{(t_j - t)^2}{(k-1)}.$$

Note that this expression is of the form s^2/n.

Suppose a three-stage design (schools, classes, and students) is used to estimate the general literacy level of 10th graders. Instead of selecting one sample of size $n = 10$ and using the exact formulas to estimate $Vâr(\hat{\bar{Y}}_{complex})$, the researchers select two samples of size $n = 5$. Table IV.C.1 displays the weighted average score attained by the students of each school (school score) and the weight attached to each school.

TABLE IV.C.1

Calculating the Estimated Sampling Variance of $\hat{\bar{Y}}$ Using Replicated Sampling

	Replicate 1			Replicate 2	
School	School score	School weight	School	School score	School weight
1001	21	16	1006	26	18
1002	27	20	1007	32	20
1003	34	16	1008	37	22
1004	38	20	1009	40	20
1005	42	20	1010	47	20
Weighted total	3,020	92		3,662	100
Weighted average	32.8			36.6	

Source: Authors' compilation.

The estimated average score for the population is

$$\hat{\bar{Y}}_{repl} = \sum_{j=1}^{2} \frac{\hat{\bar{Y}}_j}{k} = \frac{32.8 + 36.6}{2} = 34.7,$$

and the estimated sampling variance of the average score, given by the replicated sampling method, is

$$V\hat{a}r\left(\hat{\bar{Y}}_{repl}\right) = \frac{1}{k}\sum_{j=1}^{k} \frac{(\hat{\bar{Y}}_j - \hat{\bar{Y}})^2}{(k-1)} = \frac{1}{2} \times \frac{(32.8 - 34.7)^2 + (36.6 - 34.7)^2}{1} = 7.2.$$

This methodology generally gives very unstable variance estimates, because each replicate group is generally too small to provide a stable estimate on its own.

USING JACKKNIFE ESTIMATION

Resampling methods such as jackknifing and bootstrapping are frequently used in surveys with complex data. The principle of jackknife estimation is to drop, in turn, each primary unit of the sample (for example, schools); to recompute the final weights to account for the loss of one unit; and to produce an estimate of the characteristic of interest using this reduced sample. As each unit is dropped, there are as many replicates as there are primary units in the full sample. The sampling error is estimated by computing the squared differences between each of the replicate estimates and the full sample estimate (much as in the case of replicated sampling described in the previous section). If the full sample comprises, say, 150 schools, one would have to perform 150 replicate estimates and rather tedious computations.

To reduce and simplify the computations, one can overlay a "jackknife sampling design" on the original sampling design. Keeping the primary units (for example, the schools) in the order in which they appeared on the sampling frame (systematic probability proportional to size sampling is almost always used in international assessments), one pairs the first two units to form a jackknife (JK) stratum; then units 3 and 4 are paired; then units 5 and 6, and so on. At the end of the process, $n/2$ JK strata will have been formed, each containing two units. Each pair is now treated as a stratum, regardless of the original stratification (some JK strata will likely coincide with the original strata). In each JK stratum, one unit will be dropped at random, and the weight of the remaining one will be adjusted accordingly (including possible nonresponse or poststratification adjustments). The units in the other JK strata keep their original weights. Table IV.C.2 illustrates how the $n/2$ sets of JK weights are constructed (assuming no adjustments to the weights, to keep the illustration simpler).

As was done for the replicated sampling, an estimate is produced for each set of JK weights, and the variance among those estimates is computed as a basis for the sampling error. The full-sample estimate, the jackknife estimates, and the sampling variance are, respectively,

$$
\hat{\bar{Y}}_{complex} = \frac{\sum w_i \hat{y}_i}{\sum w_i}, \ \hat{\bar{Y}}^{(j)} = \frac{\sum w_i^{(j)} \hat{y}_i}{\sum w_i^{(j)}}, \ j = 1,\ldots,J
$$

$$
\text{and } \hat{V}_{JK}(\hat{\bar{Y}}_{complex}) = \sum_{j=1}^{J} \left(\hat{\bar{Y}}^{(j)} - \hat{\bar{Y}}_{complex} \right)^2,
$$

where J is the number of JK strata.

Some statisticians prefer to use the average of the replicate estimates rather than the full-sample estimate in the computation of the estimated variance. If J is large, it will not make much difference.

If n is odd, some adjustment will be required so that two units are treated as one in the random determination of the unit to be dropped or retained. A sampling specialist should be consulted in this situation.

Now the previous example can be examined using JK variance estimation rather than replicated sampling. The data table can be reorganized, and the JK replicate weights and JK estimates computed as indicated previously. Table IV.C.3 displays the 10 schools of table A4.3.1 organized in JK pairs and indicating which unit of each pair was randomly chosen to be kept or dropped. The JK replicate weights are then computed along the lines given above. With replicate 1 as an example, in JK stratum 1, JK unit 1 is dropped and its JK replicate weight becomes zero; consequently, to compensate for the loss of JK unit 1, the JK replicate weight of JK unit 2 is twice its original final

TABLE IV.C.2

Preparing for Jackknife Variance Estimation

Sampled school i	Final weight w_i	School-level estimate $\hat{y}_i$	JK stratum	JK unit	Random drop	Replicate weights		
						$w_i^{(1)}$	...	$w_1^{(n/2)}$
1	w_1	$\hat{y}_1$	1	1	1	$w_1^{(1)} = 2 \times w_1$		$w_1^{(n/2)} = w_1$
2	w_2	$\hat{y}_2$		2	0	$w_2^{(1)} = 0$		$w_2^{(n/2)} = w_2$
3	w_3	$\hat{y}_3$	2	1	0	$w_3^{(1)} = w_3$		$w_3^{(n/2)} = w_3$
4	w_4	$\hat{y}_4$		2	1	$w_4^{(1)} = w_4$		$w_4^{(n/2)} = w_4$
...	...					...	...	...
$n-1$	w_{n-1}	$\hat{y}_{n-1}$	$n/2$	1	0	$w_{n-1}^{(1)} = w_{n-1}$		$w_{n-1}^{(n/2)} = 0$
n	w_n	$\hat{y}_n$			1	$w_n^{(1)} = w_n$		$w_n^{(n/2)} = 2 \times w_n$
Estimate	$\hat{N} = \sum w_i$	$\hat{Y} = \sum w_i \hat{y}_i$				$\hat{Y}^{(1)} = \sum w_i^{(1)} \hat{y}_i$		$\hat{Y}^{(n/2)} = \sum w_i^{(n/2)} \hat{y}_i$

Source: Authors' compilation.

TABLE IV.C.3

Estimating Sampling Variance Using Jackknifing

School i	School score $\hat{y}_i$	School final weight w_i	JK stratum	JK unit	Random drop	Replicate weights				
						$w_i^{(1)}$	$w_i^{(2)}$	$w_i^{(3)}$	$w_i^{(4)}$	$w_i^{(5)}$
1	21	8	1	1	Dropped	0	8	8	8	8
2	27	10	1	2	Kept	20	10	10	10	10
3	34	8	2	1	Dropped	8	0	8	8	8
4	38	10	2	2	Kept	10	20	10	10	10
5	42	10	3	1	Dropped	10	10	0	10	10
6	26	9	3	2	Kept	9	9	18	9	9
7	32	10	4	1	Dropped	10	10	10	0	10
8	37	11	4	2	Kept	11	11	11	22	11
9	40	10	5	1	Kept	10	10	10	10	20
10	47	10	5	2	Dropped	10	10	10	10	0
Estimates		34.8				35.1	35.2	33.2	35.3	34.1

Source: Authors' compilation.

weight ($20 = 2 \times 10$). Because all other units remained untouched, their JK replicate weights are equal to their corresponding final weight. The same procedure is applied, in turn, to each JK pair.

Here, the estimated average score is

$$\hat{\bar{Y}}_{complex} = \frac{\sum w_i \hat{y}_i}{\sum w_i} = \frac{(8 \times 21 + ... + 10 \times 47)}{(8 + ... + 10)} = 34.8, \text{ the first replicate}$$

estimate is $\hat{\bar{Y}}^{(1)} = \dfrac{\sum w_i^{(1)} \hat{y}_i}{\sum w_i^{(1)}} = \dfrac{(0 \times 21 + 20 \times 27 + ... + 10 \times 47)}{(0 + 20 + 8 + ... + 10)} = 35.1$,

and the five JK replicated estimates range from 33.2 to 35.3 for an

estimated variance of $\hat{V}_{JK}\left(\hat{Y}_{complex}\right) = \sum_{j=1}^{J} \left(\hat{Y}^{(j)} - \hat{Y}_{complex}\right)^2 = 3.6$ (the esti-

mated JK variance is 3.4 when the differences are measured about the mean of the JK replicate estimates).

As mentioned earlier, one can show that jackknifing, as done here, will provide approximately unbiased variance estimates, as long as the Y quantity being estimated is a standard characteristic such as a sum, a mean, a ratio, or a correlation coefficient. Estimates of quantities such as medians, percentiles, and Gini coefficients require adjustments to the jackknife or alternative resampling methods such as balanced repeated replication.

CREATING JACKKNIFE ZONES AND REPLICATES AND COMPUTING JACKKNIFE WEIGHTS

WesVar is used with a wide range of complex sample designs where simple random sampling would produce biased estimates. You must have a data file with replicate weights before you can create a new workbook. Start by transferring data from an SPSS file to a new WesVar file. Your SPSS file should include the variables you require to conduct analyses in WesVar. You must have a data file with replicate weights before you can create a new workbook. The program can calculate these weights.

The following set of instructions guides you through the creation of jackknife weights for the two-stage survey design from the response file. Note that SPSS has been used to create the important sampling information that WesVar uses to create the replicate weights for the analysis of the national assessment data.

1. Read the SPSS response file containing the weights by following these commands:

    File – Open – Data – Look in

    ...\ *MYSAMPLSOL\RESP2STGFINALWT.SAV*

    Open

2. Because the replicate weights are created for schools, the list of participating schools can be derived from the response file. All that is required is to keep one record for each participating school.

Open **Data – Identify Duplicate Cases**, and then move **SCHOOLID** to **Define matching cases by**. In **Variables to Create**, click **First case in each group is primary**, and then click **OK**.

Then, open **Data – Select Cases** and click **If Condition is satisfied**. Click **If...** and move **Indicator of each first matching case (PrimaryFirst)** to the right-hand-side box (blue arrow). Type **=1**. Then click **Continue**. Under **Output**, click **Copy Selected to New Dataset** and type in a name, for example, **RespondingSchools**, and click **OK**.

3. Bring this **RespondingSchools** to the viewing screen. Click the **Variable View** tab at the bottom of the screen, and delete all variables but **SCHOOLID**. Return to the **Data View**; only one variable will be displayed (**SCHOOLID**), starting at 1101 and ending with 5603 as the 120th and last entry.

Now assign the JK zones and JK replicate numbers to the schools. Because 120 schools are participating, there will be 60 JK zones.

Select the commands **Transform – Compute Variable** and type **JKZONE** under **Target Variable**. Then type **RND ($Casenum/2)** under **Numeric Expression** and click **OK**.

Next, select **Transform – Compute Variable** again, and type **RANDOMPICK** under **Target Variable** and **rv.Uniform(0,1)** under **Numeric Expression**. Click **OK**.

At this point, you should see 120 schools, in 60 pairs numbered from 1 to 60, each school also bearing a random number between 0 and 1. If the random numbers are displayed as 0s and 1s, increase the number of decimal places from the **Variable View** tab. Now you can create the JK replicates.

Select **Data – Sort Cases**, then move *JKZONE RANDOM-PICK* to **Sort by**. Click **Ascending** sort and **OK**.

Now select **Data – Identify Duplicate Cases**, and move *JKZONE* to **Define matching cases by**. (If necessary, remove any other variables that may be in this panel.) In **Variables to Create**, click **Last case in each group is primary (PrimaryLast)** and **OK**.

Because WesVar expects replicates to be numbered from 1, not from 0, replicate codes need to be modified using the following commands: **Transform – Recode into Different Variables….**

Move **PrimaryLast** to **Input Variable,** and type *JKREP* in **Output Variable Name.** If you wish, you can type in a label.

Click **Change** and then **Old and New Values**. In **Old Value**, click **Value** and type *0*. In **New Value**, type the number *1* and click **Add**. Under **Old Value**, click **All other values**. Now, in **New Value**, type the number *2*. Click **Add**, **Continue**, and **OK**. Note that all **PrimaryLast** *0* values have been transformed to *JKREP* values of *1*, and all values of *1* have become *2*.

Choose **Data – Sort Cases** from the menu. Remove *JKZONE* and *RANDOMPICK* from the **Sort by** box and move *SCHOOLID* to their place; click **Ascending** and **OK**.

Save the file by using the following commands:

File – Save as – …*MYSAMPLSOL\ASSIGNJK*.

Click **Save**. You can check your solution against the backup file provided in *2STG4400*.

4. At this point, the JK zones and JK replicate numbers have been created and assigned to the participating schools; this information now has to be attached to …*MYSAMPLSOL\ RESP2STGFINALWT.SAV*, the response and weight file that you started with. If needed, open that file, or if it is already in

your workspace, bring it to the view screen and do not close the *ASSIGNJK* file.

Select the following commands **Data – Merge files – Add variables**. Choose *ASSIGNJK* from the **Open dataset** and click **Continue**.

Click **Match cases on key variables** and move *SCHOOLID* from the **Excluded variables** to the **Key variables**. If desired, move all unnecessary variables (*CLASS, PopulationSize1, SampleSize1, PopulationSize2, SampleSize2, CLASS_SIZE, CLASS_RESP,* and *NRESADJ*) from the **New active dataset** to the **Excluded variables**.

Click **Non-active dataset is keyed table** and click **OK** twice.

Save the file as *...\MYSAMPLSOL\RESP2STGWTJK*.

Close SPSS.

5. Now, the response file contains at least *STUDENTID, SCHOOLID*, the various scores, the *RESP* flag, *FINAL WEIGHT, JKZONE*, and *JKREP*. All that is left to do is to launch WesVar, compute the JK replication weights, and save that WesVar file for later use.

Launch **WesVar**. Click **New WesVar Data File**. Select the appropriate directory under **Look in**.

Select *...\MYSAMPLSOL\RESP2STGWTJK* from the directory window. All the available variables will appear in the **Source Variables** window (figure IV.D.1). (Click **Done** if **Create Extra Formatted Variables** pop up appears). Click **Full Sample** and move *FINALWEIGHT* to that window (variable name may be truncated, such as *FINALWEI*); if you wish, you can send *STUDENTID* to the **ID** box.

Click **Variables** and click **>>** to move all the remaining variables to the correct window; if desired, unnecessary variables can be moved back to the left window using **<**.

Save the file to your *MYSAMPLSOL* folder. You can use the same name because the format and extension are unique to WesVar files; they will not be confused with the SPSS originals.

FIGURE IV.D.1

List of Available Variables

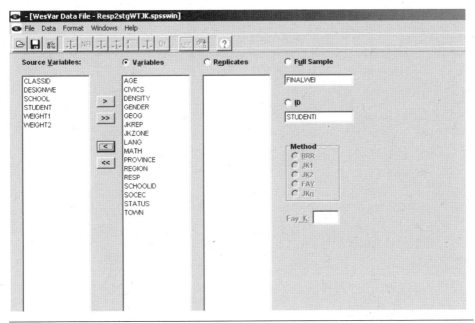

Source: Authors' example within WesVar software.

6. Now, before any table can be computed, WesVar must create replication weights to compute the sampling error.

   Still on the same screen, click the **scale** button or click **Data – Create weights**.

   From **Source Variables**, move *JKZONE* to **VarStrat**, move *JKREP* to **VarUnit**, and click **JK2** under **Method**. If you click **OK**, the **replicate prefix** will be the default *RPL* but you can change it to *JK* as shown in figure IV.D.2. Then click **OK** and accept to overwrite the file.

7. WesVar has added replication weights for the estimation of sampling error and the file now looks like figure IV.D.3.

8. Still on the same screen, click the **recode** button (the one with the downward arrow at the top of the screen), or click **Format – Recode**.

FIGURE IV.D.2

WesVar Jackknife Zones

Source: Authors' example within WesVar software.

9. Click **New Continuous (to Discrete)** to convert the math scores into a binary variable that will indicate those who scored or did not score at least 230.

10. Type **MAT230** as the **New variable name**. Highlight **MATH** in the **Source Variables** and click > to move it to **Range of Original Variables**. Type **>=230** under **Range of original variables** and type **1** under **MAT230**.

11. Move the cursor to the second line, and under **MATH>=230**, insert **MATH<230** and assign the code **0**.

12. Click **OK** and then click **OK** again to execute the creation of the binary variable. Save the file using the same name.

13. Still on the same screen, click **Format – Label**.

FIGURE IV.D.3

WesVar Replication Weights

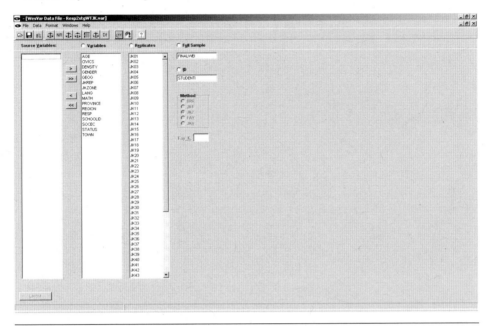

Source: Authors' example within WesVar software.

14. Highlight **GENDER** from the **Source Variables**. Type *Girl* as the label for the value **0,** and type *Boy* as the label for the value **1**; type *Total* as the label for the value **Marginal** (figure IV.D.4).

15. Highlight **MAT230** from the **Source Variables**. Type *Math score below 230* as the label for the value **0** and type *Math score at least 230* as the label for the value **1**; type *Total* as the label for the value **Marginal**.

16. Highlight **RESP** from the **Source Variables**. Type *Nonresponse* as the label for the value **0,** and type *Participant* as the label for the value **1**; type *Total* as the label for the value **Marginal**.

17. Click **OK** and save (overwrite) the file under ...\ **MYSAMPLSOL**.

18. Close this window.

FIGURE IV.D.4

WesVar: Creating Labels

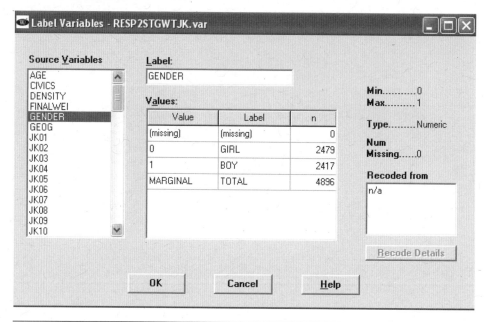

Source: Authors' example within WesVar software.

Any changes (such as recodes or format) can be made from this window by clicking **Open WesVar Data File** (on the left of the WesVar screen) and selecting the file you need.

To compute estimates, you should click **New WesVar Workbook** on the right side of the WesVar screen (figure IV.D.5). Valuable information can be found in the user's guide to WesVar.

You may now resume exercise 16.1.

FIGURE IV.D.5

WesVar: Opening Screenshot

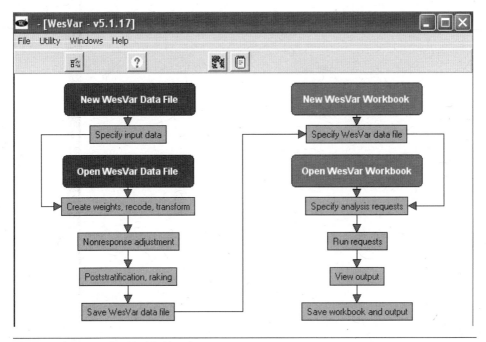

Source: Authors' example within WesVar software.

REFERENCES

Anderson, P., and G. Morgan. 2008. *Developing Tests and Questionnaires for a National Assessment of Educational Achievement*. Washington, DC: World Bank.

Cartwright, F., and G. Shiel. Forthcoming. *Analyzing Data from a National Assessment of Educational Achievement*. Washington, DC: World Bank.

Cochran, W. G. 1977. *Sampling Techniques*. 3rd ed. New York: Wiley.

Greaney, V., and T. Kellaghan. 2008. *Assessing National Achievement Levels in Education*. Washington, DC: World Bank.

Howie, S. J. 2004. "Project Plan." Unpublished document, Centre for Evaluation and Assessment, Pretoria.

Ilon, L. 1996. "Considerations for Costing National Assessments." In *National Assessment: Testing the System*, ed. P. Murphy, V. Greaney, M. E. Lockheed, and C. Rojas, 69–88. Washington, DC: World Bank.

Kellaghan, T., V. Greaney, and T. S. Murray. 2009. *Using the Results of a National Assessment of Educational Achievement*. Washington, DC: World Bank.

Keyfitz, N. 1957. "Estimates of Sampling Variance Where Two Units Are Selected from Each Stratum." *Journal of the American Statistical Association* 52 (280): 503–12.

Kish, L. 1965. *Survey Sampling*. New York: Wiley.

Lehtonen, R., and E. J. Pahkinen. 1995. *Practical Methods for the Design and Analysis of Complex Surveys*. New York: Wiley.

Lohr, S. L. 1999. *Sampling: Design and Analysis*. Pacific Grove, CA: Duxbury Press.

TIMSS (Trends in International Mathematics and Science Study). 1998a. *Manual for Entering the TIMSS-R Data* (Doc. Ref. No. 98-0028). Chestnut Hill, MA: International Study Center, Boston College.

————. 1998b. *Manual for International Quality Control Monitors* (Doc. Ref. No. 98-0023). Chestnut Hill, MA: International Study Center, Boston College.

————. 1998c. *Sampling Design and Implementation for TIMSS 1999 Countries: Survey Operational Manual* (Doc. Ref. No. 98-0026). Chestnut Hill, MA: International Study Center, Boston College.

UNESCO (United Nations Educational, Scientific, and Cultural Organization). 1997. *International Standard Classification of Education ISCED*. Paris: UNESCO.